INITIATIVES IN COMMUNICATIVE LANGUAGE TEACHING II

A Book of Readings

Edited by

SANDRA J. SAVIGNON
University of Illinois
Urbana - Champaign

MARGIE S. BERNS
Purdue University

ADDISON–WESLEY PUBLISHING COMPANY
Reading, Massachusetts • Menlo Park, California
Don Mills, Ontario • Wokingham, England • Amsterdam
Bonn • Sydney • Singapore • Tokyo • Madrid • Bogota
Santiago • San Juan

THE ADDISON–WESLEY SECOND LANGUAGE PROFESSIONAL LIBRARY SERIES

Sandra J. Savignon
Consulting Editor

CANTONI–HARVEY, Gina
Content-Area Language Instruction

CONNOR, Ulla and KAPLAN, Robert
Writing Across Languages: Analysis of L2 Text

DAMEN, Louise
Culture Learning: The Fifth Dimension in the Language Classroom

DUBIN, Fraida, ESKEY, David and GRABE, William
Teaching Second Language Reading for Academic Purposes

HIGGINS, John and JOHNS, Tim
Computers in Language Learning

MOHAN, Bernard A.
Language and Content

SAVIGNON, Sandra J.
Communicative Competence: Theory and Classroom Practice

SAVIGNON, Sandra J. and BERNS, Margie S.
Initiatives in Communicative Language Teaching I

SMITH, Stephen M.
The Theater Arts and the Teaching of Second Languages

VENTRIGLIA, Linda
Conversations of Miguel and Maria

WALLERSTEIN, Nina
Language and Culture in Conflict

Library of Congress Cataloging-in-Publication Data

Initiatives in communicative language teaching II.

(The Addison-Wesley second language professional library series)
Bibliography: p.
1. Languages, Modern—Study and teaching.
2. Communicative competence. I. Savignon, Sandra J. II. Berns, Margie S. III. Series: Second language professional library.
PB36.I586 1987   418'.007'1   86-22205
ISBN 0-201-06519-3

ISBN: 0-201-06519-3
ABCDEFGHIJ-AL-8987

Contents

iii

Introduction

Communicative language teaching is as much a focus of discussion and debate today as when the first volume of *Initiatives in Communicative Language Teaching* appeared in 1984. The range and depth of this interest is reflected in the enthusiastic response to our first collection of international case studies, a response that has brought to our attention many other initiatives in teaching contexts around the world. With the support of Byron Bush, our editor at Addison-Wesley, we are pleased to be able to offer this second collection of initiatives in communicative language teaching, initiatives that bear further witness to the vibrancy and richness of our profession.

Like its predecessor, *Initiatives in Communicative Language Teaching II* is a resource book for classroom teachers and program administrators who want to know not only *what* communicative language teaching is all about but *how* the goal of communicative competence is being met in teaching contexts similar to their own. While theoretical discussions of language and language learning are helpful in clarifying goals and issues, examples of ongoing developments in teaching and evaluation often provide the incentive needed to make changes, to modify or redesign inadequate programs and materials. Thus the emphasis in this collection remains that of the first, to provide accounts of programs that are working, reports of initiatives that are being pursued on local, regional, and even national levels to make the goal of communicative second language use a reality.

The authors of the ten chapters that comprise this volume are all intimately involved with teaching and/or program development and evaluation in either public or private language teaching contexts in Brazil, Japan, India, West Germany, Canada and the United States. The topics that they address are grouped into two major categories, "Background Perspectives" and "Approaches, Methods and Techniques."

Section I: Background Perspectives

This section presents discussions of assumptions and principles related to communicative language teaching. In Chapter 1, "Empowerment and Collaboration: A Perspective for Language Learners and Teachers," Richard Orem considers the communicative process between classroom teachers and learners. He uses the notion of "empowerment," a concept he borrows from the field of adult education, as the point of reference for his discussion. Orem illustrates how power relationships are at the heart of certain major methodological developments in language teaching and reviews recent innovations in classroom practice that are quite radical in approach and substance. In responding to a recognition of learners' needs and goals, these innovations represent empowerment for both learners and their teachers. Orem emphasizes the need for teachers to understand how the choices they make regarding what and how they teach relate to issues in society at large, a theme that is echoed in subsequent chapters of the volume.

In Chapter 2, "Language and Power: On the Necessity of Rethinking English Language Pedagogy in Brazil," JoAnne Busnardo and Denise Braga highlight two issues critical for language teaching in Brazil. The first is the rationale for teaching English, as well as other foreign languages, in a country with vast native literacy problems. Drawing from the work of Paulo Freire to establish a framework for their personal experience of the teaching and learning situation in Brazil, the authors go on to underscore the need for language learners and teachers to draw comparisons between native and target cultures. Such cross-cultural analyses promote critical thinking and provide a basis for a methodology that addresses the particular communicative needs of learners in a non-native context.

The second issue is that of the nature of prevailing language learning materials and methodology in Brazil. The authors suggest that the solution to the problems associated with current imported texts and techniques lies in teacher education, which must address the social functions of language and recent developments in psycholinguistics and sociolinguistics. Familiarity with these areas would better prepare teachers to promote communication in a genuine sense, that is, to prepare learners for the negotiation of meaning and creation of interpretations within concrete sociocultural contexts.

Concluding Section I is Chapter 3, "The Impregnability of Textbooks: The Example of American Foreign Language Education." In this chapter, Hildebrando Ruiz discusses the discrepancy between the current state of knowledge about language and the level of linguistic sophistication represented in teaching textbooks. He takes a look at the nature and content of a number of university-level Spanish textbooks in use in the United States and notes the gap between findings in linguistic and sociolinguistic research of the past 10–15 years and their applications in language teaching materials. The results of his own survey of publishers and textbook authors suggest three sources for this gap: (1) a lack of concensus as to what communicative language teaching is, (2) the omission of insights into language offered by new orientations in language study, and (3) publishers' desire to deliver textbooks that conform with teachers' expectations of what a textbook should look like and how language should be taught. Ruiz points out that the consequence of this situation is language teaching texts that do not allow communicative language teaching to play a central role in the classroom.

Section II: Approaches, Methods and Techniques

This section provides examples of ways in which teaching is becoming more reflective of the goal of communicative competence. The illustrations are drawn from foreign/second language programs at both the school and college levels in Europe and North and South America. Each offers practical guidelines and support to those who would like to bring about similar changes in their own program.

Chapter 4, "The Ontario Experience: A Modular Approach to Second Language Teaching and Learning," by Rebecca Ullmann, describes attempts to develop substantive and activity-oriented language teaching materials for Canadian elementary and secondary schools. The modular approach has been developed in connection with a long-term Core French project directly concerned with the nature of second language program content and the ways in which this content might be structured and implemented. The project's goal is to develop second language proficiency and provide expanded opportunities for communication in the classroom. Ullmann provides rationale and presents examples of modules, which serve as small multi-media units and are to be seen as complementary to regular classroom materials.

A rather different approach to the content of the language classroom is described in Chapter 5, "The Bangalore Project: Description and Evaluation." Alan Beretta reports the results of an evaluation of the Bangalore/Madras Communicational Teaching Project, a large-scale attempt to explore a new approach to language teaching methodology in South India. This project has attracted considerable attention for its foundation in the principle that form is best learned when learners' attention is on meaning rather than form and for its controversial approach to materials and methodology. To evaluate the project, the author compared the "communicational" method with a more familiar teaching method in India, a form of structural teaching. The results of the evaluation provide support for the project, which, Beretta notes, is increasingly being regarded as substantial and worthwhile.

An alternative to traditional register-bound English for Specific Purposes is described in Chapter 6, "Second Language Teaching in the Business World: Communicative English Course Content in Germany," by Stephen Smith. The author outlines a communication-based approach to the design of an English language course for managers in a German corporation. Rather than deriving the course content from particular features of language, Smith examines the nature of communication among managers in the business context. As a model for course design, Smith takes training courses in effective communication strategies conducted in the managers' first language, German. To illustrate how the principles of communication training can be realized in second language materials and content, the author includes a sample teaching unit, "The Tunnel Project."

The process of course design is addressed in Chapter 7, "A Practical Approach to Course Design: English for Computer Science in Brazil," by Miriam Solange Costa. In describing key aspects of course design, instruction and evaluation, the author places particular emphasis on the importance of constant interaction between the ESP course designer and the students and staff in the academic department to which the course content is related. This interaction, she points out, is essential to course development and evaluation because the feedback generated by this channel of communication provides a basis for modifying the course and increasing its responsiveness to actual learner needs.

Reading is the focus of Chapters 8 and 9. In Chapter 8, "Fostering Interactive Second Language Reading," Patricia Carrell describes recent research and developments in the framework of schema theory and relates them to second language teaching. She discusses the nature of *interactive* reading, which has been shown to be the most efficient means of processing written texts, and presents some of its implications and applications to second language reading pedagogy.

Chapter 9, "Getting a Better Reading: Initiatives in Foreign Language Reading Instruction," by Heidi Byrnes, suggests means of correcting the imbalance in foreign language teaching between competence in expression and competence in interpretation. She points out that in U.S. foreign language classrooms reading skills, in particular, have been neglected as a result of over-emphasis on oral communication skills. Byrnes reviews recent research in reading and illustrates how insights from this research can be applied in language teaching materials and methodology.

Her illustrations include a selection of materials for Spanish, German, and French.

Chapter 10, "Playing in English: Games and the L2 Classroom in Japan," by Marc Helgesen, discusses the value of games in second language teaching. Based on his experiences teaching English in Japan, the author provides examples of games that he has found effective in the second language classroom and offers an explanation of why these games are successful with Japanese learners of English. Helgesen encourages the recognition of games as a viable means of developing learners' overall ability to communicate in a foreign/second language.

Each contribution to *Initiatives in Communicative Language Teaching II*, as well as those in the first collection, provides a unique perspective on the possibilities for language teaching that is communicative and responsive to the particular needs of learners in a given learning context. Countless perspectives and insights remain to be explored. Therefore, it is our hope that this volume will encourage readers to take a closer look at their own teaching situation and, in turn, to pursue their own initiatives in communicative language teaching.

Glossary

Research and discussion of the concepts of communicative competence and communicative language teaching have not only resulted in an increasing number of teaching initiatives, they have also resulted in a new terminology for talking about various aspects of language learning and teaching. In an effort to provide a common basis for discussion and to promote consistent use of terms, we have included in this volume a glossary of terms. Readers are invited to refer to it as they read through the chapters.

Urbana, Illinois   Sandra J. Savignon
West Lafayette, Indiana   Margie S. Berns
1987

Section I
Background Perspectives

Chapter 1

Empowerment and Collaboration: A Perspective for Language Learners and Teachers

Richard A. Orem

Richard A. Orem is a professor of Adult Continuing Education at Northern Illinois University where he teaches adult ESL methods courses. Among his research interests are second language literacy, the influence of culture on language learning, and the impact of government and institutional policy on the professionalization of the field of adult ESL. His research has appeared in numerous ESL and adult education publications.

INTRODUCTION

This chapter is a personal view of the field of second language learning and teaching. I address this topic not as a linguist, but as an educator. This paper attempts to show how several developments in related disciplines and in society at large may shape our profession during the next 15 years.

I begin with the premise that language educators are facing a crisis in education, including language education. At the same time, our society is facing a crisis in employment that will certainly affect our students, and a crisis in the democratic governmental process that may be unparalleled in the history of this country. These crises are forcing many of us to rethink our image of the future. In developing this statement I have often found myself stepping outside the field of second language teacher education to examine my views through the filters of my training and current work in the field of adult education. In doing so, I have tried to recognize the implications of these crises for educators in general and for second language teachers in particular. Some of my remarks will be political in nature, others constitute a critique of the status quo in teacher preparation and classroom practice, the remainder issue a call to action to improve the communicative process between classroom teachers and students, and among all of us, in the field and outside it, who are in positions to influence who, what, and how we teach in the classroom.

To incorporate the theme of politics, I have reached into the literature of radical educational thought and practice and pulled out the term "empower," an increasingly popular buzz-word in the field of adult education. Education for empowerment is the process of liberating the learner from external controls to reflect on the forces that make up the problem-solving and decision-making processes. This process often leads to a transformation in the social and political environment that will better meet individual and community needs (Heaney 1982). (See Busnardo and Braga's discussion of this topic in the context of English language teaching in Brazil, later in this volume.)

This definition necessarily implies that power relationships among individuals are omnipresent in education from the primary school to the university. Indeed, such relationships make up the very heart and soul of certain major methodological developments in language teaching. Moreover, attempts to deal with these power relationships have led to several radical departures in classroom practice over the last 10 to 15 years.

Earl Stevick developed a conceptual framework for examining the student-teacher relationship within the different contexts of various methodologies. His framework was drawn from the field of transactional analysis in which interactions (whether classroom, social, family, or business) are analyzed by means of ego states called Adult, Parent, and Child.

In Stevick's (1976:66–67) words, "The Parent ego state draws on early memories of how things were in the great, overwhelming world outside the skin of a very young child. Numerous clues indicate the moments when a person is probably under the control of his Parent ego state. Some nonverbal clues are a furrowed brow, a pointing index finger, a 'horrified' or disapproving look, sighing, and patting another person on the head. Some verbal cues are 'always' and 'never,' which are consistent with a long-standing system of conclusions which are not open to new data; evaluative words, both favorable and unfavorable; 'If I were you . . .'; 'should' and 'ought.'" Stevick is careful to point out that the Parent ego state is not a totally negative state. "To the extent that its data are consistent with present reality, it is useful in controlling and protecting the Child, and in saving the Adult from overwork."

Stevick describes the Child ego state as one that "comes out of memories about how we thought and acted before approximately age five, and particularly how we felt. There are numerous signs that the Child has been activated. Display of emotion, either pleasant or unpleasant, is one of them. Some specific nonverbal signs, in American culture at least, are rolling eyes, shrugging shoulders, downcast eyes, and raising the hand for permission to speak. Verbally, where the Parent makes sweeping and judgmental statements, the Child is likely to emphasize his lack of responsibility by using such words as 'I wish' and 'I dunno'" (pp. 67–68).

Finally, Stevick quotes from Berne (1972:11) in describing the Adult ego state as the one in which a person "appraises his environment objectively, and calculates its possibilities and probabilities on the basis of past experience." The Adult is the Self reaching out and trying to make sense of the outside world. At the latest, this ego state appears as soon as an infant is able to move about, and must thus begin to choose among alternatives. The Adult is the ego state most likely to be swept aside by the others under pressure of external events (Stevick 1976).

Stevick continues in his analysis to point out the varieties of power structures that exist both in the language classroom and in society at large. Stevick calls the teacher the "most powerful" single person in the classroom, and states that "the personal style with which he wields that authority is a principal determinant of the power structure of the class" (p. 91).

Stevick then applies this conceptual framework to a critical analysis of Audio-Lingual Methodology, Counseling-Learning/Community Language Learning, the Silent Way, and several other lesser known approaches. Remember that at the heart of this analysis are the concepts of power and the power relationship between teacher and learner. The methodologies that most successfully met Stevick's criteria were the ones that seemed to invest more power in the learner and saw teacher and learner as continually moving toward equality. The major difference between the power relationships implied in Stevick's discussion of language teaching methodology and the power relationships referred to in the literature of liberating education, or education for empowerment, lies in the essentially apolitical nature of the language teaching act and the very political nature of education for empowerment.

One of the underlying assumptions of my view of the teacher-learner relationship in any educational context, and certainly in language teaching, is the presence of a power relationship that *is* political in nature. I am certainly not alone in this perception. A growing number of educators, both within and outside of the language teaching profession, are beginning to look more closely at this politically based power relationship, to consider how it enhances or impedes learning, and to study its effect on curriculum development. Perhaps what we need is research leading to a psycho-socio-cultural-political model of second language acquisition.

A key element of empowerment is the shift in the responsibility for decision making, from what has traditionally been considered a function unique to the teacher to a role shared by the teacher and the learners. Ultimately, the process of empowering teacher and learners will dramatically shift responsibility for decision making to the learners with the aim of raising the learners' consciousness of their political, cultural, and social environment. In the process, we need to examine more closely how this changing relationship will affect the learning capacity of the learners, in our case second language learners. Also, we must examine how this changing capacity to learn may enable learners to actively transform their environment, both in and out of the classroom, rather than adapting passively to what may be perceived as unchangeable. This passive stance on the part of learners predominates in today's language classrooms.

Where should this change take place? Education has traditionally been regarded as the primary vehicle for achieving change within our society. Schools are viewed as the formal institutions of education. But over the last 10 or 15 years, institutionalized schooling has come under increasing criticism by the general public (often in the form of editorials designed to sell newspapers) for failing in its mission to educate. This view was reinforced by the publication of the report of the President's Commission on Excellence in Education, one of many reports that have described the American educational process as a disaster. In his analysis of a number of critical reports on education, Karp (1985) characterized schools in the United States as "suffering from 'stifling corruption'" (p. 73). Ironically, in the eyes of many critics, our schools have failed most noticeably to achieve a goal found in most mission statements of school systems throughout this country, namely, to teach students civic awareness of the democratic process and the right and responsibility of every citizen to participate in the decision making process, either by standing for election to governing bodies or by voting for others to represent them. Too often schools ignore or deny the participants in the process of education, the students, their right to express their views. In the language of empowerment, students become simply objects, not agents, in this academic and political process. By discouraging their participation, we are promoting a society of civic illiterates.

Because much of our work as language teaching professionals is carried out in institutions such as public schools, community colleges, and universities, we, too, are guilty of failing to promote a sense of civic literacy. By not actively involving our students in the curriculum building process, we neglect to teach them what is meant by the democratic process. I believe that student involvement should be a daily process. Handing out an evaluation form once a year or once a term and asking students to evaluate the teacher can be very intimidating, and does not constitute involvement in the democratic process.

Again, none of this is new. Critics of the educational process have long assailed schools for not promoting civic responsibility. In my view, the concept of collaborative learning is the key to understanding empowerment of learners and teachers, thereby encouraging civic responsibility. Collaboration lies at the heart of the empowerment model and is not restricted to collaboration among learners, but extends to collaboration between learners and teachers, and among teachers themselves. In addition to promoting collaborative learning, teachers should also seek to identify experiences that provide common reference points between teacher and learner, since these can lead to more productive materials development and more effective learning. What motivates someone to want to learn to read and write, for example? Smith (1984:7) characterizes this motivation as a need to be a "member of the club." In order to learn how to read, one must want to become a member of the club of readers. To do so implies some sharing of goals, and perhaps of strategies. In other words, being a member of the club involves some amount of collaboration, of seeking help from and giving help to one's peers as well as consulting one's designated teachers.

It is quite natural for youngsters to want to imitate and actually to try to teach other youngsters. Likewise, it is natural even for adult learners to seek help from and provide help to other learners in the classroom. In a not uncommonly heard anecdote, students who seemingly can't learn from the teacher appear to relate and to understand better when taught by other students.

Yet, teachers often discourage collaboration in the classroom. They do not allow students to help others who are stuck. They quiz students and then penalize those who seek help from another student. In the American value system this is called cheating. Yet, study after study has shown that students do not learn significantly from tests. Instead, they learn most successfully when allowed to work with others.

How does collaboration apply to teachers? More programs are discovering the benefits of providing opportunities for teachers to learn from each other. I am personally acquainted with several large adult-education ESL programs in northern Illinois where whole staffs are periodically brought together, where teachers teach other teachers, or where there is simply a free-flowing discussion of problems. Teachers often leave those sessions remarkably stimulated by the insights of their peers, or at least heartened by the fact that the problems they face in their classrooms are not unique to them. This raising of personal awareness and of the concept of group is the first important step toward achieving program-wide success. Unfortunately, it often happens that if teachers are brought together at all, it is only to be lectured on or informed of new policies and procedures, imposed on them and their students, that interfere with the educative process. The results are growing frustration, cynicism, and a breakdown of communication among teachers and between teachers and administrators. These negative factors are easily transferred to the classroom.

A growing body of professional literature speaks to the issues to which I am alluding. Goodlad (1983:552) has provided some disturbing but not too surprising findings regarding what really happens in the K–12 classroom. Overall, his rather pessimistic assessments include such observations as:

1. Teacher-talk is by far the dominant classroom activity. Teachers rarely encourage student-to-student dialog or provide opportunities for students to work collaboratively in small groups, to plan and set goals, or to determine alternative ways of achieving these goals.

2. The emphasis of the curricular process is on recall, not on problem solving or inquiry. Again, students work primarily alone or in large-group settings—rarely collaborating on tasks requiring division of labor, integration of effort, and shared rewards for accomplishment.

These observations are not limited only to K–12 schooling, but extend to higher education and adult education as well. Goodlad concludes his report with a series of recommendations. Among these, making greater use of peer teaching (students teaching students) is perhaps the most pertinent to this discussion.

Certainly those who work within the public school context must be familiar with the issues Goodlad addresses and realize how much they apply to their particular context. Those who spend most of their time in higher education should also be aware of these issues. I often like to think that those who have pursued the adult-education route have overcome the problems faced by the public school teacher. But many get swallowed up by traditional models of instruction that simply look upon adults as grown-up kids, and so continue to dominate the learner with teacher-talk. This phenomenon occurs frequently in community colleges, universities, and public school programs. The only glimmers of hope I see consistently are those offered by nonschool, community-based organizations that provide an alternative model more teachers and program administrators need to consider. Ironically, many of the "teachers" in these programs have had no formal training in language teaching.

In light of all this, it should not be surprising that educational leaders in some developing countries are taking a long, hard look at the effects that traditional schooling has on the education of young and old. There is increasing interest in nonformal education, that is, education received outside the formal structures of schools, in contexts that are more relevant and informal: health education and family planning, community development, literacy, vocational skills training, and many more. However, in most cases these alternatives are considered complementary rather than replacement models for formal education.

This raises the question: Where are educational programs going and how do language teachers fit in? In the March 1983 issue of *The Learning Connection,* a periodical intended primarily for adult educators, my attention was drawn to a review of *Megatrends* (1982) by John Naisbitt. This bestseller contains information of extraordinary relevance for anyone in education, at any level and in any discipline.

Naisbitt has an interesting occupation. He is paid $15,000 a year by each of many corporations to tell them what he reads in the newspapers. Over the last 12 years he has read a lot of newspapers and has found a number of trends. When a trend becomes very important, he labels it "megatrend." Megatrends are not necessarily new, but their implications for education and for our changing society are surprising, provocative, and in some cases most disturbing. The implications discussed in Naisbitt's review of current *Megatrends* were meant primarily for adult educators, but several are relevant to language learners and language teachers in the context of this discussion of empowerment. To give an idea of where Naisbitt is coming from, here is a list of his ten "megatrends:"

1. Although we continue to live in an industrial society, we have in fact changed to an economy based on the creation and distribution of information.

2. We are moving in the dual directions of high tech/high touch, matching each new technology with a compensatory human response.

3. No longer do we have the luxury of operating within an isolated, self-sufficient, national economic system; we now must acknowledge that we are part of a global economy.

4. We are restructuring from a society run by short-term considerations and rewards in favor of dealing with things in much longer-term time frames.

5. In cities and states, in small organizations and subdivisions, we have rediscovered the ability to act innovatively and to achieve results— from the bottom up.

6. We are shifting from institutional help to more self-reliance in all aspects of our lives.

7. We are discovering that the framework of representative democracy has become obsolete in an era of instantaneously shared information.

8. We are giving up our dependence on hierarchical structures in favor of informal networks.

9. More Americans are living in the South and West, leaving behind the old industrial cities of the North.

10. From a narrow either/or society with a limited range of personal choices, we are exploding into a freewheeling, multiple-option society.

For the purposes of my argument, I would like to focus on the first two of these megatrends, discussing their implications for language teachers, for students as language learners, and for the concept of empowerment.

The first megatrend has very serious implications for the educational process: "Although we continue to live in an industrial society, we have in fact changed to an economy based on the creation and distribution of information." It is interesting to note that the number-one occupation in the U.S. in terms of total numbers employed is "clerk." In 1900 it was "farmer," in mid-century it was "laborer." Today the leading occupation is "office clerk." The second largest classification is "professional." Farmers now constitute only 3% of the work force. More people are employed full time in universities than in agriculture. Just 13% of our labor force is engaged in manufacturing, and that figure is destined to decline as well. Finally, of the nine million new workers added to the labor force from 1969–76, no new jobs were created by the Fortune 1,000 largest industrial concerns. Six million new jobs were created by small businesses, and in fact, today's entrepreneurs are creating new businesses to the tune of 600,000 a year. This figure represents six times as many new businesses as were created 30 years ago. The other three million new jobs were created by local and state, but not federal, government.

Since a recent trend in language instruction involves the study and teaching of language in the workplace, it seems that we must readjust our view of the employability of many of our students. The many linguistic minority students who continue to prepare for jobs in heavy industry and manufacturing will continue to suffer the frustration of unemployment as that sector of the U.S. economy declines. Therefore, our focus might be better placed on building their basic literacy competencies in preparation for work in service industries. A walk through the publisher's exhibits at any recent TESOL convention will confirm that there is a movement toward high technology within the field. However, it is still unclear whether computers are being used by programs and curriculum designers as tools to replace teachers in the instructional program, or whether computers are being introduced as instructional aids for students, with part of the instruction including the use of computers in the workplace and in the home.

One especially disturbing aspect of this trend is that the general level of basic competencies possessed by high school graduates in the United States has been steadily decreasing. This fact has prompted Naisbitt to observe that "the generation graduating from high school today is the first generation in American history to graduate less skilled than its parents" (p. 31).

As the schools turn out increasingly unskilled learners, more corporations are deciding to enter the education business. Some 300 of the nation's largest companies operate remedial courses in basic math and English for entry-level workers. Just when offices are demanding more highly skilled workers, to operate word-processing machines, for example, what they are finding are graduates who would have a hard time qualifying for jobs that are already technologically obsolete. I have also observed in higher education that an increasing number of the students enrolling in high-tech disciplines are not Americans, but foreign-born. Often, the foreign-born student who lacks adequate oral skills preparation is superior in those basic literacy and computation competencies required to operate in a high-tech industry. Although computer use in public education is still in its infancy, schools around the nation are beginning to realize that in the information society, the two required languages will be English and computer.

But for those who fear a return to an overwhelming reliance on machines in the classroom, reminiscent of the audio-lingual era, there is still hope, for Naisbitt observes that with the growth of high-tech industry comes the growth of high-touch work. This combination of high tech and high touch is Naisbitt's second megatrend. There will still be a need for people to work together, and to convene at conferences and workshops. In terms of language teaching and in light of Naisbitt's observations, it is understandable that methodologies such as Community Language Learning, Silent Way, and Total Physical Response have gained in popularity within a society that seeks high touch.

If these trends are indeed accurate descriptions of where society is going, then teachers had better reflect on how students are being helped to prepare for what appears to be a less industrialized and more computerized society. Helping students to become aware of and to acquire these necessary skills will enable them better to control their own future. This self-control is central to the issue of empowerment. Given the rising number of functional illiterates in this country among both native and non-native English speakers, the growing reliance on information, and the increasing feasibility of instantaneously transmitting information to those who have access, it seems that we are creating another case of the "have's" and "have-nots," of those who have the power to make decisions and of those who must simply submit to the imposition of those decisions. Language is at the center of this issue of who controls information. And that is why the language teachers' role is so vital in an information society.

This brings me to what I have labeled the "Call to Action." Again, I want to stress that what has been reported so far are largely personal reflections based on my perceptions of the profession and other people's perceptions of the larger society. My hypothesis is that language teaching is a political process that is largely exploited by the controllers, the institutions in which we operate. This is manifested in their determination of curricular content, scheduling of classes, and promotion of certain classroom practices without regard for the learners' needs and goals. Teachers and students alike must take control over what is being taught and learned by engaging more actively in this decision-making process.

It is urgent that teacher training programs prepare teachers better to cope with the political realities of the educational process. Likewise, teachers must prepare learners to deal with the political and social realities of the greater society in which they hope to participate. I am encouraged by recent developments in language teaching methodology that attempt to shift the responsibility of learning from teacher to learner. This is a preliminary and most necessary step in the process of involving learners actively in learning. This process is best promoted through collaborative, not competitive, efforts by teachers and learners to identify and to achieve common goals. Rather than simply focusing learners' attention on features of language, it implies engaging them in the reflective process of choosing what language they want and need to learn. It may also mean identifying problems that need to be addressed in the larger community outside the classroom, such as adequate education, improved health care, better housing, fire and police protection, or more responsive government. This raising of consciousness may be seen as a threat by those who possess control over these institutions, but the democratic process should ensure that all students have a voice in the decision-making process.

Finally, the whole point of encouraging collaborative efforts among students and teachers and among teachers themselves is to improve communication. This collaboration need not be limited to the classroom teacher and student. After all, that is why we educators have had so little impact on the political process that affects us daily. We must also seek out and communicate with legislators, professional organizations, and community leaders, for true empowerment of learners and teachers will only come through the collaborative efforts of all of us.

REFERENCES

Berne, Eric. 1972. *What Do You Say after You Say Hello?* New York: Bantam.

Goodlad, John I. 1983. "A Study of Schooling: Some Implications for School Improvement." *Kappan* 64 (8):552–558.

Heaney, Thomas W. 1982. *Adult Learning for Empowerment: Toward a Theory of Liberatory Education.* Reston, Virginia: Latino Institute, Research Division.

Karp, Walter. 1985. "Why Johnny Can't Think: The Politics of Bad Schooling." *Harper's* 270 (1621):69–73.

The Learning Connection. 1983. 4 (2):4, 15.

Naisbitt, John. 1982. *Megatrends: Ten New Directions Transforming Our Lives.* New York: Warner Books.

Smith, Frank. 1984. "The Promise and Threat of Microcomputers for Language Learners." In Jean Handscombe, Richard A. Orem, and Barry P. Taylor (eds.), *On TESOL '83.* Washington, D.C.: TESOL.

Stevick, Earl W. 1976. *Memory, Meaning, and Method: Some Psychological Perspectives on Language Learning.* Rowley, Massachusetts: Newbury House.

Chapter 2

Language and Power: On the Necessity of Rethinking English Language Pedagogy in Brazil

JoAnne Busnardo
Denise B. Braga

JoAnne Busnardo is a member of the faculty at the Institute of Language Study, State University of Campinas, in Campinas, São Paulo, Brazil, where she teaches English and Applied Linguistics. She has published extensively on the teaching of reading in both Portuguese and English, and is currently engaged in research on reading and cross-cultural communication in language teaching.

Denise B. Braga teaches English at the Institute of Language Study, State University of Campinas, in Campinas, São Paulo, Brazil. Among her publications are articles on the teaching of reading in Portuguese. Her present research focus is reading comprehension and retention in school-aged children.

INTRODUCTION

What justification is there for the teaching of foreign languages, and of English in particular, in a country with vast educational and native-language literacy problems? Reflecting on our own experience as professors of English at one of the major Brazilian universities, we have attempted to formulate an answer to this question. We take into consideration certain broad issues that some may judge better left to sociology or educational philosophy, but that we have come to see as central to any serious reflection on the role of foreign language teaching and learning in countries such as Brazil. In this reflection on the nature and implications of English language teaching within a concrete Third World context, our starting point is a complex of educational principles that we believe complement and support certain recent views on the nature of language, language acquisition and use, and the role of language in society.

Informing all of our views on language pedagogy is the basic concept that language acquisition does not occur in a vacuum. To learn a language implies contact with the referential contents and cultural values characteristic of the people who use that language. It implies equally the negotiation of meaning and the creation of interpretations within concrete sociocultural contexts, processes in which the continuous comparison between native-culture and target-culture experiences is fundamental. In creating and evaluating meaning in English, Brazilian undergraduates must often deal with their own attitudes toward this very prestigious foreign language, since the hegemony of English is part of the concrete context in which they learn and use English.

One of the most common arguments for teaching English in Third-World countries has to do with the concept of that language as the necessary instrument of international communication. In particular, Reading for Special Purposes is often presented as the only possible antidote to alienated teaching and learning, because it permits access to badly needed information in the areas of modern science, technology, and the humanities. This study on the nature of English language pedagogy in Brazil grew out of our own experience with, and critical assessment of, ESP. Our conviction that this methodology was often inadequate to the needs of undergraduates and resulted in passive reception of information rather than in "international communication" triggered our search for a language teaching methodology that would promote critical thinking through cross-cultural contrast and comparison. In other words, we were seeking a language teaching methodology that would promote communication in a genuine sense.

Our general dissatisfaction with most prefabricated language teaching materials, discussed in detail in this chapter, led us to the conclusion that the solution to many of our problems lies not in them, but in teachers with a sound understanding of the social functions of language, and knowledge of recent developments in psycholinguistics and the sociology of language. To illustrate and defend this position, we begin our discussion with a personal account of the language learning and teaching situation in which we are involved as professionals: a situation we characterize as "dominant foreign language learning" that must be analyzed in the context of language and power. Using this reflection on the power function of language and the educational implications of foreign language teaching as a starting point, we examine what we see as the contribution of prefabricated materials in general, and imported materials in particular, to an already difficult situation. We then go on to examine some local solutions that have been proposed for the teaching of English.

Finally, we outline a proposal for the teaching of English at the university level in Brazil, based on three key principles. First, language is never acquired in a vacuum, and the solution to many of the problems associated with the teaching and learning of English in Brazil depends upon the development in both teachers and students of a critical and comparative understanding of the target culture—this is, in fact, one of the most urgent "needs" to be met. Secondly, language teachers must take themselves seriously as educators in the Brazilian context, and to this end they should not be naive to the social and educational consequences of certain language teaching materials and methodologies. Thirdly, one of the best justifications for the teaching and learning of foreign languages is the development of sensitivity, not only to the processes and pains of language acquisition and use, but above all to the understanding and interpretation of human differences, essential to the mature evaluation of one's own language and culture.

LANGUAGE AND POWER: ENGLISH AND ENGLISH TEACHING IN BRAZIL

Many students and teachers in Brazil perceive the knowledge of English to be somehow essential for general scientific and technological development, or even for purposes of individual advancement through employment in multinational firms. At the same time, they cannot ignore the fact that Brazilian culture often seems relegated to a subordinate status in the present scheme of things. Many believe that a progressive decharacterization of national values and aspirations is linked to a political and economic dominance concretized in the hegemony of the English language. This complex situation has led some of us to question the role of our profession within the Brazilian context. Are we indirectly contributing to a situation of dominance and dependence when we teach the English language? Or are we promoting development and independence by giving access to information in the fields of science, technology and the humanities?

This description of the conflict experienced by both students and teachers of English is certainly simplistic; one must ask, for example, what is *meant* by development, modernization, and the like. Nevertheless, it does capture the general outlines of an "existential crisis" not uncommon in our profession, especially in our concrete historical circumstances. This conflict is at the root of the extreme positions of idealization and radical rejection of target language and target culture frequently assumed by learners and even teachers of the English language. Such positions are generated in reaction to the status of English as a language of prestige in Brazil today. The language that is the object of our teaching and research has become a foreign status symbol, a magic talisman believed to confer status even on those who, pathetically, have little, and an important instrument in the selling of an idealized "American way of life" completely absurd and out of place in the Brazilian context.[1] This idealized image, created and transmitted by the mass media, is very often appropriated and explored by the proliferating private schools of English. In reaction to this situation, and in particular to the uncritical perception of the target culture that it encourages, many Brazilians end up by rejecting altogether the teaching and learning of English. We believe this rejection of English as an object of study, although entirely comprehensible, is a naive reaction to the perceived hegemony of English in the world today.

We cannot ignore English, for this would imply, among other things, ignoring the vast bibliography published in English, including translations from other languages. It would also imply an increased Brazilian fragility vis-a-vis Anglo-American dominance, for one cannot be critical of, or even dialogue with, that which one ignores. Unfortunately, our experience as teachers of English suggests that extreme positions, in the form either of idealization or of rejection of the target language, are becoming increasingly common. Only a more profound sociolinguistic analysis of the language learning and teaching situation in which we are involved can create an English language pedagogy that does not depend upon, nor encourage the formation of, superficial, ingenuous and idealized images of Anglo-American culture and know-how. Such an analysis is urgently important in situations like our own, in which the target language is perceived as somehow "dominant."

We can only sketch here some lines of thought which, it seems to us, should be included in any analysis of the situation described above. First of all, languages are not limited to their referential function. They have also a power function in that they communicate to the hearers the position that the speakers either occupy or think they occupy in the society in which they live. As Gnerre has observed:

> ". . . not all members of a society have access to all varieties of the language spoken, and much less to all referential contents. Only some of the members of complex societies, for example, have access to the 'cultured' or 'standard' variety, considered generally to be 'the language,' associated typically with contents of prestige. . . . A linguistic variety 'is worth' what its speakers 'are worth' in their society, that is, it reflects the power and authority which they possess in economic and social relations. This affirmation is valid, obviously, in 'internal' terms, when we confront varieties of the same language, and it is valid in 'external' terms, due to the prestige of languages internationally. There was a time when French occupied the highest position in the international scale of values; after that, it was the turn of English to ascend" (1985:4, our translation).

These comments furnish us with several concepts important for any analysis of the situation of English in Brazil, and consequently for language pedagogy in that context. The basic questions seem to be the following: How do we, teachers and students, relate to English as a language of power? How do we understand the opposite poles of idealization and rejection?

If a foreign language reflects the power of those who speak it, and if knowledge of the language is perceived as access to that power, it is easy to understand why some Brazilians would be highly motivated to study and even to teach English. The nature of this motivation becomes even clearer when we recall the parallel of "internal" and "external" dominance referred to by Gnerre. Just as a certain international reality explains the idealization of target language and culture by Brazilian elites, and their often uncritical adoption of foreign models, so the internal Brazilian reality explains a superficially high motivation to learn English among persons in lower socioeconomic brackets whose chances of ever using the English language are in fact very small. In both elites and non-elites, we have a curiously similar desire for status and power together with a lack of perception of the facts of dominance. If one adopts this line of analysis, hostility towards English seems inevitable among those who, regardless of their particular political persuasion, wish to contest a general pattern of dominance. And so we return to one of the first questions posed in this paper. Given this historical context of constant alienation and hostility, why teach English in Brazil?

We believe that arguments *can* be made for teaching English in this context, and that the creation of a more productive attitude depends on our capacity and willingness to rethink both language pedagogy and the status of English in Brazil. Furthermore, we believe that the teaching of English imposes itself, not in spite of the hegemony of English, but because of that very hegemony. As long as the order of things remains as it is, a critical pedagogy of the English language will be imperative. Those of us who teach at the university level must ask ourselves what kind of pedagogy is appropriate for our students, themselves an elite in Brazil. We would like to suggest that the language classroom must become a space for critical reflection, and that this is especially important for university students, who at every turn run great risks of becoming mere appliers and reproducers of foreign models. The type of critical reflection we have in mind is in the (Brazilian) tradition of Paulo Freire, whose theories we believe to be just as pertinent to dominant foreign language learning as they are to other pedagogical situations in contexts of dominance. Freire has pointed to critical reflection as an integral part of "problem-posing education," in which creative, active subjects in concrete historical circumstances transform reality through interaction and dialogic processes. In other words, critical reflection is an antidote to alienation. Unfortunately, language pedagogy based on prefabricated materials has often either contributed directly to alienation or at best made critical reflection almost impossible in the language classroom.

IMPORTED AND NATIVE
MATERIALS AND METHODOLOGIES

It is our contention that the widespread, uncritical adoption of imported language teaching materials and methodologies is exacerbating the difficult situation described above. In a sense, all prefabricated materials, regardless of their origin, are attempts to crystallize and simplify the complex and extremely variable language learning process. We do not deny the attraction that such prefabricated materials exert on language teachers. They facilitate our task enormously, and we all feel a very great temptation to return to them, after having experienced the hard work and frustration that often accompany language teaching without their support. For teachers abroad who are not native speakers, they are hard to resist: they relieve the insecurities we feel regarding our competence in the language, they plan our classes for us, some of them seem to work. Why not take advantage of them? We believe that, in spite of the hard work and frustration involved, it is worthwhile to try to get along without them, or at least to adopt only those that permit the development of critical reflection in the classroom. It is worthwhile because, in the long run, it will contribute to the development of independent, active, critical teachers and students who are true participants in a process, and this is fundamental to the type of language learning situation we advocate.

The utilization of *imported* prefabricated materials, be they structuralist or functionalist, is doubly problematic, simply because course content is then predetermined abroad, without consideration of all the implications for the situation we have named "dominant foreign language learning." In our view, teachers have the responsibility of evaluating all materials and methodologies within this context. This evaluation goes beyond the narrow view of teachers as mere "language trainers" and presupposes the wider perspective of "educators within the Brazilian context."[2] The observations that follow are intended above all to illustrate the ways in which different types of language teaching materials that suggest different underlying methodological principles and presume different concepts of language and language acquisition, often obstruct equally any kind of critical reflection in the classroom. In other words, we do not intend at this point to engage in the standard debate on structuralism versus functionalism, but wish rather to reflect on the problems that structuralist, functionalist, and other types of imported materials pose for our concept of language pedagogy.

One of the first problems we would like to discuss involves the fragmentation of the target language for pedagogical purposes that is characteristic of so many commercial language teaching methods. One hears frequently the argument that such fragmentation is inevitable, because "one cannot teach all of the language at once." Although some sort of selection and organization of course content is obviously necessary, it is imperative for the development of critical reflection in the language classroom that this organization be realized at the level of cohesive, coherent *texts* in the target language. When the unit of organization is at a lower level—language structure in many audio-lingual methods, speech acts in many functionalist methods—meaning itself is fragmented and trivialized, and mature reflection and even normal language-acquisition processes such as hypothesis-formulation are effectively blocked. We emphasize that this is the case not only for methods based on structuralist principles, but also for those functionalist methods in which communicative function is conceived as a simple speech act conventionally realized in certain structures of the target language. In both cases, the essential task of the student is the same: to manipulate and, it is hoped, to incorporate one by one a series of *items*, whose assimilation may be verified at any point in time by an evaluation of competence. In other words, instruction concentrates on individual structures, or on individual acts like greeting, apologizing, asking directions, etc., relying on the students' ability to apply this accumulated knowledge in some future opportunity for "real communication." While this concentration on single, predetermined items is one of the most generalized and accepted solutions to the problem of teaching oral production in a foreign language, it is not evident that students ever get beyond the memorization of a list of structural or functional items.

In a sense, then, these types of imported materials often imply what Freire has called a "banking" concept of education, in which "the scope of action allowed to the students extends only as far as receiving, filing, and storing the deposits." Freire observes that in this type of education students have only the opportunity "to become collectors or cataloguers of the things they store. . . . The more they work at storing the deposits entrusted to them, the less they develop the critical consciousness which would result from their intervention in the world as transformers of that world. The more completely they accept the passive role imposed on them, the more they tend simply to adapt to the world as it is and to the fragmented view of reality deposited in them" (1972: 58–60). We would like to point out that these observations are especially relevant to Third World English language pedagogy, which depends on imported materials.

If imported structuralist materials are to be condemned because they imply a view of language and language acquisition in which the human subject as active acquirer, user, and communicator is simply not considered, we believe that the implications of certain imported functionalist materials are even more sinister. For, although it is true that the learner implied by structuralist materials is extremely passive, the functionalist theories of language as use, as human action, which seem to defend the centrality of the learner in language acquisition, mask the fact that the imposition of language functions via imported functionalist materials violates the rights of learners to participate in topic and need definition.

One may contend that many such methods are based on a "common universal core" of language functions that any student in any country of the world would have to master in order to gain reasonable competence in English. However, we question the validity of this concept of language learning, since it minimizes cultural peculiarities and ignores the concrete needs of learners that functionalism supposedly advocates. It is our experience that "common core functions" contribute to the abstraction of course content, alienating concrete learners in concrete contexts. In both structuralist and common-core functionalist materials, the language tends to be fragmented and decontextualized. Certain "situational" methods have attempted to solve these problems through verisimilitude of situation and discourse. On closer examination of such materials, however, one discovers that the language is often presented in situations that are basically very attractive, but virtually unattainable for the majority of Brazilian young people. Thus, we examine method after method based on situations in which young foreigners travel, work, study, and enjoy leisure in the United States and England, in scenes that contain much real detail, but that can only be understood in the actual Brazilian context as a kind of manipulation of patterns already idealized by many Brazilians. In other words, whereas structuralist and "common-core" functionalist materials may alienate learners because they lack concrete, relevant content, "situational" materials often reinforce tendencies already present in the society to idealize the target culture. We also believe all three types of materials block the perception, action and participation of the subject-learner at various levels.

In general, Brazilian attempts at remedying the problems posed by foreign materials have proposed two types of solutions. The first, preoccupied above all with the reinforcement of Brazilian cultural identity through locally created language teaching materials, has tried to bypass what is viewed as an invading foreign culture, choosing instead the vehicle of Brazilian themes, characters and cultural contexts to present the English language. The second focuses on problems of needs analysis within the Brazilian context.

The first type of solution, often proposed for a younger or more general public, is especially concerned with the problem of alienation from Brazilian reality, and the concomitant idealization of target culture. It is an innovative solution, not only because of its implicit position against cultural colonialism via language training, but also because of its utilization of the subject-learner's prior discourse and cultural knowledge in the acquisition process. Nevertheless, we believe that this type of locally produced material may have a counterproductive effect. In the first place, it is not clear, from the point of view of needs analysis, why a Brazilian of any age should, for example, read Brazilian folktales in English.[3] More importantly, this type of material masks the fact that language is not learned in a sociolinguistic vacuum. The presentation of traditional Brazilian figures speaking English seems to suggest that language is neutral, acultural, when in fact English in Brazil is laden with sociolinguistic implications. Our task as language teaching professionals should be to unmask these implications, not to cover them up. Indeed, we have a responsibility to make explicit the language/culture connection.

The second type of local solution to the impasse created by imported materials was inspired by the English for Specific Purposes approach. At the university level, especially, this approach has taken the form of various types of reading instruction to enable students to access bibliographies in their areas of academic interest. In contrast to commercial, functionalist materials imported from abroad, texts for Instrumental English (as it is often labelled) promise to "individualize" learning to a great degree, since they are selected to meet specific academic needs; moreover, the emphasis often laid on the importance of students' prior discourse and encyclopaedic knowledge in the formulation of reading hypotheses suggests that such "global" approaches to foreign language comprehension represent a truly subject-centered functionalism. In a sense, this seems to answer the problems associated with the "banking concept" of language learning, and its passive, accumulating subject-learner. Although that may be true to a great extent, we believe that foreign language reading instruction, especially of the "instrumental" type, could benefit from a sociolinguistic analysis of the status of English in Brazil and its relationship to the status of Anglo-American technological and scientific know-how.

Gnerre (1978) has observed that languages of prestige, whether standard dialects or dominant foreign languages, represent status and access to "referential contents of prestige," and that these languages and contents of prestige are very closely associated with written language. This sociolinguistic notion can surely contribute to a more profound understanding of our students' fragility *vis-à-vis* written texts in English: to the undergraduate's usual credulity concerning written language in general, we have added the overwhelming attraction and prestige of English. This fragility is exacerbated by the erroneous belief that science and technology are somehow "universal" or "neutral." As Alptekin (1974:57) points out in a very perceptive analysis that seems to coincide perfectly with what we have observed in Brazil, "developing countries exposed to the omnipotent forces of image-making and consciousness-shaping of the Anglo-American communications technology" are very often simultaneously victims of the belief that technology "provides the grounds for a cultural and ideological neutrality on which the acquisition and use of English can be promoted rather easily." In fact, technology is "laden with norms and values often reflecting the ideological constraints and cultural priorities of the Anglo-American world." Reading teachers must be conscious of the fact that reading is not simply access to, and absorption of, "neutral" information. To assume the role of educator in the broad sense, one must be aware of the sociolinguistic status of English and of the fact that texts in any given language transmit cultural and ideological assumptions. It is our belief that a sociolinguisitic perspective is urgently necessary in our particular context, and that such a perspective would lead to a reformulation of foreign language reading instruction of the "instrumental" type. Above all, it would lead us to rethink the concept of student *needs*, so closely associated with problems of learner attitude and motivation.

Recent studies carried out at the Universidade Estadual de Campinas suggest that learner needs and attitudes with regard to foreign language reading are not as static as traditional "needs analyses for specific purposes" would seem to imply.[4] We have discovered that needs must be seen as dynamic, changing, eminently negotiable; that students' ambiguous attitudes towards the language, even within the framework of Instrumental English, are to be expected. But more importantly, we have come to understand that the involvement of the subject-learner cannot be advocated at the level of prior discourse and encyclopaedic ("area") knowledge without consideration of cultural identity and values; indeed, it was precisely as we observed our students omitting themselves as Brazilians that we came to recognize the seriousness of our situation.

Our most urgent problem thus arises from the lack of a *status of equivalence* between learners and target culture.[5] However, this lack of a status of equivalence leads not only to poor acquisition due to social and psychological distance (Schumann 1978; Alptekin 1974, 1981), but also to the even greater problem of cultural alienation, in the form of the Brazilian's uncritical identification with and reproduction of the prestigious "other." In fact, we have come to the point of asking ourselves whether the most alienated are not at times the best "acquirers" of English (Sabinson 1983). At any rate, our priorities as educators within the Brazilian context seem clear: first of all, the rejection (or non-naive use) of language teaching materials that mask the sociolinguistic implications of the status of English; secondly, the development of a language pedagogy in which questions of cultural identity and values are posed openly, as a central point of reflection.

TOWARDS A CRITICAL/COMPARATIVE UNDERSTANDING OF THE FOREIGN LANGUAGE AND CULTURE

We can only sketch briefly here some of the directions that we believe English language pedagogy should take at this moment. First of all, even though acquisition may be very possible in situations in which the language learner overidentifies with a dominant foreign culture, it is our position that a need exists in our context to rethink language pedagogy in terms of a desired status of equivalence. This conviction has led us to draw inspiration from the educational philosophy of Freire, on the one hand, and from interactional psycho- and sociolinguistics on the other. What these theories have in common is a central preoccupation with the activity of the human subject and his or her interaction with other subjects in the acquisition and use of both linguistic and nonlinguistic knowledge. Specifically, interactional psycho- and sociolinguistics contribute to our understanding of how all types of language acquisition involve necessarily active subjects in interactive contexts of use, and how language use involves necessarily sociocultural presuppositions and values, together with questions of social identity and social roles. Such theoretical foundations are crucial for those who opt to promote a status of equivalence. Like the work in psycho- and sociolinguistics mentioned above, the educational philosophy of Freire takes as axiomatic the point that the acquisition and use of knowledge involve interaction among active subjects. However, the value of Freire's work for our proposal lies, above all, in the fact that it contains concrete suggestions for promoting "discourse among equivalent subjects" where it does not exist. (See Orem, this volume, for a related discussion.)

It is our belief that this promotion of discourse among equivalent subjects should be one of the central concerns of English language pedagogy in Brazil. In the words of Freire, our ideal should be to move from the "antidialogic" situation which now exists, to a "dialogic" situation. By this we mean, of course, not only a dialogic situation in the classroom, but also *vis-à-vis* the target culture and the objects it produces, such as written texts. We believe that this move from an "antidialogic" to a "dialogic" situation will be facilitated by procedures that attempt to *demythologize* the target language and culture. To demythologize is to contest the extreme idealization of the target culture present in Brazilian society; this is perhaps the single most important step in the development of genuine cultural contact and dialogue. Teachers should be prepared to transmit a more realistic picture of the target culture, including perceived shortcomings and contradictions; students should be constantly called upon to contribute with their own past knowledge and experience to the formulation of interpretations and the evaluation of target culture experiences, stereotypes, and values. It is our experience that these educational objectives cannot be attained via traditional language teaching methodologies and most prefabricated materials.

To demythologize target language and culture, to go beyond the fragmentation of language, the trivialization of meaning, and the imposition of content inherent in most prefabricated materials, two principles recommend themselves:

1. Thematic Organization of English Courses

Work in grammar and language function should be dependent on what Freire calls "the investigation of meaningful thematics with students."[6] The themes should not be imposed upon students, but worked out with them. This search for thematic units of interest to both students and teachers is fundamental to what Freire refers to as "problem-solving education," in which teacher-student and student-teacher combine their cognitions of the same object, and in which investigation is based on reciprocity of action. Thematic organization is important both for reasons of language acquisition and for the attainment of the educational objectives proposed here. From the point of view of language acquisition, it is our experience that units consisting of several types of authentic written text, organized around themes that genuinely engage student interest, allow the natural development of a satisfactory linguistic repertoire in the target language. This procedure may be complemented by work on grammar in context at several stages. From the point of educational objectives, thematic investigation and organization are especially important in the creation of more "dialogic" classroom interaction and cultural contact, simply because students must no longer remain passive receivers of fragmented, predetermined, and irrelevant content. Envisaged as one possible solution to the problems of foreign language communicative needs in situations of dominance, *thematics* should precede narrowly functionalist-utilitarian concerns in language courses, even for students of exact sciences. It is often through the investigation of significant themes, in dialogue with other students and the teacher, and in texts in *both* Portuguese and English, that the students begin to discover authentic needs and interests.

2. Questioning and Comparison: Strategies That Make Evident Cultural and Ideological Presupposition

The basic question, "Is it so?", is one that students must learn to direct at the interpreters of Anglo-American culture. It is also one that teachers, be they native speakers of English or of Portuguese, have the right and responsibility to direct at students engaged in the interpretation of Brazilian and non-Brazilian realities. The foreign language classroom, it seems to us, should become a space that fosters reflection in a broad, humanist sense. To demythologize is to encourage students to question, to evaluate, and to accept or reject target-language solutions and experiences on Brazilian terms.

One of the most efficient strategies for making explicit cultural and ideological presupposition is comparison: to compare native and target languages and cultures is to prepare the way for the critical reflection necessary for any kind of true autonomy *vis-à-vis* the target culture. It is this comparative perspective that also allows one to discern more clearly the profile of one's own culture, its contradictions and shortcomings, as well as its originality. An important resource for the development of self-perception, comparison leads eventually to a more mature assessment of all human culture. As Freire points out, students presented with "pictures of reality unfamiliar to them" could "compare this reality with their own and discover the limitation of each." This possibility, however, depends crucially on the students not being "in a state of submersion" with respect to their own reality (1972: 107). In other words, foreign language instruction, even of the kind we are advocating, cannot presume to take the place of a general education for critical consciousness with its aim of a profound understanding of Brazilian reality. Nevertheless, we are convinced that foreign language pedagogy *can* make an important contribution to this general educational aim, if it will only make serious comparative work a central part of methodology.

For our particular language learning situation—formal, non-immersion language instruction—work with written texts seems to be one of the most efficient and economical ways of bringing students into contact with the target language and culture in an active, critical way. We understand reading to be an interactive process in which an active subject, making use of all kinds of prior knowledge, interacts with texts in the construction of interpretations and the generation of new knowledge and experience.[7] In this interaction the active, knowing subject must also be seen as a social subject with a sociocultural identity, beliefs, and values. Nevertheless, most ESP reading methodologies do not make this a central concern, and many seem to reflect an underlying concept of language in which communication is reduced to the recuperation of information. In situations of cultural asymmetry, it is essential to go far beyond this concept, and emphasize the social aspects of reader/text interaction. Comparative work can make this side of reader activity explicit to the student. Prior investigation of themes in Portuguese prepares the student to take a more active part in the evaluation of cultural and ideological differences. This work is continued at a later stage through the comparison of texts in English and Portuguese in the same thematic field; it is our experience that the comparison of texts in the two languages constitutes excellent training in the art of "dialoguing" with foreign language texts.[8] Many other types of comparative work could be mentioned. Among them are two that seem particularly well-suited to the development of critical/comparative understanding: the use in the classroom of English language newspaper clippings relating Brazilian current events with which the students are acquainted; and the use of translation in the study of cultural and ideological presupposition. In the latter type of work, the comparison of English translations of Brazilian works with the Portuguese originals permits the examination of translators' interpretations in terms of cultural and ideological assumptions.[9]

It is our hope that through the various types of procedures discussed above students will become more critical in their reading, that they will question foreign language texts on the basis of their Brazilian experience, and that the fundamental question, "Is it so?", will become second nature to them. We hope above all to make clear to our students that the reader who reads creatively, who does not merely reproduce and passively absorb but who synthesizes new insights, knowledge, and solutions from interaction with a text, must be involved with the text not only on the cognitive level but on the social level as well. In contexts of dominance, the involvement of social identity in the interpretation of the foreign culture is especially crucial if we wish to avoid the double bind of alienation and naive rejection. One can neither idealize nor ignore "dominant foreign cultures." Nevertheless, the dilemma of many students, and even teachers, with respect to English language training still remains very real. It should not surprise us that this dilemma involves complex attitudes of attraction and repulsion. We remain convinced that the only possible solution lies in a profound knowledge of the prestigious other, and an even more profound self-knowledge.

CONCLUSION

We have presented our case in favor of an English language pedagogy based on the development of critical reflection. To the question "What is the most functional English for Brazil?" we wish to reply, "That which responds to the broadest needs, defined in terms of the concrete Brazilian context." These needs cannot be met through the accumulation of English structures and functions alone. The central, urgent need vis-à-vis English language and culture is for a process of critical reflection, which we believe may be facilitated through critical/comparative work of various sorts.

One of our main concerns as university teachers of English is to encourage our students in their questioning of the target culture. We are also fully conscious of the impact of the *foreign monolingualism* represented by English in Brazil, so perceptively described by Ballalai.[10] It is clear to us that any proposal that seeks to defend national autonomy and freedom of option vis-à-vis foreign models and access to foreign information must take a position in favor of the pluralization of language study. However, we should point out that pluralization alone cannot be expected to provide the ultimate solution to the problems discussed here. Although it would perhaps facilitate access to non-Anglo-American models and patterns of thought, there is no guarantee that it would put an end to the cultural colonialism that has for so long been part of Brazilian reality. For this reason, we believe that *all* language pedagogy should attempt to develop in students a critical perception of both Brazilian and foreign realities.

Finally, it is important to point out that for those of us who are native American teachers of English in Brazil, this proposal in no way implies uncritical self-denigration. Rather, it implies the rejection of aggressive ethnocentricity. Furthermore, it implies a certain vision of our own culture. Above all, it implies an ultimate belief in the possibility of communication without dominance.

NOTES

1. The selling of English through an appeal to status is a constant in Brazil, where it is becoming more and more common for the proliferating private English language schools to make reference to "coming up in life" in their commercial propaganda. We are personally acquainted with several examples of parents who are willing to spend a good part of their minimum wage on English language training for their children. Prospective English language learners, however, are not always naive with respect to the status of English; Scaramucci (mimeo) cites examples of Brazilian university students who consider English to be "bitter medicine," "um mal necessário," ("a necessary evil.") The magazine VEJA (October 19, 1983) makes reference to a high school student determined to spend precious wages on an English course because: "Tudo mundo diz que os americanos estão tomando conta de tudo. Eu, pelo menos, eles vão ter que dobrar no papo," ("Everybody says that the Americans are taking over everything. With me they'll have a hard time, because they'll have to convince me verbally.") (25).

2. We would like to recognize here our debt to our colleague Lígia Fonseca Ferreira, whose pioneering essay "Ensino de línguas estrangeiras e identidade cultural" makes explicit the necessity of going beyond mere "language training" to a broader concept of "education in the Brazilian context."

3. We have in mind here several methods for teaching English to Brazilians developed by Instituto de Idiomas Yázigi, whose apparent objective is to reinforce Brazilian cultural identify (see Zelio 1982).

4. On the concept of need negotiation, see Otoni 1983. On the complex problem of motivation and attitudes in Brazilian undergraduates, see Scaramucci 1983.

5. According to Schumann's "Acculturation Model" for language acquisition, poor language learning can be expected in situations in which the target language is dominant with respect to the language learner. Alptekin, in his extension of Schumann's model, observes: "Given the massive exposure of the Third World to the institutions and patterns of the Anglo-American system, the *status of equivalence*, which is one of the vital parameters of a successful language learning situation, is superseded by one of cultural and ideological dominance" (54). Alptekin goes on to suggest that "true dialogue" with the target culture could solve many of the problems of poor language learning in such contexts. However, he does not touch on the fact that most concerns us here: identification with the dominant culture may actually take place in situations of "nonequivalence" in Third World contexts.

6. We would like to point out that two of the "generative themes" that Freire considers to be "central to our age," *dominance* and *nature-and-culture,* are very pertinent to foreign language reading in Brazil. Seen against the background of foreign language reading in a context of dominance, work with these themes suggests that man, as an active, transforming, autonomous subject, has a right to intervene as a social being in the reading of text (and the world), creating something new: new knowledge, new perceptions, new solutions.

7. Much of our own work at UNICAMP has concentrated up to now on the relationship between area and discourse knowledge and the development of reading competence in foreign languages. (See Galves and Busnardo 1983, Busnardo and Galves 1983, and Busnardo and Moraes 1983.)

8. One type of comparative work is that which is carried out on the level of language use and discourse structure by moving from native to foreign discourse (both oral and written texts). For the theory and practice of "comparative discourse," see Gumperz 1982 and Moirand 1982. It is our belief that such approaches should be complemented on the level of cultural and ideological content.

9. This type of work has been carried out by Eric Sabinson with students of language and literature at the Universidade Estadual de Campinas. It is based on the fact that translations manifest the cultural and ideological "filters" of translators.

10. Roberto Ballalai suggests in his perceptive analysis of *foreign monolingualism* in Brazil that a solution to the problems of foreign language pedagogy may be sought in the *pluralization of language study* combined with the use of written texts, in other words, access to information in different languages. We agree entirely with his analysis, but insist that it is only a partial solution to the more general problem of cultural colonialism.

REFERENCES

Alptekin, Cem. 1974. "Cultural Dominance and EFL." *Canadian Modern Language Review* 39(1):56–62.

———. 1981. "Sociopsychological and Pedagogical Considerations in L2 Acquisition." *TESOL Quarterly* 15(3): 275–284.

Ballalai, Roberto. 1982. "Línguas estrangeiras e ideologia." In R. Nasr et al. (eds.). *Foreign Language Teaching and Cultural Identity.* São Paulo/Brussels: Instituto de Idiomas Yázigi/AIMAV.

Busnardo, JoAnne and Charlotte C. Galves. 1983. "Leitura em língua estrangeira e compreensão e produção de textos em língua materna." *Redação e Leitura,* PUC São Paulo, 305–311.

Busnardo, JoAnne and Maria da Glória de Moraes. 1983. "Negociano o sentido (Elogia da ignorância)." *Trabalhos em Linguística Aplicada I.* IEL/Unicamp/Funcamp, Campinas, S.P., 9–37.

Fonseca Ferreira, Lígia. 1982. "Ensino de línguas estrangeiras e identidade cultural." In R. Nasr et al. (eds.). *Foreign Language Teaching and Cultural Identity*. São Paulo/Brussels: Instituto de Idiomas Yázigi/AIMAV.

Freire, Paulo. 1972. *Pedagogy of the Oppressed*. (Translated from the original Portuguese manuscript, 1968.) New York: Herder and Herder.

————. 1973. *Education for Critical Consciousness*. (Translated from *Educação como prática da liberdade*, Editora Paz e Terra: Rio de Janeiro, 1969.) New York: Herder and Herder.

Galves, Charlotte C. and JoAnne Busnardo. 1983. "A vulgarização científica no ensino de línguas (funcionamento discursivo e situação de enunciação)" *Estudos Linguísticos VII*. Anais do GEL. GEL/FAPESP, 221–245.

Gnerre, Maurizio. 1985. "Linguagem, poder e discriminacão." In M. Gnerre. *Linguagem Escrita e Poder*, Martins Fontes: São Paulo, 3–24.

Gumperz, John. 1982. *Language and Social Identity*. New York: Cambridge University Press.

Moirand, Sophie. 1982. "De la communication à la compétence de communication." In S. Moirand. *Enseigner à communiquer en langue étrangère, recherches/applications*. Paris: Hachette, 8–20.

Otoni, Paulo. 1983. "A '(re)negociação' no ensino da leitura em língua estrangeira." *Trabalhos em Linguística Aplicada I*. IEL/Unicamp/Funcamp, Campinas, S.P., 39–56.

Sabinson, Eric M. 1983. "Foreign Language Acquisition: Identification and Realpolitik." *Trabalhos em Linguística Aplicada I*. IEL/Unicamp/Funcamp, Campinas, S.P., 153–172.

Scaramucci, Matilde. 1983. "Contribuições para um estudo de aspectos motivacionais de atitudes de alunos brasileiros com relação ao inglês." Mimeo, IEL, Unicamp.

Schumann, John H. 1978. "The Acculturation Model for Second-language Acquisition." In R. Gingras (ed.). *Second-language Acquisition and Foreign Language Teaching*. Washington, D.C.: Center for Applied Linguistics.

————. 1978. *The Pidginization Process: A Model for Second Language Acquisition*. Rowley, MA: Newbury House.

Zelio. 1982. "A interferência da industria da cultura no ensino de línguas." In R. Nasr et al. (eds.). *Foreign Language Teaching and Cultural Identity*. São Paulo/Brussels: Instituto de Idiomas Yázigi/AIMAV.

Chapter 3

The Impregnability of Textbooks: The Example of American Foreign Language Education

Hildebrando Ruiz

Hildebrando Ruiz is a professor of Spanish linguistics at the University of Georgia. In addition to teaching courses in theoretical and applied linguistics, he is responsible for the training and supervision of graduate teaching assistants in the Spanish program. His research interests and publications concern Spanish linguistics, teacher training and foreign language teaching models and materials.

INTRODUCTION

The title of this study is ambiguous. It could suggest that textbook writers in North America are, regrettably, too conservative or too slow to perceive and to implement advances from recent theories on language and language acquisition. Or it could mean, on the other hand, that American writers of teaching materials know what they are doing and thus are not about to give in to fashionable but unproven approaches to language learning and teaching.

The discussion that follows will show that the first interpretation is the intended one. This study demonstrates the need for a restructuring of foreign language textbooks as we know them today if communicative language teaching (CLT) is to play a central role in the language classroom. Three factors are identified as important obstacles to the production of texts that facilitate CLT. First, there is a lack of consensus as to what CLT is. Second, there is a lack of understanding of new linguistic orientations and recent proposals of syllabus design. Third, there is publishers' conservatism, reflected in their low interest in risk-taking with regard to truly innovative manuscripts.

This study begins with consideration of the putative correlation between textbook development and related disciplines, such as descriptive linguistics and language learning theories. Examples of currently available Spanish texts provide illustrations and data for this discussion. Following an exploration of possible sources of information for the textbook author, there is a consideration of the pedagogical principles and research findings that authors claim have influenced their work. As a follow-up, three selected formal features of Spanish are critically considered to determine what effect, if any, current theory has had on their treatment in language teaching texts. This leads to an examination of the broader question of whether communicative language teaching is possible within the present context of classroom instruction in the United States.

Throughout this discussion, it is assumed that in most foreign language (FL) departments of American universities, the textbook is not only a basic form of course design, but most often the only form of organization and sequencing, particularly in multi-section programs. The textbook predetermines what should be taught and learned, and in what order, and becomes a binding document to which most teachers voluntarily subscribe.

An examination of the principles of language theory and the assumptions about language learning processes that underlie the organization of currently available college textbooks is a step in considering the general nature of these foreign language materials and their pervasive influence on teaching programs.

RATIONALE

The rationale for this study can be stated by paraphrasing Richards (1984): when one understands the role of language and language acquisition theories, as well as instructional theory and the limitations of textbook writing, one gets to know the "secret life" of textbooks, which tend to proliferate without apparent evolution.

It should be made clear at the outset that a one-to-one correlation of teaching materials with each and every one of the current theoretical tenets of language and language acquisition theories should not be expected. In fact, teachers as well as materials designers would be ill-advised to access linguistic theories and research findings in language acquisition and teaching uncritically, without first determining their relevance. Gomes de Matos (1983) provides insightful examples illustrating the distinction between being "up-to-date" and being "trendy." The latter term refers not only to the use of terminology but also to the hasty application of concepts from theories in disciplines that, although adjacent to language teaching, are pedagogically undesirable. The same applies to the findings of language acquisition research.

Johnson (1982:10) has observed that "it is natural for the language teacher to regard linguistics as something of a mother discipline." A large number of textbook writers are also language teachers. Thus it seems fair to assume, at least *a priori*, that current Spanish teaching materials reflect at least two alternative sets of attitudes and beliefs about FL teaching in terms of emphasis on language structure vs. emphasis on language use. As reasonable as this assumption might be, the conclusions of this study indicate that the state of the art in textbook writing is suspiciously uniform. That is, the ongoing wealth of methodological and instructional proposals that we witness in the FL journals, as well as the implications from general linguistics, have had little impact on the design and organization of Spanish textbooks.

FRAMEWORK

Textbook writers need a strategy to determine what aspects of descriptive linguistics and various approaches to the psychology of L2 acquisition can be modified for pedagogical purposes and how this modification can be achieved. My analysis of current Spanish teaching materials adopts the working assumption that the field we call applied linguistics must provide textbook writers with principles for relating descriptive grammars to processes of language acquisition. Only then will we be in a position to evaluate empirically and either endorse or reject claims made in the introductory pages of pedagogical materials.

Following Noblitt (1972:316), I find it necessary, to distinguish between the term *pedagogical grammar,* which is at the very least "a theoretical statement that accounts for second language acquisition in a formal or structured learning situation . . .," and the term *pedagogical text,* which is the actual reproduction of formal statements, examples and exercises in accordance with tenets of pedagogical grammar. I further subscribe to Noblitt's characterization of the components of a pedagogical grammar, in which descriptive and contrastive analysis are tasks charged to the linguist, while the analysis of tasks, performance and objectives comes under the responsibility of the psychologist and educator. These components are, in my view, minimal sources of information for the textbook writer, and I have attempted to determine to what extent they have been integrated in the development of teaching materials.

Along with the Chomskyan approach to linguistic inquiry and its subsequent modifications, which have dominated American linguistics for the last 20 years, a more inclusive type of linguistic thought is beginning to catch the attention of language educators. By inclusive I mean linguistic endeavor that refuses to consider language in a sterile vacuum. Language is viewed instead as "a way of behaving and making others behave" (Firth 1951), that is, as interaction or interpersonal activity, always constrained by social and spatial contexts and used by flesh and blood speakers rather than ideal ones. This approach to language, generally associated with the British tradition of linguistics, provides the theoretical foundation for so-called functional approaches to language teaching. Given that functional approaches to language teaching have served as the basis for change in language teaching materials for more than a decade, there has been sufficient time for authors of Spanish teaching textbooks to design materials reflecting the influence of functional approaches to linguistics and language teaching. A cross-section of such materials serves as the basis for this study.

A LOOK AT
SPANISH TEXTBOOKS

The first and most prominent feature of the materials studied is the multiplicity of interpretations of the term "communicative language teaching," which has been used loosely to signal a reaction against the inadequacies of structural syllabuses in preparing learners to use their new language beyond the classroom. For some, it means a slight expansion of audiolingual-type activities in which an individual interacts with another, mainly for the purpose of practicing sentences as abstract manifestations of the linguistic code. For others, it means providing group activities, such as games, or various informal instances of exposure to the target language.

Another feature is the use of the terms "notional" and "functional." While both terms are used in a few Spanish texts, there is no evidence of any significant influence from the philosophical foundations of these labels, nor assurance of a sufficient understanding of their origin as technical terms. One author promises that the textbook gives opportunities for learning Spanish unconsciously as well as consciously. This statement is apparently an effort to convince prospective users that recent theories of language learning and acquisition such as those espoused by Krashen (1981) have guided the organization of the book.

Other theories and research findings that authors of Spanish textbooks strive to acknowledge can be summarized as follows: There is a general acknowledgement that knowledge of the linguistic system (competence) is not a sufficient condition for successful language use (performance), especially when this is understood as interpersonal activity within the framework of social context. Instruction and syllabus design gravitate around the learners' needs in an effort to make FL learning pertinent. Instructional theory, in particular, is characterized by an unprecedented degree of flexibility that allows authors from the outset to subscribe to the position that seeking "the best method" is a chimera. Error correction is promoted only to the extent that it does not interfere with efforts at communicating, or getting messages across. Finally, there is an implicit acknowledgement of differences in learning styles: Some individuals have a greater dependency on the conscious application of grammar rules (monitor-users), while others prefer a less systematic approach and thus opt for "picking up" language.

The following quotations from a 1983 publication are not only representative of a large portion of the Spanish materials studied, but also accurately portray the desire of authors to reflect current trends in language teaching and learning:

> . . . [it is] a textbook that blends opportunity for genuine communication with mature topics and a comprehensive approach to learning . . ., written with a concern for the student's interests and attitudes, current instructional goals and research in the field . . ., the only introductory Spanish textbook to provide opportunities for meaningful and real use of the language from the very beginning of every chapter . . . instead of promising students that they will be able to communicate *someday* the activities of this book create an opportunity to communicate *immediately* . . . [This book] has been designed to allow both conscious learning and unconscious acquisition to occur. [This book] . . . is designed to accommodate diverse instructional needs rather than to impose a single methodology; its flexible format can be easily adapted to different teaching styles, student preferences and course objectives (Labarca 1983: xi, xvii).

Additional pedagogical principles are outlined in the introduction more or less along the following lines: a) learners are active participants in or initiators of the communicative process; b) when learners feel comfortable, they are more likely to take risks during communication; c) error correction made in discreet and unobtrusive ways encourages learners to use the language freely and to accept errors as a natural part of learning a language.

In short, if the preceding statements were representative of current efforts to produce materials that facilitate the attainment of the desired results, we would conclude that the intense activity in the field of foreign language teaching has had a direct impact on commercially produced teaching materials. As we shall see below, this does not turn out to be the case. In fact, the organization of the table of contents, teaching units and learning activities is frequently in conflict with the underlying trends of such philosophical stands.

A TRADITION THAT LINGERS

Most standardized sets of procedures or principles of language teaching have as their ultimate goal the creation of opportunities for the development of communicative competence. Differences in procedures almost always correspond to differences in the perspective taken on language. Thus, when language is viewed as the ideas, notions, or norms of social and linguistic behavior identified with and by the members of a speech community, the organization of pedagogical materials will have a better chance for success if it is based on functional principles and the integrative presentation of the formal system. The term "functional," as used here, should be understood as a cover term for the concept of language as a means of interaction and communication.

On the other hand, if language is perceived as a taxonomy of discrete units such as person/tense morphemes, gender/number markers, sentence connectors, and sentence types, these units will be the cornerstone for syllabus design. There is no question that this conception of language underlies the history of language teaching in North America. It remains in force today, despite a recent trend towards emphasizing the utilitarian value of studying foreign languages that can be traced back to the enactment of the National Defense Education Act (1958) and the assumption that foreign language learning was in the national interest.

A cursory examination of the table of contents and the lesson structure of selected textbooks indicates that structural taxonomy of language is a prevailing paradigm and serves as the theoretical foundation of these materials. Because discrete units of syntax, morphology, and phonology are available for direct observation by both the teacher and the learner, they have also become language teaching units. As Rutherford (1983:16) puts it, "A long characteristic of language pedagogy has been the conversion of observable discrete language entities into observable discrete language material. . . . Such practices even at best reveal an impoverished view of what [a] language system is . . . ."

This view is reflected in the practices of those colleagues who still cling to the objective of teaching Spanish as a means of developing the agility of college students' minds, thereby increasing their intellectual powers. In such cases, the language teacher is a trainer whose task is to discipline the learner through a series of rigorous exercises in order to "practice" the talent and the unused power of the mind (Herron 1982). In the opinion of some, this view of foreign language learning as an intellectual activity has been one reason for students' failure to attain even a working knowledge of language for communicative purposes at the beginning level (Terrell 1982). Curiously, this situation still prevails at a time when the declared rationale for language teaching is more concerned with cross-cultural understanding through language than with learning about language.

AN INFORMAL QUESTIONNAIRE

Having considered practices and traditions evident in some Spanish textbooks, we can address two questions: Are Spanish textbook writers in the United States in tune with what I have chosen to call "inclusive linguistics," and are textbook writers aiming at a communicative approach to language teaching?

Responses to a questionnaire that was sent to the authors and publishers of 20 Spanish textbooks provide a basis for answers to these questions. The questionnaires were designed to assess authors' and publishers' perceptions of their products, the most widely used Spanish textbooks over the past 5–8 years.[1]

While the format for responses to questions and statements addressed to authors and to publishers was the same (respondents could express their views on a scale from 1 to 5), the contents of questions were necessarily different. Questions to authors inquired about, among other things, the factors contributing to their decision to write a text for a given level, their degree of autonomy in its organization and contents, their awareness of recent pedagogical trends and the extent to which their text reflects them, and the components of the text that leave the author with the greatest sense of accomplishment.

Questions for the publishers included statistical information about proposed and accepted or rejected manuscripts for each level. Other questions inquired about the publisher's own preferences, the language in which the greatest variety of proposed titles had been received (French, German, Italian, Spanish), the reasons for rejecting manuscripts, interest in manuscripts on foreign language for specific purposes, the relevance of components such as contents, organization, emphasis on activities as opposed to grammatical information, and the amount and nature of input from language teachers in the decision-making process.

Judging from the responses to my questionnaire, all authors and publishers, without exception, are familiar with recent trends in linguistics. Some even expressed enthusiastic adherence, while others expressed various degrees of caution. All claimed commitment to a communicative approach, as indicated by references in their responses to real/genuine/authentic communication, language use, genuine self-expression, or spontaneous/everyday/real-life conversation. This common denominator of objectives should not be surprising, especially if one takes communication to mean any form of manipulation of language. However, this interpretation is not that generally accepted when we speak of the notional/functional syllabus.

According to Richards (1984:10), notional syllabuses, as proposed by Wilkins (1976), van Ek (1975) and others, reflect "a movement from a grammatical to a communicative account of what it means to know a language." The implication is that the content of a program is no longer identified with the vocabulary, grammar and, perhaps, the situations used to teach Spanish for general purposes. Rather, the program must be organized around content variables, whose nature depends upon the determination of the learner's communicative needs. To my knowledge this type of program organization has not been done for Spanish in the United States, in spite of the increasing use of the language.

One explanation for the absence of a functionally organized syllabus for Spanish as a foreign language may be our difficulty in specifying the communicative needs of learners in general language courses like those that satisfy university FL requirements. This problem, however, is neither the most serious nor the most immediate. There are others.

SOME "WELL-KNOWN" DIFFICULTIES

The change from structurally based to communicatively based language instruction presupposes not only reassessment of the teacher's role and restructuring of the classroom environment, but also and more importantly, clarification of theoretical accounts of communicative competence of the type done by Savignon (1983). Aside from this work, the framework we have so far is tentative and incomplete, especially when compared with the pre-transformational models offered by structural linguistics.

What I have called inclusive linguistics has aroused interest in theories of speech acts, pragmatics, and discourse analysis in general. But very little from these sources, relevant as they are for the purposes of negotiating meaning, has reached current commercial Spanish textbooks. Noticeably absent are, for instance, statements about particular formal features of Spanish that are relevant to the implementation of grammar in discourse, i.e., above the level of the sentence. I will now address several instances of such features, all familiar to learners of Spanish.

The first is the symmetrical and asymmetrical use of the pronouns of direct address, *tú* and *usted*. These pronouns are uniformly introduced in the first lesson, and drills are designed to achieve mechanization of their use. After significant effort on the part of the learners, the textbook typically tells them that Spanish does not frequently use subject pronouns. The point omitted, of course, is that subject pronouns are used to satisfy such specific functions as contrast, stress, or disambiguation.

Furthermore, the *tú*/*usted* distinction is oversimplified by associating *usted* with formality, deference and social or psychological distance, and *tú* with informality. Solé (1978) has pointed out, accurately I believe, that such clear semantic differentiation does not hold during actual conversation since "formality" and "informality" are not values inherent to the pronouns *usted* and *tú*. Rather, such values are a function of the sociolinguistic context in which the pronouns are used. In other words, form cannot always be equated with function. Likewise, manifestations of social distance and power related to the appropriate choice of either *tú* or *usted* are not necessarily attributes of particular individuals (Brown and Gilman 1960). Rather, they are interpretations of a relationship that can change depending on a variety of factors in a given context.

It appears, then, that Spanish textbook writers have been ignoring an implication that is central to functional approaches to language study; namely, that people speak to one another with intent. They intend not only to communicate a specific message associated with a referent, but also to influence their interlocutors in some way. They may wish to establish and maintain a relationship or to acknowledge the parameters of an existing one (i.e., I perceive you (*usted*) as socially distant and perhaps more powerful than I). Undoubtedly, forms of address are at the heart of this matter.

A different kind of problem is that exemplified by the terms "preterite" and "imperfect." One source of difficulty in the teaching and learning of the aspectual differences implicit in these terms is the piecemeal fashion in which textbook authors treat this distinction. Their approach denies the fact that time and aspect reference is not an entity composed of subconstituents, but part of a network system that operates throughout the language to express an important form of cognition. In this respect, authors fail to point out, for instance, that so-called changes of meaning caused by preterite/imperfect opposition in verbs like *conocer* (*conocí* "I met"; *conocía* "I used to know"), *saber* (*supe* "I found out"; *sabía* "I knew") or *poder* (*pude* "I managed, was able to"; *podí* "I was able to, had the ability to") are not really differences at the lexical level but rather are part of the same network of aspectual oppositions and relations operating with the rest of the Spanish verb system.

Actually, aspectual distinctions in Spanish are appropriate illustrations of the inability of pedagogical texts to assimilate insights from inclusive linguistics, such as the role of discourse in the negotiation of meaning. It is an established fact that the more abstract a grammatical category is, the more it draws upon context for its interpretation. Aspectual distinctions are highly abstract. As Hopper (1982) pointed out, the verbal category of aspect defines the perspective from which the speaker views a state, event or activity. Two Spanish sentences like *Ese estudiante nunca faltó a clase* and *Ese estudiante nunca faltaba a clase,* are both rendered in English as 'That student never missed class.' Teachers and learners of Spanish are usually at odds in trying to understand or explain the difference between these two constructions. Actually, the preterite morpheme in *faltó* stresses the final outcome or *perfect record of attendance.* The pragmatic implication is therefore, that classes are over, and such a statement is a truthful assessment of the student's attendance. On the other hand, the imperfect morpheme in *faltaba* stresses another aspectual dimension of the event, namely, the *habit of attending regularly.* The discourse function of these aspectual distinctions is to focus the listener's or reader's attention on relevant points of the message, and to relate states and events to whatever precedes or follows (linguistic context) by making some verbal actions more prominent than others.

It is therefore axiomatic that the aspectual meaning of an utterance has to be derived from the entire context of situation. The components of this context include not only the physical environment, but also the perspective of the speaker. These components make it possible to refer to the same action first as a perfective form, and then as an imperfective one, without being contradictory (Hopper 1982). Consequently, the preterite/imperfect distinction needs to be derived from the whole, from the context, and not from abstract and isolated utterances, as is usually the case in language texts.

Two other formal features found in the Spanish texts considered here deserve our attention. One is the tripartite distinction among noun, adjective and adverbial clauses as a necessary condition for dealing with the indicative/subjunctive distinction. In view of recent as well as long-established linguistic characterizations of Spanish mood, these distinctions only increase the grammatical apparatus to deal with an already complex notion.

The other feature is Spanish word order, the primary function of which is to signal pragmatic relations rather than grammatical ones. For example, the "unmarked" (i.e., normal) word order of a Spanish sentence like *Yo voy al laboratorio todos los días* ("I go to the lab every day"), places the adverbial *todos los días* at the end of the string. However, it is also possible to give prominence to this information by moving it towards the beginning of the sentence, as in *Yo voy* todos los días *al laboratorio,* and even more prominence in *Yo* todos los días *voy al laboratorio.* This dislocation of the pronoun and the verb by an adverbial is a "marked" (i.e., less common) word order systematically used by speakers to give prominence to certain information in the sentence. Although Spanish word order has clear communicative value, textbook writers pay little attention to it.

I do not intend to criticize unduly the quality of grammatical information in current Spanish texts. After all, authors must constantly struggle with the dilemma of linguistic truth vs. pedagogical utility. The end result is frequently a product of compromise. Nor do I want to underestimate the pedagogical usefulness of isolating structural features of language for the purpose of making grammatical information more accessible to the learner. However, given the uniformity of the presentation of linguistic form in the textbooks studied, we can conclude that the presentation of their grammatical content has been shaped by the authors' views of what language is and how it is put together. In the materials considered here, the authors' views appear to be based on structural linguistics. Furthermore, it is clear that the number of grammatical generalizations and insights available in the various linguistic analyses of Spanish is significantly greater than that which actually makes its way into published teaching materials.

In light of available insights into the nature of language use, a description of grammar solely in terms of discrete units and definable boundaries and constituents is conspicuously insufficient. It not only leads to the paradoxical situation of breaking down language for students to reassemble or to synthesize, but it also leaves the false impression that language learning is the additive learning of grammatical structures (Newmark 1979; Rutherford 1983).

In order for language to serve the needs of language learners, it must be presented in a way that makes the principles of discourse apparent; many of these principles are not observable in the forms of the language at the sentence level and cannot be isolated as autonomous discrete units. Nonetheless, they are present in the speech act. Their inclusion in the teaching syllabus implies a *restructuring of textbooks as we know them today.* Learners need to be aware of the various functions of sentences in discourse, as well as the various sociolinguistic markers and means of influencing the behavior of one's interlocutor. The "new" textbook author will have to move away from a conception of grammar in terms of constructions and rules towards a conception of grammar as the formal realization of meaning at the level of discourse.

ON "SCHOOLS" AND "TRENDS"

The next question to address is related to the current environment of FL learning in the United States. Is it suitable or even realistic to attempt communicative language teaching? Valdman (1978:568) has observed that ". . . in North America, foreign languages are taught in a nonsupportive environment, created by suspicious or hostile attitudes on the part of the parents and school administrators, unrealistic expectations on the part of the learners themselves, [and the] low value assigned to a knowledge of foreign languages by the community." Compared with the high return value of FL learning in Europe, the scarcity of opportunities that Americans have to engage in authentic speech acts indicates that the implementation of communicative language teaching is not an immediate concern.

Before responding to this observation, it is necessary to describe what is meant by communicative language teaching. Let us begin by distinguishing between a communicative "school" of language teaching and a simple "trend" towards communication. In the former case (according to Ross's (1981) characterization, and Raimes's (1983) analogies), we are dealing with a paradigm in the Kuhnian sense (1970), that is, with practitioners who hold a common denominator of assumptions and beliefs. The communicative paradigm has pedagogical principles based on humanistic, learner-centered teaching and syllabus design, and a set of broad methodological practices consistent with aspects of the language learning process. Communicative language teaching presupposes a common theoretical linguistics background in the British tradition, which includes among others, the names of Firth, Sweet, and Halliday. Syllabuses consistent with the communicative paradigm are generally organized around uses of languages, as in a notional syllabus, or around tasks and activities that engage learners in language use, as in a procedural syllabus. (See Beretta, this volume, for a description of this syllabus type.)

Given the characteristics of current Spanish textbooks described above, we can conclude that Spanish textbooks are not a by-product of this paradigm for two compelling reasons: First, the contents of these materials are organized around sentence-level features of language, which thus become the primary teaching units. Second, the presentation of the standard language variety implies that other subsystems are not legitimate varieties. This narrow view conflicts with the philosophical foundations of the communicative "school," which views language fundamentally as interaction, as "a way of behaving and making others behave."

In contrast to the communicative school, the "trend" towards communication in the classroom does not have the rigor of a theoretical model, nor does it aim at methodological purity. It is instead a set of responses to a specific problem commonly associated with grammar-based teaching of language. Grammar-based language teaching fails to take into account that knowledge of a language is not the same as the ability to use it. The resulting problem is the detachment of language from the world beyond the classroom or from the learner's immediate needs.

THE COMMUNICATIVE TREND AND SPANISH TEXTBOOKS

Since there are no examples of university level texts solidly based on the principles of the British tradition of linguistics, our review of Spanish texts is limited to those more appropriately associated with the trend toward communicative language teaching. These materials fit Raimes's (1983) description of textbooks that offer *ad hoc* solutions to the problems associated with structurally-based materials. As has already been pointed out, one solution has been simply to express adherence to the notion of language as communication in the text's introductory pages. Another strategy is the adoption of labels such as "functional approach" that convey the state-of-the-art nature of the materials. However, while the table of contents is organized around so-called functions of language, one can easily identify the terms of the structural syllabus upon examination of the chapters in question. For example, the chapter on "expressing disagreement" is actually a lesson in expressing negation with "no." Likewise, "describing yourself and others" is a lesson on the verb *ser* and adjectives; "describing people and things" is a lesson on noun/adjective agreement; and, "saying what you do in school" is really an introduction to *-ar* verbs.

To label such materials "functional" is misleading; what the author has in mind is a particular structure, not a function of language. While a given notion such as likes/dislikes can be expressed in a variety of ways, the author is not interested in presenting a cluster of structurally unrelated constructions, even if they belong in the same time and place in view of their relationships to a particular "notion." Another more common strategy is to add to the old components a new one with communicative "overtones"; thus adhering to tradition while at the same time projecting the idea of evolution and change. The rules of use and the learner activities presented throughout these texts differ little from those of texts available before 1976 when Wilkins, *Notional Syllabus* was published.

In scrutinizing what is typically offered in currently available Spanish texts, we can observe almost without exception that the presentation of a grammar point and drills involving repetition, fill-in-the-blanks, sentence conversion, dehydrated sentences, and simple and multiple substitutions are followed by a section entitled variously as "Conversación," "Comunicación," "A hablar," "A conversar," or "Situaciones." These sections are designated as the time to use language spontaneously, creatively, and meaningfully. Allegedly, this is the opportunity for learners to be themselves, to learn about themselves and about each other, and at the same time to express their own view of the world. It is their opportunity to interact.

The following examples of opportunities for interaction are representative of the kinds of strategies for developing communicative skills found in most currently available Spanish texts.

Situations

What would you say in the following situations?

a) Someone offers you a piece of cake: Say that you are not hungry and that you have just eaten.

b) Someone asks you about your vacation: Say that you learned how to swim and ride a horse and that you caught an enormous trout.

(¿Cómo se dice . . . ? 2nd ed., D. C. Heath, 1982)

It is difficult to argue that a genuine exchange of information takes place in this exercise. While it invites the learner to imagine a hypothetical situation, the "wings of imagination" are promptly clipped by instructions that decide in a dictatorial manner what should be imagined and what should be said. Consequently, the learners have no opportunity either to be themselves or to be creative. In essence, this is essentially a translation exercise with a hidden agenda of conversion from indirect to direct speech. While potentially valuable as language practice, this exercise is not communicative.

Interview

Ask a classmate the following questions. Then report the information to the class.

– Do you prefer to travel by plane, by train or by boat? Why?

– What kind of clothes do you take in your suitcase when you go on vacation?

(¿Habla español? 2nd ed., Holt, Rinehart and Winston, 1981)

There is a purpose behind these questions and the students do in fact practice structures used in communication. However, the problem with this exercise is its lack of authenticity, meaningfulness, and spontaneity. First, an interview is not just a series of questions directed to the interviewee without communicative purpose or interest in the information sought. In this exercise the interviewer knows that the answer to the question will not be true. Both the interviewer and the interviewee know also that the information requested is irrelevant for the continuation of the dialog. In short, what is lacking is context. A person cannot truthfully answer a question concerning preferences about means of travel without knowing the destination, the distance, the availability of options, money, time, and weather conditions. The same holds true for the kinds of clothes a person puts in a suitcase before going on vacation. Furthermore, artificiality is evident from the start, since these questions have not been created by the interviewer, but rather have been given to the learner by the author.

Politeness

Imagine that you need help in a Hispanic country or in a Hispanic area of an American city. How would you ask the following questions politely?

¿Poder/ usted/ decirme/ dónde está el correo?

¿Poder/ usted/ ayudarme/ con estos documentos?

(*Invitación*. CBS College Publishing, 1983)

This exercise deals with the relationship between the indirectness of a request and varying degrees of politeness, which is an important feature of successful communication. However, in reality it involves little more than the rather mechanical manipulation of a particular morpheme attached to the verb *poder,* and it differs little from the standard dehydrated sentence type. To claim that it involves any real exchange of new information among the participants is therefore arbitrary.

One of the most obvious flaws in all of these activities is that they do not allow for the free exchange of information. Not only does the listener know what is going to be asked, but the questioner already knows the answer. In order to establish a need and a purpose for the exchange, an "information gap" must exist between speaker A and speaker B that motivates the interaction. (See Helgesen, this volume, for use of this notion in classroom activities.) Without this information gap, an exercise does not simulate real life, a necessary condition for meaningful practice.

To summarize, an exercise is not communicative because its creator decides it is so. It must conform to several criteria set in accordance with a minimum of empirical evaluation. We have mentioned here the information gap as a condition for the exchange of information. Other evaluation criteria have been suggested by Berns (1984) and Johnson (1982).

Gomes de Matos (1983b) suggests challenge as a necessary feature if exercises are to arouse competitive interest and thought. He also stresses the value of problem solving activities that involve decision-making. Such activities make language use truly interactive and at the same time inspire enthusiastic participation among learners.

SOLUTIONS THAT ARE NOT SOLUTIONS

Since I am not looking for "the ideal text" (nobody does any more!), I could conclude on the basis of the present analysis that the textbooks scrutinized here have come a long way in comparison to materials developed 15 or more years ago. Unfortunately, the findings of my study do not support the various authors' contentions that the materials present opportunities to learn language meaningfully. The profession's realization of the inadequacy of teaching language for its own sake and heightened awareness among teachers of the general need for communication skills have led authors and publishers alike to opt for solutions that are unconvincing or misleading.

We can turn again to responses from the questionnaire for an explanation of this state of affairs. Authors' and publishers' responses clearly indicate that the proliferation of FL texts is not necessarily a response to recent findings of theories on language and language acquisition. As they openly acknowledge, authors and publishers aim to reach the largest public. Therefore, the word "flexibility" is found with a frequency second only to "communication" in current textbook rationales. The success of a textbook is clearly determined by its ability to please the majority of teachers. Any innovation encountered in a particular manuscript that could prove threatening to established teaching practices results in the manuscript's rejection.

The notion that textbooks are products of compromise is strongly supported by the responses to the questionnaire. For example, none of the publishers responded affirmatively when asked if manuscripts are geared toward specific geographical areas of the United States. Statistics concerning the language and the levels for which the greatest number of manuscript proposals were received indicated also that economic variables determine the extent of publishers' willingness to experiment with new forms of curriculum design. This reticence on the part of publishers does not exclusively affect language textbooks, but is paralleled in general throughout the publishing industry. The following anecdote summarizes this situation well. When asked by a journalist to explain 13 previous rejections of William Kennedy's novels, including his Pulitzer Prize winning *Ironweed*, the representative responded: "Publishing is above all business." In other words, the publisher had no guarantee that the themes and characters predominant in Kennedy's novels (winos, losers, "splendid nobodies," "underrated scoundrels," and a variety of similar characters set against the backdrop of Albany, New York) would ensure financial success. Actually, only after the strong endorsement of a Nobel Prize laureate was *Ironweed* published. The point is that the inherent merits of Kennedy's novels and his talent as a writer were not reason enough for acceptance of his work by a prospective publisher. Economic contingency could have deprived readers of the genius of a prize winner.[2]

Thus economic and political realities constitute the basis underlying the complex process of textbook writing and publishing. The outcome of this situation is exactly what we have noticed in the texts studied in this investigation, namely, homogeneity among the various publications and their uniform focus on language forms rather than on principles of language use. Although strategies for the design of learning activities reflect interest in student-to-student interaction, practice in constructing sentences as abstract manifestations of the language code still dominates the nature of most of the classroom activities profferred by textbooks.

It is feasible to adopt modest but attainable goals for the development of communicative skills. If the notion of communicative competence is understood to include interacting by means of oral and written language as well as nonverbal communication, which together contribute to the successful expression, interpretation, and negotiation of meaning (Savignon 1983), then communicative skills may be seen as a continuum along which degrees can be identified. Perhaps, this notion is what textbook planners need most to bear in mind when they attempt to incorporate the entire grammar of a language into one or two levels and consequently make misleading promises to prospective users.

SUMMARY AND RECOMMENDATIONS

While researching for this study, I have found that there is no shortage of Spanish textbooks for the beginning and intermediate levels. I have also found that their organization and the contexts they present are distressingly similar from one to another. Today's Spanish textbooks offer no apparent response to recent linguistic and pedagogical trends. Rather, these materials illustrate adherence to a philosophy of textbook writing that treats language units as teaching units, and presupposes knowledge of the linguistic code as a prerequisite to classroom activity involving language use. As a result, problem solving activities, strategies for interaction, principles of negotiating meaning, and many other features that contribute to the development of communicative competence are not well represented.

Since publishers are understandably interested in marketing their product, they research carefully the wishes and preferences of the consumer. It is no small wonder that language teachers, a prime source of consumer information, are visited so regularly by publishing house representatives. While some publishers' representatives seem genuinely interested in learning about the realities of classroom language instruction, many seem primarily intent on learning what kind of book best fits the teaching style of the greatest number of teachers. However, should teaching styles be regarded as the basis for the development of materials that promote communicative competence?

If we accept communicative competence as a broad and complex concept consisting of grammatical, sociolinguistic, discourse, and strategic competence (Canale and Swain, 1980; Savignon, 1983), the FL textbook must evolve to become a facilitator of effective teaching and learning. It should not be viewed as the source for a description of the linguistic code but rather as a repository of conditions and opportunities for learners to engage in activities that genuinely expose them to many of the intangibles of communicating through language.

Although language teachers can provide publishers with invaluable input, information about teaching styles is not a sufficient criterion by which to evaluate the inherent merits of a textbook manuscript. Furthermore, it is axiomatic that sound professional training for language teachers must develop their potential to restructure materials. The training of language teachers should not consist merely of familiarization with a variety of classroom techniques and procedures of the type to which beginning graduate teaching assistants in language departments cling desperately. While such strategies are certainly useful, they are usually valid for specific contexts only. Of greater relevance is an awareness of the rationale for and the implications of using certain techniques. Teacher training should prepare individuals to continue learning about the nature of their task. Language teachers trained in this way will be in a far better position to assist in the production of language teaching materials. Otherwise, as long as the reviewers of text manuscripts, who are often classroom teachers themselves, continue answering yes/no questions about a manuscript's potential interest and length, and the points of grammar that need to be added, omitted, simplified or expanded, textbooks with no apparent rationale will continue to be produced. Sound teacher training can in fact become a deterrent to what may otherwise become an applied linguistics industry.

This investigation has attempted to analyze the textbooks currently used in the United States to teach Spanish as a foreign language at the college/university level. I have departed from my initial assumption that some impact from current syllabus design and linguistic and methodological trends should be evident among the materials available at this level. That assumption proved to be unsubstantiated since most of the texts turned out to be not only uniform in their organization, but also a continuation of the language teaching tradition that bases the sequencing of content and the overall organization and selection of teaching activities on linguistic forms. While the trend towards communicative language teaching has been found by publishers to be intuitively appealing, the materials considered here did not provide significant evidence that the basic parameters of CLT, desirable though they may be, have found their way into commercially produced materials.

The current textbook situation is obviously not the most desirable. As I have illustrated, the observed and perhaps premature willingness of some textbook writers to make communicative competence the objective of language teaching is to some extent the result of either misinterpretation of new theoretical perspectives or failure to adapt them to the pedagogical realities of FL instruction in college. Since teachers play an important role in the marketing practices of publishers, it is to be hoped that those teachers involved in training will recognize their responsibility to develop teachers' potential to evaluate materials critically and to advocate principled reorganization and modernization of foreign languages texts.

NOTES

1. My purpose is not to isolate a particular title for criticism. When I refer to a specific text, it is only for the sake of illustration. In these cases my comments should not be taken as a judgment on the entire work, but only as a critique of the point in question. Some of my observations apply to texts that, although near completion, had not reached the market as of the moment in which this study was written. No identification of such works is given.

The following titles and publishers were included in this investigation: *Adelante: A Cultural Approach to Intermediate Spanish.* Scott, Foresman (1977); *Beginning Spanish: A Concept Approach.* 5th ed. Harper & Row (1983); *¿Cómo se dice?* 2nd. ed. D. C. Heath (1982); *Comunicando: A First Course in Spanish.* D. C. Heath (1979); *Communicating in Spanish: A First Course.* 2nd. ed. Houghton Mifflin (1984); *Dicho y hecho. Beginning Spanish: A Simplified Approach.* Wiley & Sons (1981); *En marcha: Español para niveles intermedios.* Houghton Mifflin (1983); *La lengua española: Gramática y cultura.* 3rd. ed. Scribner's (1983); *En contacto: A first course in Spanish.* Houghton Mifflin (1980); *Español en la comunidad.* Holt, Rinehart & Winston (1984); *Español a lo vivo.* 5th. ed. Wiley & Sons (1982); *El español y su estructura: Lectura y escritura para bilingües.* Holt, Rinehart & Winston (1983); *Foundation Course in Spanish.* 5th. ed. D. C. Heath (1981); *¿Habla español? Essentials.* 2nd. ed. Holt, Rinehart & Winston (1982); *Invitación: Spanish for Communication and Cultural Awareness.*

Holt, Rinehart & Winston (1983); *Pasaporte: First Year Spanish*. 2nd. ed. Wiley & Sons (1984). *Puertas a la lengua española: An Introductory Course.* Random House (1982); *Puntos de partida: An Invitation to Spanish.* Random House (1981).

2. The publishing company in question was Viking Press and the journalist was Diane Sawyer from the Columbia Broadcasting System (CBS), for the program *60 Minutes,* broadcast on December 23, 1984.

REFERENCES

Berns, M. 1984. "Functional Approaches to Language and Language Teaching: Another Look." In S. Savignon and M. Berns (eds.) *Initiatives in Communicative Language Teaching.* Reading, Mass.: Addison-Wesley.

Breen, M. and C. Candlin. 1980. "The Essentials of a Communicative Curriculum in Language Teaching." *Applied Linguistics* 1:89–112.

Brown, R. and A. Gilman. 1960. "The Pronouns of Power and Solidarity." In T. Sebeok (ed.). *Style in Language.* Cambridge, Mass.: MIT Press.

Brumfit, C. 1982. "Methodological Solutions to the Problems of Communicative Teaching." *On TESOL '81.* Washington, D.C.: TESOL.

Canale, M. and M. Swain. 1980. "Theoretical Bases of Communicative Approaches to Second Language Teaching and Testing." *Applied Linguistics* 1:1–47.

Firth, J. R. 1951. "Modes of Meaning." *Essays and Studies of the English Association,* N.S. 4:118–149. London: Oxford University Press.

Gomes de Matos, F. 1983a. "It Pays to Be Up-to-date, but Let's Not Be Too Trendy." *Gaikokugo Kyoiku Kiyo* 9:1–4. Nagoya Gakuin Daigaku.

———. 1983b. "Constructing and Using Challenging Exercises." *World Language English* 2:105–110.

Herron, C. 1982. "Foreign Language Learning Approaches as Metaphor." *The Modern Language Journal* 66:235–242.

Hopper, P. J. (ed.). 1982. *Tense-Aspect: Between Semantics and Pragmatics.* Amsterdam: J. Benjamins.

Johnson, K. 1982. *Communicative Syllabus Design and Methodology.* Oxford: Pergamon.

Krashen, S. 1981. *Second Language Acquisition and Second Language Learning.* Oxford: Pergamon.

Kuhn, T. 1970. *The Structure of Scientific Revolutions.* Chicago: University of Chicago Press.

Labarca, A. 1983. *Invitación. Spanish for Communication and Cultural Awareness.* New York: Holt, Rinehart and Winston.

Newmark, L. 1979. "How Not to Interfere with Language Learning." In C. Brumfit and K. Johnson (eds.). *The Communicative Approach to Language Teaching.* Oxford: Oxford University Press.

Noblitt, J. 1972. "Pedagogical Grammar: Towards a Theory of Foreign Language Materials Preparation." *International Review of Applied Linguistics* 10:313–331.

Raimes, A. 1983. "Tradition and Revolution in ESL Teaching." *TESOL Quarterly* 17:535–552.

Richards, J. 1984. "The Secret Life of Methods." *TESOL Quarterly* 18:7–23.

Ross, D. 1981. "From Theory to Practice: Some Critical Comments on the Communicative Approach to Language Teaching." *Language Learning* 31:223–242.

Rutherford, B. 1983. "Functions of Grammar in a Language Teaching Syllabus." In M. Saltarelli, (ed.). *The Foreign Language Syllabus: Grammar, Notions and Functions*. Urbana-Champaign: University of Illinois Language Learning Laboratory.

Savignon, S. 1972. *Communicative Competence: An Experiment in Foreign Language Teaching*. Philadelphia: Center for Curriculum Development.

―――. 1983. *Communicative Competence: Theory and Classroom Practice*. Reading, Mass.: Addison-Wesley.

Solé, Y. 1978. "Sociocultural Determinants of Symmetrical and Asymmetrical Address Forms in Spanish." *Hispania* 61:940–949.

Terrell, T. 1982. "The Natural Approach to Language Teaching: An Update." *The Modern Language Journal* 66:121–132.

Valdman, A. 1978. "Communicative Use of Language and Syllabus Design." *Foreign Language Annals* 11:567–578.

Van Ek, J. 1975. *Threshold Level English*. Oxford: Pergamon Press.

Wilkins, D. 1976. *Notional Syllabuses*. Oxford: Oxford University Press.

Section II

Approaches, Methods and Techniques

Chapter 4

The Ontario Experience: A Modular Approach to Second Language Teaching and Learning

Rebecca Ullmann

Rebecca Ullmann is a former Research Associate at the Modern Language Centre, the Ontario Institute for Studies in Education in Toronto, Canada and now heads her own consulting firm in Toronto. Her research interests and publications concern the relationship of multiculturalism, curriculum design, program implementation, and classroom observation to second language program evaluation. She has also published several multi-media modules for French instruction.

INTRODUCTION

For several decades second language educators have grappled with the challenge of how to develop second language proficiency in the face of a variety of limitations and constraints. In Canada, recent developments in materials and methods and an increase in the amount of contact time for instruction in French as a second language have helped alleviate some of these constraints. However, the second language teaching profession as a whole still faces the challenge of developing interesting and worthwhile second language (L2) programs that will achieve appropriate and satisfying levels of proficiency and still be usable in limited time frames.

The most common French as a second language (FSL) program found in Canadian schools is the Core French program. In this program French is taught as a subject for a defined period of time, usually 20–40 minutes a day at the elementary level and approximately 40–45 minutes per day at the secondary level. The starting point for these programs varies from province to province, and within provinces from school board to school board. The Ontario Ministry of Education (OISE) has suggested that 1,200 hours of French instruction can be attained by students in Core French programs. They have suggested that the second language proficiency of these students should include "a fundamental knowledge of the language—its grammar, pronunciation and idiom . . ." (Ontario Ministry of Education 1977). In addition, these students should be able to "participate in simple conversation . . . read, with the aid of a dictionary, standard texts on subjects of interest . . . and be able to resume the study of French in later life . . ." (Ontario Ministry of Education *op.cit.*).

The issue of what constitutes appropriate and satisfying levels of L2 proficiency at particular stages of learning is far from clear and deserves careful study in its own right. However, if goals such as those suggested above are to be attained, it seems important to adopt an approach to L2 curriculum development that accepts the limitations within which most Core French programs operate. Such an approach would aim for program improvement within these limitations.

This paper reports on a long-term Core French (FSL) project in Canada that has focused on second language curriculum issues. The project has addressed itself to questions dealing with the nature of L2 program content and the ways in which this content might be structured and implemented. A major goal of the project has been to further the development of L2 proficiency and provide expanded opportunities for communication in the second language classroom.

THE MODULE-MAKING PROJECT

In 1969–70 an L2 curriculum project for French as a second language, the Module-Making Project, began experimenting with a new concept of curriculum planning and development. We wondered if it were possible to develop small multi-media units (modules) that would be defined by clearly stated goals and that could be added to existing FSL programs in order to supplement these programs. We were in fact suggesting an alternative approach to the large, sequential L2 programs then in use. Since these large programs focused mainly on the formal features of the second language, the supplementary materials we intended to develop were to provide additional material of a more substantive and activity-oriented nature that would be complementary to the program. In this way it would be possible to broaden the L2 curriculum base and at the same time expand the opportunities for communication in the L2 class. We hoped to make the materials sufficiently flexible in format and content to meet the varying needs of students and teachers in both elementary and secondary schools, and thus to provide a degree of flexibility lacking in conventional lock-step L2 programs. We envisaged that carefully developed modules leading to language *use* and to the communication of *ideas* and *information* within the L2 classroom setting would have a lasting educational impact on the learner. And we anticipated that this impact could take place within the existing FSL administrative structures with a minimum of disruption. In this way we did not seek to radically alter the existing teaching and learning framework for FSL but to adapt it to current curricular innovations.

A large-scale survey of Core French teachers at the onset of the project indicated a growing need for readily usable classroom materials containing authentic information about "la francophonie au Canada." This survey determined the topics, thematic content, and modular design the project was to pursue.

Over the years modules have been developed for FSL programs from Grade 1 to Grade 13. Some modules, especially at the primary and junior levels, contain picture flashcards or flannelgraph figures as well as puppets. On occasion patterns are included for making stuffed toy animals, which young students can then manipulate during their language learning experience. Obviously, these modules for younger students focus on the more experiential, activity-oriented approach to second language learning.

Other modules, usually for older students with more second language background, contain tapes of authentic speeches and conversations with their corresponding transcript booklets (to be read while listening to the tapes), or reading materials such as folktales, adapted from original sources. Some modules contain excerpts of historical narratives that students will be required to read and then discuss in class. All these more senior materials are reinforced with additional writing exercises and project work.

Every module contains a teacher's guide that states the overall purpose of the Module-Making Project, and the aims and objectives of the specific module at hand. These aims and objectives are outlined in detail so that it is clear to the teacher from the outset what students are expected to *know* and what students are expected to be able to *do* in the second language after using the module. In addition the guide contains extensive background information for teachers, suggestions for using the various components of the module, and selected references. In effect the teacher's guide accomplishes two purposes. Not only does it provide a framework to help teachers organize their lesson, but it also expands teachers' own substantive knowledge about the thematic context within which the target language is being taught. Although it has not been our intention to develop "teacher-proof" material, a great deal of time and thought has been spent in preparing the teacher's guide, and when modules are presented during in-service workshops, teachers are urged to make full use of the material in the guide.

Through the development of modules, a systematic set of procedures for materials development was to emerge that stressed *research* on the information to be contained in these curriculum materials and *formative evaluation* of the materials prior to their publication.

Materials evaluation has been an essential part of module development. Certain aspects of the formative evaluation procedures used by the project relate to the framework and practical guidelines for materials evaluation discussed in the *Handbook of Curriculum Evaluation* (Lewy 1977), and have been refined by the project over time. A developers' questionnaire assisted the project in deciding on testable objectives and an appropriate evaluation scheme for the module in question. Then, during the draft stage of module development, pilot trials were conducted, usually by project staff members or by volunteer test-teachers. Teacher and student questionnaires were used during this stage. In the case of some modules, the pilot trials were considered sufficient.

Once revisions suggested by the pilot trials had been made, the module was sent out to test-teachers in schools throughout the province of Ontario for field trials. The instruments adapted to the module during the pilot phase served to evaluate the module at this stage. Students and teachers were asked to rate the components, content, and activities of the module in terms of their appropriateness, importance and worthwhileness, interest, and degree of difficulty. Teachers also provided information about class characteristics and the activities carried out during the teaching of the module.

These extensive evaluation procedures helped the project determine the adaptability and flexibility of modules to various teaching situations, and indicated whether the modules provided a genuine motivation to communicate. The results of the evaluation were incorporated in the final version of the materials prior to publication.

SOME THEORETICAL CONSIDERATIONS

Since issues related to the language syllabus have traditionally been most clearly elaborated, it is hardly surprising to find that the language syllabus is the most fully formed of all areas of syllabus development. Likewise, it is not surprising that a fair majority of the FSL programs used in Canada focus on and promote the achievement of grammatical competence in L2 students. However, as indicated in the literature (e.g., Canale and Swain 1980; Savignon 1983) it is becoming increasingly evident that grammatical competence does not necessarily lead to communicative competence. We are of the view that, while a grasp of grammatical structures is a necessary condition for the attainment of L2 proficiency, it is not a sufficient condition. Substantive content and natural communication in the L2 class are equally essential factors leading to L2 proficiency. This view concurs with that of others (e.g., Krashen 1982) and is perhaps best expressed in the efforts to develop new syllabuses and L2 methodologies in recent years (Wilkins 1972; Johnson 1979; Breen and Candlin 1980; Savignon 1983; Savignon and Berns 1984). In keeping with these new developments, and in conjunction with the work of the Modules Project, movement has been made in the direction of a curriculum framework that posits a much broader view of the L2 curriculum than is currently in use. This framework is based on the view that the potential for improving learning in the L2 classroom is ignored if too much emphasis is placed on the formal language domain within the L2 curriculum. The framework described below presents an alternative, multi-dimensional conceptualization of the curriculum, and outlines a broadened context for L2 teaching and learning.[1]

A Broadened Curriculum Framework

In this framework "curriculum" and "syllabus" are defined as distinct from each other. *Curriculum* is used as a general term for the entire organized teaching plan of a subject. *Syllabus* refers to a sub-area or smaller division of the curriculum. A curriculum can therefore consist of a number of syllabuses.

Figure 1. *The L2 Curriculum Framework*

Content of L2 curriculum	Objectives of a second language curriculum				
	Proficiency	Knowledge	Affect	Transfer	Teaching strategies
Language syllabus	▓▓▓				Formal study and practice
Communicative activity syllabus	▓▓▓				Functional activities (communicative)
Culture syllabus		▓▓▓			Formal study (knowledge about) Functional activities (experiences)
General language education syllabus				▓▓▓	Spontaneous or planned

Key: Major Focus

Minor Focus

Adapted from H. H. Stern (1982) R. Ullmann (1982), Modern Language Centre, Ontario Institute for Studies in Education, Toronto, Canada

The content of the L2 curriculum framework seen in Figure 1 is expressed as four syllabuses: the language syllabus, which deals with the formal aspects of language, including speech acts, notions, and functions; the communicative activity syllabus, which parallels the formal language syllabus and provides natural situations for language use; the culture syllabus, which provides an authentic context for the communication of ideas and information within the second language learning setting; and the general language education syllabus, which makes room for aspects of language phenomena and language learning strategies as an integral part of the L2 curriculum.

Each syllabus mentioned above is characterized differentially by four major objectives in varying degrees of focus. These objectives or "student learning outcomes" are:

proficiency (understanding of and an ability to communicate in the L2);

knowledge (specific experience with and knowledge of a target language and its people);

affect (positive attitudes towards the L2 and towards learning it);

transfer (general knowledge about language and language learning, the ability to apply L2 learning strategies in new settings, and the ability to apply knowledge, attitudes, and skills learned in the L2 setting to other subject areas of the curriculum).

Figure 1 arranges these objectives from the most language specific to the most general. Proficiency, knowledge, and affective objectives apply to the specific L2 setting. Transfer has a high degree of generalizability to general language learning settings and to settings outside the domain of language. Affect is concerned with the positive attitudes and values one wishes to see develop in L2 learners. This objective can be applied to all areas of the curriculum.

It is important to consider the four syllabuses as closely integrated entities that together form the basis for the expanded L2 curriculum framework. Likewise, the objectives that have here been presented separately for discussion purposes should be thought of as integrated. The four objectives are related to each content syllabus in terms of their varying degree of emphasis. Thus, while the proficiency objective forms the major focus of the language syllabus, it is also an appropriate objective for other syllabuses in the framework, although it may have lower priority. Similarly, while knowledge is the central objective of the culture syllabus, affect, transfer, and proficiency are also relevant. Figure 1 illustrates the varying degrees of importance of the objectives to each syllabus within the curriculum model.

The multidimensional L2 curriculum framework described here has strong potential. Taken as a whole, the framework can provide more flexibility to the L2 curriculum and a greater variety of second-language learning experiences for the student. In addition, each syllabus can provide clearly enunciated objectives to guide L2 methodologies and, by extension, L2 materials development. For example, the language syllabus as it is defined in our framework implies formal study and practice strategies, whereas the communicative activity syllabus suggests a more functional or experiential approach to L2 teaching. Syllabus content and methodologies should, in turn, guide the development of related teaching materials.

THE L2 CURRICULUM FRAMEWORK AND THE MODULE-MAKING PROJECT

The L2 framework has provided an important construct for work in the Module-Making Project. We have used this framework in an attempt to broaden the currently accepted L2 curriculum base and to develop prototype modules that focus on culture and communicative activities. In essence, the project has endorsed a thematic and activity approach to promote the development of communicative competence on the part of the L2 student.

Although a few French as a second language (FSL) programs that are communicatively based have been developed to date, they are not in widespread use in Canada. The modular approach provides an additional example of material with communicative content and methodology. We have suggested that the criteria of relevance, worthwhileness, and comprehensibility, which provide an incentive for communication, can be met at least in part by a study of the cuture of the target language. The teaching of culture, a potentially important content area of the L2 curriculum, is too often overlooked as a source of comprehensible input in actual classroom practice. Cultural content in the L2 curriculum can provide a forum for a great deal of communicative language development. It can provide an environment for the emotional and intellectual involvement of students in their language program that is a necessary stimulus for language learning (Nemetz-Robinson 1981). Worthwhile cultural activities can at the same time be educationally stimulating and promote the development of communication in the L2 classroom.

Twenty-five modules have been published for elementary and secondary FSL programs. When several of these modules are used over an extended period of time, the expanded substantive content that they contribute to the L2 program helps develop L2 proficiency in students and orients teaching in a more communicative direction. The following description of how the modules were prepared and what they contain may serve to illustrate this point.

Culture Modules[2]

A first step in the preparation of the series of culture modules based on the theme "La francophonie au Canada" was to select and categorize relevant topics and subtopics that reflected contemporary French Canadian culture. This was no easy task, as current, carefully compiled information tended to be difficult to find. Indeed, some recent literature on the content of the L2 curriculum (Stern 1984) presents a strong argument in favor of more systematic research on the contemporary nature of French Canadian society to serve as a data base for further curriculum and materials development.

In spite of the difficulties, attempts were made to fill in the gaps by developing a unique categorization scheme of information gathered from the well-developed and readily accessible francophone media in Canada. French radio, television, magazines and newspapers, and government publications dealing with the contemporary culture of Quebec were all consulted, analyzed, and categorized. Because the largest group of French-speaking Canadians is found in the province of Quebec, we focused our initial endeavors on the francophone culture of this province. A thematic chart highlighting certain key features of Quebec society in the early 70s was prepared. This chart served as a guide for the development of modules and dealt with such topics as the music and literature of French Canada, famous personalities and their impact on contemporary Canadian society, peer group issues and viewpoints, and so on. The chart supplied essential information about sources and resources. This information was used to validate the authenticity of the cultural content we intended to include in the modules. In addition, the chart was helpful in pointing out possible thematic overlapping in the event that individual modules were unified for presentation in a series. In later years, as the project expanded its work to include elements of the Acadian francophone community in Canada, a similar schematic chart was developed for Acadia.

Modules dealing with famous personalities and their impact on the anglophone and francophone societies of Canada have been developed in a variety of ways. For example, several modules present the lives and views of important Canadian political figures. One module, *René Lévesque et le séparatisme*, shows René Lévesque as the spokesman for Quebec nationalism and independence. Another module, *Trudeau et le fédéralisme*, presents Pierre Elliot Trudeau as the spokesman for unity and Canadian federalism.

The issues presented in these two modules cross subject-matter boundaries and serve to integrate Canadian studies with French instruction. Both modules use historical and contemporary information to promote discussion of issues that tend to recur on the Canadian political scene from generation to generation. English-French relations and the nature of Canadian unity are presented through authentic, first-hand sources, both written and oral. A conscious attempt has been made not to indulge in editorial comments and to allow these famous personalities to speak for themselves via their eloquent writings and speeches.

Humorous political cartoons are included, however, to provide a counterbalance to the views so eloquently and convincingly expressed by both Lévesque and Trudeau.

The materials in these modules are challenging because they contain no ready-made answers. Their open-ended quality is conducive to question, debate, discussion, and even argument. The supplementary content that they bring to the L2 program leads students in a search for meaningful responses to real-life issues. Students arrive at their responses through informed discussion and serious reflection.

Excerpts of the Prime Minister's country-wide radio and television speech of November 24, 1976, concerning the election of a separatist Parti Québécois government in Quebec.

While the transcript follows the speech as delivered, slips of the tongue are not reproduced.

. . . La question, la question essentielle qu'il faut se poser, c'est la suivante: les Francophones du Québec peuvent-ils considérer le Canada comme leur pays? Ou doivent-ils se sentir chez eux seulement au Québec?

Il est certain qu'un nouveau partage des pouvoirs entre Ottawa et les Provinces ne fera jamais, par lui-même, qu'un Francophone se sente plus à l'aise à Victoria ou à Toronto qu'à Québec. Ce problème cherche une autre réponse.

Pourquoi? Parce que les Québécois sont fiers. Ils veulent s'épanouir libres et indépendants.

La seule question qui importe, c'est la suivante: qui du Canada ou du Québec peut le mieux assurer leur épanouissement dans le respect de la liberté et de l'indépendance? [. . .]

A mon avis, le Canada ne peut pas, ne doit pas survivre par la force.

Ce pays ne restera uni que si l'ensemble des citoyens veut vivre ensemble, dans une même société civile.

L'histoire a créé ce pays de la rencontre de deux réalités, deux réalités très fortes, très caractérisées: l'anglaise et la française.

Ces deux réalités se sont enrichies, comme on le sait, par la suite, par l'apport de beaucoup d'autres réalités, des gens venus des quatre coins du monde.

Mais cette rencontre, parfois dure à accepter et difficile à vivre, cette rencontre est devenue l'étoffe même de notre vie comme nation, la source de notre originalité et la fondation même de notre identité comme peuple. [. . .]

Mon désaccord avec Monsieur René Lévesque depuis dix ans vient de ma conviction qu'il y a place au Canada pour tous les Canadiens; alors que lui, probablement à regret et peut-être même avec mélancolie, est convaincu du contraire.

Trudeau states that the essential question one should ask is whether francophones in Quebec can feel at home anywhere in Canada or only in Quebec.

Trudeau expresses the view that the central question is whether the growth of freedom and independence for Quebeckers is best assured by Canada or by Quebec alone.

Trudeau is referring to the historical antecedents which have characterized Canada; the meeting of the English and the French, who were later joined by people from all parts of the world.

Trudeau contrasts his viewpoint with that of René Lévesque, the newly elected Prime Minister of Quebec and leader of the separatist party. Trudeau expresses the belief that Canada is for all Canadians and suggests that M. Lévesque believes the opposite.

Moi, je crois qu'on peut être à la fois bon Québécois et bon Canadien, et je me battrai jusqu'au bout contre ceux qui voudraient m'empêcher d'être l'un et l'autre.

Je parle aujourd'hui à tous les Canadiens comme je le fais depuis que j'occupe mon poste. Je vous parle comme à des *concitoyens*. Je vous parle d'une fra-

> Trudeau expresses the view that for him being a good Québécois and a good Canadian are not mutually exclusive.

> *concitoyens*, m.pl.—fellow citizens

ternité beaucoup plus large que celle du sang, une fraternité humaine fondée sur l'espérance, fondée sur la charité au sens biblique; car je crois profondément que si la nation canadienne doit survivre, ce ne saurait être que dans le respect et l'amour des uns pour les autres.

> Trudeau asks Canadians to consider a brotherhood more encompassing than blood; a human fraternity based on hope and on charity in the biblical sense. He expresses the view that the Canadian nation will only survive in mutual respect and in love for one another.

Excerpt from tape transcript in *Trudeau et le fédéralisme* (OISE 1978 pp. 3–5).

René Lévesque et le séparatisme (OISE 1979)

PYGMALION

Trudeau et le fédéralisme
(OISE 1978)

The musical heritage of French Canada is a unique feature of the Canadian cultural setting. In our work we chose to demonstrate the impact of this heritage on French Canadian society in two modules: *Gilles Vigneault—l'homme et l'oeuvre* and *L'Acadie d'Edith Butler: chansons et réflexions*.

Gilles Vigneault—l'homme et l'oeuvre treats this famous singer as both *chansonnier* and poet. His poem-songs are presented on tape and are explored as contemporary Canadian poetry. Detailed *explications de texte* give students the opportunity to learn about Quebec culture through the eloquent language of one of its native sons. As students hear Vigneault sing or recite and discuss his song-poems, they have the opportunity to attain an in-depth understanding of the sincerity and emotion these songs convey. This understanding enables anglophone students to grasp the popularity of Vigneault and his contemporaries and to appreciate more fully the impact of the *chansonnier* movement on Quebec society in the 60s and 70s.

In *L'Acadie d'Edith Butler: chansons et réflexions,* extensive interviews convey the personality of this famous Acadian singer. Throughout the module she discusses the significance of being an Acadian in the twentieth century, the trials and tribulations of her chosen career as an Acadian *chansonnière*, and some interesting personal accounts of her historical antecedents.

Édith Butler parle de l'Acadie
BANDE 1, CÔTÉ A

Le mascaret

Mon père sur la mer il m'envoie,
Le soir à terre il vient vers moi,
Il veut savoir si je m'en émois,
Des déportés qui furent noyés

Pensez-vous, ma fille, qu'ils seront vengés?

I: Nous avons commencé notre émission aujourd'hui avec la musique d'Édith Butler. Bonjour Édith.
É: Bonjour.
I: Bienvenue à Toronto.

Le mascaret—tidal wave or tidal bore
A brief biography of Edith Butler and her feelings about her Acadian heritage.

This section of the tape, in which Édith Butler speaks about Acadia, presents her personal view of Acadian history and the events that have significance for Acadia today.

É: Merci beaucoup. Ça me fait plaisir d'être ici.

I: Édith, c'est qui au juste Édith Butler?

É: Ah, c'est pas tellement difficile à définir. Disons que c'est la fille à Johnny Butler et de Lauretta Godin. J'ai venu au monde dans un village qui s'appelait Paquetville, près de Caraquet. Ça c'est au nord-est du Nouveau-Brunswick et puis ce que je fais actuellement, disons, les chansons que je chante qui parle de l'Acadie moderne et aussi de l'Acadie traditionelle c'est tout simplement, je pense, le reflet de mon village et aussi le reflet de ce que j'ai vécu et ce que je vis encore—la culture acadienne.

Parce que quand j'étais jeune, quand j'étais petite, disons, on n'avait pas la télévision dans la maison. Alors on faisait beaucoup de musique, et la musique qu'on faisait c'était la musique qui nous était donnée, disons, par nos parents, par nos grand-parents et par les voisins. C'est la culture traditionelle.

I: Um hm.

É: Et actuellement, je continue ça. J'essaie de garder au présent toute cette culture qui m'a été transmise, disons, depuis des générations.

• • •

I: Tu sais, je suis extrêmement intéressée à l'histoire acadienne. Pourriez-vous nous dire qui au juste étaient les Acadiens?

É: Disons que les premiers qui sont arrivés c'était avec Champlain en 1604. Je pense que la plupart des gens venaient soit de la Picardie, du Poitou, peut-être aussi de la Bretagne et de la Normandie.

Et c'était des gens qui sont venus s'établir là pour un peu fuir le régime français, mais je pense qu'ils sont pas restés tellement longtemps parce qu'il y a eu beaucoup de problèmes de scorbut. À la première année ils vivaient sur l'île Sainte-Croix, une toute petite île. Il y a eu beaucoup, beaucoup de maladie et on a perdu plus que la moitié des hommes.

I: Oui.

É: Après ça ils sont revenus en 1608, je crois c'est en 1608, ils se sont établis à ce moment-là à Port Royal et de là la colonie est partie de là. Et ensuite s'en est suivi plusieurs mouvements, disons, de colons qui sont venus s'établir dans cette région-là.

• • •

Quand ils se sont établis ils s'appelaient les Français neutres. Ils voulaient pas être ni sur le côté des Français, ni sur le côté des Anglais.

• • •

The French you hear on the tape is the natural, spontaneous speech of Édith Butler and the interviewer. When following along in your Transcript Booklet, you may notice certain features typical of conversation. For example, there are repetitions and hesitations when the speakers search for the right word. At times the grammar does not correspond with what you have been taught. Some of these features occur frequently in oral French. Others are slips of the tongue. Still others may be typical of Acadian speech.

This section of the tape deals with the early history of the Acadian people and their settlements.

Picardie, Poitou, Bretagne, Normandie are regions in France.

scorbut—scurvy

Ils voulaient pas être ni sur le côté des Français, ni sur le côté des Anglais—a reference to the frequent wars between the two big colonial powers of the day.

Et je pense qu'il fait aujourd'hui qu'un Acadien est un Acadien c'est son histoire, c'est les difficultés qu'il a eues, c'est la déportation, c'est sa façon de penser. . . .

la déportation—In 1755 the Acadians were forced to leave their settlements and their lands over the question of Acadian allegiance to the British, who controlled the colony at that time.

• • •

[Les Acadiens] ils ont été déportés très loin en Louisiane, même en France, en Angleterre, dans tous les États-Unis, dans le Maine, Massachusetts, en Georgie, dans les Carolines du Nord et du Sud, et il y a beaucoup de ces gens-là qui après sont partis à la recherche de leurs parents, sont montés vers le nord pour revenir s'établir dans la terre d'Acadie. Mais pas sur leurs anciennes terres parce qu'ils étaient déjà pris par les Anglais.

Mais beaucoup se sont établis pas tellement loin des Anglais comme à Church Point, ensuite à Comeauville, à Digby. . . .

• • •

Puis le roman d'Antonine, le dernier roman qui a gagné justement le prix Goncourt, s'appelle *Pélagie-la-charrette*. Et c'est l'histoire de cette femme qui est partie de la Georgie après la déportation avec sa grande charrette à la recherche de toute sa famille. Puis en montant d'un état à l'autre, là, des États-Unis, elle a retrouvé des parents, des cousins, des gens, des déportés. Puis quand elle a fini par arriver en Acadie elle avait avec elle tout un peuple. C'est une très, très belle histoire . . .

Antonine—Antonine Maillet, an Acadian author who, in 1979, won the Prix Goncourt, a coveted French literary prize, for her novel, *Pélagie-la-charrette*.

L'Acadie d'Edith Butler: chansons et réflexions (OISE 1982, pp. 1–2, 5).

Students have the opportunity to listen to authentic Acadian French music, to consider the little known history of the Acadians, and to discuss many issues that relate the main events of Acadian history to similar world events of more recent times.

FOLLOW-UP DISCUSSION AFTER THE PRESENTATION OF THE TAPES

The following are suggestions which the teacher may use after the presentation of the tapes to stimulate discussion. The first three suggestions are most closely related to the first tape, Side A ("Édith Butler parle de l'Acadie"). The fourth suggestion relates more directly to Tape 1, Side B, and Tape 2, Sides A and B.

1. Discutez ce qui, au cours des siècles, a permis aux Acadiens de subsister même dans l'adversité (par exemple, le souvenir de la déportation, leur langue, le rôle de la musique). Décrivez

certains aspects de la culture moderne des Acadiens.

2. Renseignez-vous sur d'autres peuples qui ont connu une histoire pleine de perturbations (par exemple, les Cambodgiens, les Arméniens, les Juifs, les Indiens de l'Amérique du Nord, "les réfugiés de la mer"). Comparez et mettez en contraste leur expérience avec celle des Acadiens.

3. Bien que de nos jours certains Acadiens au Nouveau-Brunswick insistent pour que leurs droits soient reconnus davantage, le mouvement séparatiste en Acadie a été moins fort que le mouvement séparatiste au Québec. Comment expliquez-vous cette différence?

4. Que révèle Édith Butler au sujet du rôle de la musique comme moyen de conserver une culture?

L'Acadie d'Edith Butler: chansons et réflexions (OISE 1982, p. 19).

The lives and views of famous and eloquent personalities can be a powerful stimulation for communication, particularly at the secondary school level. However, we felt that it should also be possible to stimulate communication in FSL senior classes by using authentic data about peer groups from other cultural environments. To give the L2 program relevance and an up-to-date quality, we considered it advisable to prepare materials that reflected current peer group issues and tastes. We experimented with this concept in our design of *Devant le micro,* a module for senior anglophone students, and found that the use of authentic peer group data across cultures leads to interesting results in the L2 classroom.

The substantive content for *Devant le micro* was based on interviews with francophone teenagers. The materials include three taped interviews, tape transcript booklets, biography booklets, and a teacher's guide. Since we wished to base our module content on real-life conversations with francophone teenagers, it was necessary to find an appropriate peer group of francophone students and interview them on an individual basis in a setting that would not intimidate them, but that at the same time would be conducive to broadcast quality recording. Fortunately, the Modern Language Centre (OISE) has a recording studio of high caliber. However, it was clear that such surroundings might intimidate teenage speakers and that their language style might change from informal speech to a more formal, stilted speech. We were concerned that in extreme cases some speakers might become completely inhibited. In order to overcome these potential problems the following plan was proposed. First, a professional interviewer, who was herself a French Canadian, was hired. She was provided with general background information about each teenager in the sample and also a list of themes to be discussed during the interview, but no structure for the interview beyond that point. Secondly, a party was held for all the teenagers in the sample. While the teenagers were enjoying themselves at the party, they were each taken aside to the studio for an interview on a one-to-one basis.

This strategy seemed to work. The French Canadian teenagers responded comfortably to the interviewer and were able to express personal views about their schooling, way of life, hobbies, and career aspirations. As a result, the conversations used in the materials were live and unrehearsed, a fact not lost on the anglophone students. The views of the young francophones were expressed in a spontaneous and natural style, and provided a strong stimulus for open-ended discussion in the senior L2 class.

Chantal: Comment est-ce que ça se passe à l'école? Quelle sorte d'école est-ce? C'est *une école*. . . .

une école privée—a private school

Judith: *Privée.* Disons c'est une école—premièrement c'est juste des filles—j'aime pas ça. C'est une bonne école, premièrement, mais c'est réputé comme étant une école de snobs. C'est vrai—la majorité sont, sont des snobs. Il y en a d'autres *au travers* qui sont, sont gentils disons.

au travers—among (them)

Chantal: Qui est-ce qui enseigne? Est-ce que ce sont *des religieuses?*

des religieuses f.pl.—nuns

Judith: Non. Il y a quelques années c'étaient des religieuses, mais présentement c'est presque tous *des laïques.*

des laïques m. & f.pl.—people (here, specifically teachers) who do not belong to a religious order

Chantal: Est-ce que la discipline est très sévère?

Judith: Disons que c'est sévère au point de vue costume, parce qu'on porte *un costume*. On a une belle petite jupe et un petit *"blazer"* vert. Mais à part ça, pour la discipline, non, c'est pas trop sévère.

un costume—a uniform
"blazer" m.—blazer (anglicism)

Chantal: Est-ce que vous aimez ça, avoir un uniforme?

Judith: Non. Disons que l'uniforme est beau, quand c'est juste une personne qui le porte, mais quand ça fait deux mille qu'on voit passer avec la même jupe et le même "blazer" là—ça, ça commence à être *énervant.*

énervant—irritating

Chantal: Le côté snob, la réputation de cette école-là, est-ce que ça se sent dans l'enseignement?

Judith: Non, je croirais pas. C'est pas de la manière qu'ils nous enseignent qui fait que c'est un, un collège de réputation snob. C'est plutôt parce que, tous ceux qui vont là là—et pas tout le monde, mais—la

majorité sont des gens qui sont très, très riches. Il y a
beaucoup de filles de mon âge là qui ont seize, dix-
sept ans qui ont leur auto, et puis, qui ont leur
cheval—et puis ils font rien que de parler de ça. Par
exemple, il y en a certaines qui parlent des fins de
semaine à New York—juste pour la fin de semaine—
ils nous disent, *"Où que t'as passé la fin de semaine?"*—
bien, moi je dis, "Je suis allée à Trois-Pistoles."

où que t'as passé—"où est-ce que
tu as passé"

Chantal: Est-ce que vous habitez à l'école?

Judith: Non. Euh, j'habite avec ma soeur dans une
maison.

Chantal: Alors vous êtes très *libre?*

libre—free

Judith: Oui. Mes parents ont décidé de, ont acheté
une maison à Québec parce que, on était trois, et puis
au lieu de payer pour trois *pensionnaires* ça, *ça revenait
moins*—et puis je reste avec ma soeur—mon frère est
en appartement présentement, juste depuis cette
année—et puis je reste avec ma soeur depuis quatre
ans dans cette maison-là avec—et puis il y a d'autres
chambres pour des étudiants de l'Université Laval
parce qu'on est juste *en face.*

pensionnaires m. & f.—boarders
ça revenait moins—that cost less

en face—opposite

Chantal: Qu'est-ce que vous avez comme *passe-temps?*

passe-temps m.inv.—hobby,
hobbies

Judith: La musique. J'adore la musique.

Chantal: Est-ce que ça laisse le temps à, pour des
sorties avec les garçons?

Judith: Pendant la semaine durant l'année scolaire,
disons je sors pas tellement, parce que je, je suis,
j'arrive de l'école, et puis j'ai mon piano—et puis
après ça, ça, bien, disons que j'ai pas, *je sens pas le
besoin de sortir trop trop* puisqu'on est quinze en tout
dans la maison—*des gars* et puis des filles—ça fait que
c'est pas, c'est pas un problème. Mais la fin de
semaine, disons que j'ai le temps de sortir, et le
piano, je le mets un peu de côté, et puis, je sors.

*je sens pas le besoin de sortir trop
trop*—I don't feel too much need
to go out
des gars m. inv.—boys, guys

Chantal: Mais dites, dans une maison comme ça,
mixte, à seize, dix-sept ans, est-ce que c'est pas un
peu dangereux?

Judith: Tout le monde pense ça mais c'est quand on—
moi je pense que c'est quand on est libre de faire ce
qu'on veut qu'on fait rien. Disons c'est un risque pour
mes parents O.K., quand ils nous ont envoyés là—
mais la première chose, la première année que j'étais
là mon frère avait vingt-trois ans, et puis c'est lui qui,
qui *surveillait* tout, et puis disons que c'est *un genre*
assez, et puis je dirais même trop sérieux—ça fait

surveiller (surveillait, 3rd pers.
imp.)—to supervise, to keep an
eye on

qu'il y avait pas aucun danger. Et puis, aussi mon père monte très souvent, et puis ma mère monte *faire le ménage* des fois. Mais disons que présentement il y a aucun danger dans la maison parce qu'on est tous *des amis*—ça reste au *niveau* ami—et puis, chacun de la maison a ses amis en dehors de la maison.

un genre—a type
faire le ménage—to do the housework

des amis—pals
niveau m.—level

Chantal: Est-ce que vous avez voyagé beaucoup jusqu'à maintenant?

Judith: Disons pas tellement, mais j'aime bien ça—je suis allée—avant de venir en Ontario travailler ici, j'ai fait toutes les provinces maritimes avec quatre autres de mes amis—et puis, disons que je, j'ai bien aimé ça.

Interview excerpt from *Devant le micro*. (OISE 1977 pp. 7–8)

As we discovered during the evaluation procedures, this type of material provided interesting insights for the anglophone peer group. "The francophone students are just like us," they told their teachers. "Only the language separates us." It seems that materials prepared in this manner can be effective in sensitizing students across cultures. Obviously, both cultural similarities and differences come into play.

Communicative Activity Modules

Second language educators have always accepted the fact that the target language can be used to deal with the study and enjoyment of literature. Recently, however, the communicative approach to second language teaching has stressed the importance of using language in authentic and natural contexts. This trend has created a need for activity-oriented materials in which language learning could be treated in an experiential manner. Several of the activity modules, such as *Le Hockey,* a module for junior and intermediate level students, reflect this experiential approach. In *Le Hockey* students are required to use French in order to play two language games: a card game that simulates the challenge of the hockey experience and a picture-recognition game. The basic premise underlying the activities in this module is that the learners' own perception of the *usefulness* of the language they are learning can be a powerful motivating force that will foster the development of language proficiency and encourage communication, even at fairly rudimentary levels of L2 instruction.

In order to use this module it is essential that students learn to use approximately thirty-two specialized language items related to ice hockey, a favorite sport in Canada. The standard, traditional approach to teaching new vocabulary would soon leave the students floundering or disinterested. But by allowing students to *learn while playing* teachers soon notice that learners can assimilate and use a large amount of new French vocabulary in an astonishingly short period of time.

Six basic language items and the sequence essential for scoring a goal are introduced by flashcards. The remaining items, learned by playing the card game, provide many opportunities for exchanges between students. During this interaction students often have chances to communicate. For example, they can request information, give explanations, and express joy or dismay as the game progresses. They are motivated to learn this substantial amount of new French quickly because they want to succeed, and in order to succeed they need to know and to use a certain number of French expressions. Repeated visual clues on flashcards and in the card game provide a learning aid.

The second game, *Jeux Croisés*, helps students use and perfect the French they have already encountered while playing the card game. It challenges them to understand increasingly complex hockey expressions that resemble more and more what they would actually hear in a broadcast play-by-play.

When students have mastered this task they are encouraged to use their new knowledge to listen to hockey games in French, first by using the simulated taped broadcast in the module and then by extending their listening activities to authentic radio and television broadcasts in French. Expanding the curriculum content in this way leads students to transfer their FSL experience to the broader setting in the world outside the classroom.

Le Hockey is an example of communicative materials that increase students' proficiency in French in a variety of ways: through listening, speaking, and reading. However, the goals go beyond the development of proficiency skills. Students want to play and win a game; to listen and understand a French broadcast. French is the tool to help them achieve these goals. Experience with *Le Hockey* suggests that it is necessary to introduce nontrivial thematic content and authentic language at all levels of instruction in order to engage students' interest and motivate them to communicate in the L2. Since educators generally accept that it is important to capture students' interest from their first contact with the new language, building on previous knowledge in order to expand the content of our programs seems to be a powerful strategy that can help establish a productive setting for communication in the L2 classroom.

IMPLICATIONS OF THE MODULAR APPROACH FOR PROGRAM PLANNING

In the preceding discussion modules were described primarily as individual units that can supplement existing programs. However, we also

Jeux croisés   1

	A	B	C	D
1				
2				
3				
4				

SCRIPT FOR *JEUX CROISÉS*

Jeux croisés 1

	A	B	C	D
1	La *mise au jeu* en zone torontoise (1)	Une passe à Doh-erty (4)	*Un lancer frappé* (7)	*Le disque est bloqué* par le gardien (10)
2	Et c'est *Noritz* des Memorials qui *entre en zone adverse* (2)	*Une passe* jusqu'à Eadie—ratée (14)	*Belle accélération!* (9)	*Un tir* au but—bloqué (10)
3	Noritz fait *une passe* à l'ailier McInnes (4)	*Un tir—bloqué* (10)	Oh belle *mise en échec* donné par Cornwall (6)	*Le tir* de La-tour—ah—*trop haut* (11)
4	*Un tir qui rate* le but (12)	*Le défenseur va derrière son but* (15)	*Une passe à Lee jusqu'à McInnes* (13)	Et voilà un *but!* (8)

Le Hockey (OISE 1979, p. 5)

envisage a more extended use of the modular approach where teachers select and group modules from a data bank according to theme or skill focus, and prepare mini-programs that relate in a very direct way to the needs and interests of particular L2 classes. The concept of a data bank of modules is based on two premises: first, that a systematic, ordered core of structures and vocabulary is available for the development of the linguistic syllabus in the L2 curriculum, and secondly, that a sufficient number of modules is available to permit the selection and grouping of these materials in a flexible manner. Obviously a large number of modules is needed if a bank of modules is to operate successfully.

The publication of twenty-five modules for French as a second language provides the beginning of a data bank for French instruction. An opportunity now exists to select material according to the age level, general interests, background knowledge and particular stage of linguistic development of specific target groups. Modules can now be organized according to their thematic or substantive content with a view to expanding an issue already encountered in the main program of study. Likewise, modules can be selected and grouped in various ways to introduce topics that have not been discussed to date in the regular program.

Teachers are beginning to experiment with this approach to L2 curriculum planning. They are developing their own mini-programs based on the available data bank of modules. It begins to seem quite possible that in the near future several L2 programs at the same grade level will share a basic core of linguistic features, and yet differ in substantive content as teachers choose a variety of modules to adapt their program to different student interests and needs. For example, one teacher may choose to focus on the development of cultural enrichment in the L2 program and plan a mini-program dealing with the music of French Canada. Another teacher may opt for an interdisciplinary, team-teaching approach. In conjunction with the History Department this teacher may select modules that develop a mini-program integrating Canadian Studies and French language instruction. A third teacher may prefer a business skills orientation and develop a mini-program that gives students some practical experience in the area of bilingual careers. The possibilities for flexible program development will be constrained only by the type and number of modules available for selection.

The L2 framework presented earlier ventured suggestions about the nature of the curriculum *content* that should form part of a second language program. The module bank approach discussed here offers an organizational principle for curriculum planning. This principle suggests that the L2 curriculum could be made more flexible and adaptable by organizing the program content around a central core of systematically ordered linguistic features enhanced by the addition of modules at particular points in the program when they are deemed suitable by the L2 teacher. Curriculum guidelines developed by Ministries of Education and many published L2 series have provided substantial assistance in organizing the basic linguistic core for L2 programs. The modules available to date provide a *point de départ* for experimenting with this new, expanded planning concept.

FUTURE DIRECTIONS

While it is evident that a start has been made in the development of a modular approach to L2 teaching and learning, much more needs to be done. The potential of this approach as an aid to curriculum planning warrants further exploration. Likewise, more modules must be developed, not only in the areas of culture and communicative activities but in other areas of the L2 curriculum as well. And of course, while the focus of this discussion has been on the development of French programs, it is clear that the modular approach should be equally applicable to other languages.[3] In addition, there is a need to evaluate the impact of this approach on students' attitudes toward L2 learning and toward the target culture. Finally, it seems important to monitor the L2 achievement of learners who use modules.[4]

This report will conclude with the suggestion that expansion of the curriculum content in accordance with the preceding discussion and use of the concept of a data bank of L2 modules to organize this expanded curriculum more flexibly will provide a more interesting L2 experience for our students. The result should be an increase in L2 proficiency and a corresponding increase in communication in the classroom.

NOTES

1. For more details regarding the L2 framework the reader is referred in particular to the work of H. H. Stern, founder and former director of the Modern Language Centre, OISE. See Stern 1982, 1983 a, 1983 b and 1984 and also Ullmann 1982 and 1983. For a somewhat different approach to the issue see also the curriculum model described in Allen 1983.

2. Further information concerning these modules and others can be found in Stern et al. 1980; Ullmann and Balchunas 1979; Ullmann 1981 and 1983.

3. More information about modules for English as a second language can be found in Allen and Howard 1981.

4. For some interesting observations regarding the importance of formative and summative evaluation see Allen et al. 1984.

REFERENCES

Allen, J. P. B. 1983. "A Three-Level Curriculum Model for Second Language Education." *The Canadian Modern Language Review* 40(1):23–43.

Allen, J. P. B. and J. Howard. 1981. "Subject-related ESL: An Experiment in Communicative Language Teaching." *The Canadian Modern Language Review* 37(3):535–550.

Allen, J. P. B., J. Howard, and R. Ullmann. 1984. "Module-making Research." In *Issues and Education Policies.* C. Brumfit (ed.). Oxford: Pergamon Press, 83–98.

Breen, M. P. and C. N. Candlin. 1980. "The Essentials of a Communicative Curriculum in Language Teaching." *Applied Linguistics* 1(2):89–112.

Canale, M. and M. Swain. 1980. "Theoretical Bases of Communicative Approaches to Second Language Teaching and Testing." *Applied Linguistics* 1(1):1–47.

Johnson, K. 1979. "Communicative Approaches and Communicative Processes." In C. J. Brumfit and K. Johnson (eds.). *The Communicative Approach to Language Teaching.* Oxford: Oxford University Press, 192–205.

Krashen, S. D. 1982. *Principles and Practice in Second Language Acquisition.* Oxford: Pergamon Press.

Lewy, A. (ed.). 1977. *Handbook of Curriculum Evaluation.* New York: Longman; Paris: UNESCO.

Nemetz-Robinson, G. L. 1981. *Issues in Second Language and Cross-Cultural Education.* Boston, Mass.: Heinle & Heinle.

Ontario Ministry of Education. 1977. *Teaching and Learning French as a Second Language: A New Program for Ontario Students.*

Savignon, S. 1983. *Communicative Competence: Theory and Classroom Practice.* Reading, Mass.: Addison-Wesley.

Savignon, S. and M. Berns (eds.). 1984. *Initiatives in Communicative Language Teaching.* Reading, Mass.: Addison-Wesley.

Stern, H. H. 1982. "French Core Programs across Canada: How Can We Improve Them?" *The Canadian Modern Language Review* 39(1):34–47.

———. 1983a. "Towards a Multidimensional Foreign Language Curriculum." In R. G. Mead (ed.). *Foreign Languages: Key Links in the Chain of Learning.* Middlebury, VT.: North East Conference, 120–146.

———. 1983b. *Fundamental Concepts of Language Teaching.* Oxford: Oxford University Press.

———. 1984. "A Quiet Language Revolution: Second Language Teaching in Canadian Contexts—Achievements and New Directions." *The Canadian Modern Language Review* 4(4):506–523.

Stern, H. H., R. Ullmann, M. Balchunas, G. Hanna, E. Schneidermann, and V. Argue. 1980. *Module Making: A Study in the Development and Evaluation of Learning Materials for French as a Second Language.* Toronto: Ontario Ministry of Education.

Ullmann, R. 1981. "A Thematic and Activity Approach to Communicative Language Teaching in Second Language Classrooms." *The Bulletin of the Canadian Association of Applied Linguistics* 3(2):183–194.

———. 1982. "A Broadened Curriculum Framework for Second Languages." *English Language Teaching Journal* 36(4):255–262.

———. 1983. *The Module Making Project and Communicative Language Teaching in the Core French Program*. Modern Language Centre, Toronto: Ontario Institute for Studies in Education.

Ullmann, R. and M. Balchunas. 1979. "Modules for Today: Implications for the French Curriculum of Tomorrow." *Orbit* 10(1):21–23.

Wilkins, D. A. 1972. "Grammatical, Situational and Notional Syllabuses." *Proceedings of the Third International Congress of Applied Linguistics,* Copenhagen, 1972. Heidelberg: Julius Groos Verlag. Reprinted in C. J. Brumfit and K. Johnson (eds.) 1979, *The Communicative Approach to Language Teaching.* Oxford: Oxford University Press, 82–90.

Chapter 5

The Bangalore Project: Description and Evaluation

Alan Beretta

Alan Beretta has taught English as a Second/Foreign Language in West Germany, Britain, Greece, and Saudi Arabia. At present, he is a professor at Sultan Qaboos University, in the Sultanate of Oman, where his duties primarily involve evaluation and research. He is also carrying out doctoral research under the supervision of the University of Edinburgh, Scotland. He has published articles on evaluation in TESOL Quarterly *and* Language Learning.

INTRODUCTION

The Bangalore/Madras Communicational Teaching Project (CTP) has aroused a great deal of professional interest in recent years. It constitutes a (strong) form of a communicative curriculum. Initiated and developed by N.S. Prabhu[1] in South India, in far from ideal circumstances and in actual school settings, it has subjected to thorough examination a major current model, one that stresses the value of unconscious assimilation in language learning.

To date, the most accessible discussions of the CTP in the literature are found in Johnson (1982) and Brumfit (1984a, 1984b). Detailed reports are available in the series of newsletters and bulletins issued by the Regional Institute of English (RIE), Bangalore. Apart from these publications, there is only scattered comment. However, a number of talks at various conferences and seminars have increased awareness of the project (see especially Allwright 1982; Prabhu 1982, 1983, 1984a and 1984b).

Early in 1984 I had the opportunity to carry out an independent evaluation of the CTP (Beretta 1984) following a feasibility study by Davies (1983). (See Beretta and Davies 1985 for a brief report.) This paper provides both a description of the project itself and an account of that evaluation. Its intention is to draw further attention to an enterprise that is increasingly being regarded as substantial and worthwhile.

DESCRIPTION

Background

The CTP began life as a local response to a local problem. It grew out of a sense of professional disenchantment with the prevalent structural approach that had failed to yield satisfactory results.

In the early 1950s the first structural syllabus was introduced in South India, but several years later it was observed that many teachers had merely applied grammar-translation methods to this new syllabus (Patel 1962; Smith 1962). The result seemed to be a case of innovation without change, and the subsequent campaign to rectify the situation has become almost legendary. The "Madras Snowball," as it became known, was an attempt to retrain over 30,000 teachers of English according to structural principles (Smith 1962, 1968). However, although structural teaching was apparently implemented with considerable determination, by the late 1970s dissatisfaction with it led Prabhu and his colleagues to cast about for alternatives that might promote more effective language learning.

Notional/functional syllabuses were considered at a seminar in Bangalore in 1978, but it was concluded that a change in syllabus-content would be unhelpful. Such a change would merely substitute one set of objectives for another: control of the semantic structure of the language for control of its grammatical system. The project team believed from the beginning that the generative nature of grammatical structure was a powerful argument in favor of its centrality as a goal in language teaching (RIE 1980b). Although the goal was never in doubt, the question of how best to arrive at it remained. Thus an exploration of methodology commended itself more convincingly than did the adoption of an alternative syllabus. Clarity on this issue has been in my opinion one of the abiding strengths of the project.

The catalyst that gave direction to this methodological exploration came at a seminar in Bangalore in 1979, chaired by H. G. Widdowson. Discussion of the use/usage distinction (Widdowson 1978) raised questions about the acquisition of usage itself, from which it emerged that usage might be enlarged by use-based language behavior. In other words, the structure of the language might be acquired through communicative activity (see Prabhu 1981). This implied a basic methodological principle: not "English for communication" but "English through communication"; not "learn English so that you will be able to do and say things later" but "say and do things now so that as a result you will learn English" (Prabhu 1980a:23). Hence the term *communicational* rather than "communicative" was used to characterize the project.

The guiding principle of the CTP was that form is best learned when the learner's attention is focused on meaning. To experiment with this principle a series of activities were tried out in the classroom (RIE 1979:10). A process of trial and error revealed that role-playing and dramatization did not work; nor did the narration of stories without endings that the pupils were to complete. The most promising results were obtained with tasks that involved problem solving. Consequently, tasks of this type came to dominate and eventually to oust other procedures.

Given that the central tenet of the evolving methodology was that form is best learned when the learner's attention is focused on meaning, any syllabus based on a focus on form would directly conflict with it. It was argued that a syllabus that specified linguistic behavior would make nonsense of a methodology that stipulated meaning-based activities (Prabhu 1980; see Prabhu 1984a for an example). Thus the notion of a linguistic syllabus was abandoned in favor of a syllabus dictated by the methodology, and the CTP opted for a task-oriented or procedural syllabus.

Developments in other parts of the world, notably studies in second language acquisition and interlanguage (Corder 1981), offered both empirical and theoretical support for the hypothesis being tested in South India. When the annual review seminar was held in 1981 the CTP had completed almost two years of experimental teaching and a level of coherence had been achieved which suggested readiness for a wider audience.[2]

I have maintained a retrospective attitude so far to emphasize the evolutionary development of the CTP. It is worth stressing that the project was not brought about by an imported ideology used as a coarse template for circumstances for which it was not designed. On the contrary, it was a locally inspired, independently developed initiative that constituted a practical manifestation of an emerging, world-wide consensus. Thus the main CTP principles, far from being doctrinal, are deeply rooted in classroom practice.

Consolidation

The assumption that focusing on meaning facilitates the assimilation of structure implies that to a great extent language structure can be acquired and operated subconsciously. This perspective is, of course, hardly new (see, for example, Palmer 1921/1964). Perhaps the best known readoption of this view in recent years is found in Krashen's work (1981, 1982). To my knowledge, however, Prabhu has not annexed the word "learning" and narrowed its scope; he has not implied that what is learned consciously cannot seep into the subconscious. Prabhu's reason for avoiding explicit attention to language is that this concept may conflict with the learner's constant process of hypothesis construction and revision. This is tantamount to saying that there is no reason to assume that the linguist's generalizations about language structure parallel whatever generalizations are actually involved in the learner's grammar construction. Conscious learning is based on a fully formed competence that is likely to be at odds with the learner's formative, transitional competence. In this sense, conscious learning can be regarded as a hindrance to natural learning. By contrast, what is learned naturally is considered more readily available for deployment:

> In the Bangalore Project . . . we concentrate on the ability to communicate, and assume that the acquisition of structure will arise out of this, and, furthermore, that the kind of structure acquisition that arises from this is a better form of competence, is more dependable than the kind of structural competence that results from teaching of structure itself. [Prabhu 1980b:161]

Linguistic specification is therefore abjured. By the same token, no provision is made for pre-selection of language for any particular lesson, nor for classroom activities that focus on language. In their place, the project proposes reasonably challenging problem solving activities that promote an understanding, and this involves an incidental struggle with language use. The learners' attempts to cope as well as possible with the language required are thought to be essential to the process of grammar construction. This implies that the linguistic resources required for the completion of a task are best perceived and internalized when the mind is engaged in analyzing.

CTP lessons comprise three stages: (1) pre-task (2) task and (3) feedback. The pre-task makes known the nature of the task, brings relevant language into play, regulates the difficulty level of the task, and allows some learners to learn from attempts made by others. The task itself is a period of self-reliant effort by each learner to achieve a clearly perceived goal (e.g., interpreting a schedule or a map). The feedback gives an indication to the learners as to their success at the task.

The pre-task is essentially a rehearsal during which the teacher's help is overt. The further the actual task is from the pre-task, the greater the challenge, and vice-versa. Achieving the appropriate regulation of the level of challenge is crucial to the success of the methodology. If the task is too difficult or too easy, interest flags and the learners' minds fail to become engaged. The criterion used by the CTP teachers is that at least half the class should succeed in performing at least half the task. One teacher stressed that if the level of the task was ill-suited to the class pandemonium ensued (Bose 1980:86–87).

I mentioned earlier that the CTP opted for a syllabus of tasks. This type of syllabus was essential to ensure a sense of continuity and sequential progression. In more concrete terms, it provided a framework in which each task could be translated into a lesson plan. The sequencing is partial: tasks dealing with the same general topic are divided into several cycles that recur intermittently throughout the course. A task cycle consists of three to five sequential lessons on one theme. Teachers determined that if the cycle were any longer learners suffered from what has been labelled "task fatigue" (see, for example, Elia 1981:32).

It has been charged that a procedural syllabus of this kind does not ensure adequate coverage of the language. Prabhu (RIE 1980b) counters this objection with the assertion that any element of language not covered during the course of a year or two of communicational teaching must be peripheral. Even so, as Johnson pointed out in a discussion (RIE 1980c), the tasks themselves are all cognitive (apologizing, for example); and, one might add, in general they involve affective language that has little scope for development. To this Prabhu answers,

There is no real danger because learners will be learning to learn; if they listen to apologies they will pick [the relevant language] up. Form through meaning is necessarily cognitive. Otherwise we shall end up with form in relation to meaning (RIE 1980c:153).

I find this response is interesting for two reasons: first, because it rejects an appeal to linguistic prediction and the inevitable next step, pre-specification; and secondly, because it reaffirms the Humboldtian dictum that language makes "infinite use of finite means." Let us now consider each point in turn.

First, the attack on coverage focuses attention on the difference between a "communicative" approach and a "communicational" approach. The former preselects language, for example, in terms of notions or functions, while the latter relinquishes this level of control. As soon as provision is made for certain areas of language (like apologizing) to be made available as input, the approach ceases to be communicational. Although the immediate intention might be not to "teach" such items by planning for activities to relate to language categories, eventually the syllabus becomes linguistic. Thus if the CTP is to remain consistent, such appeals are rightly resisted.

They may be resisted also on the grounds that "grammar is enough," which is the second point. The reaffirmation of the centrality of grammar has an air of paradox in a context where structural syllabuses have been abandoned. But the paradox disappears if the senses of the term "grammar" are considered:

> When statements are made of the form "when grammar is taught, grammar alone is learnt," the word 'grammar' is being used with unhelpful ambiguity. If the grammar learnt is being equated with the grammar taught, then that knowledge of grammar cannot represent grammatical competence in the sense of an internally constructed and unconsciously deployed system. . . . [Prabhu 1984b]

Moreover,

> . . . arguments on the lines of "grammar is not enough" may be taking too restricted a view of what grammatical competence involves and the achievement of grammatical competence in a truer (more deployable) form may itself mitigate the problem of communicative ability. [Prabhu 1984b]

Prabhu maintains that grammar, in the sense of an unconsciously derived, internalized, generative system, is available for deployment in communication. Therefore, it is unprofitable to make special arrangements for certain areas of language use. (Such examples as Newmark's (1966) asking for a light in perfectly grammatical but inappropriate language are dismissed as hard to find [Prabhu 1984b].)

But having discussed and quoted at some length to help illuminate just how seriously the question of avoiding linguistic predetermination is taken, I must now say that there is, after all, some language control.

The language that forms the classroom input is controlled by the teacher. But again, this does not necessarily imply predetermination of content. Much is made of the teacher's capacity to exercise "natural" language control, that is to say, a continually modified, intuitive judgment as to what the learner can manage at any given stage. The learner's mind engagement then makes the input available for intake. It is not assumed that the intake will be uniform in any way, so errors are not treated as such, but are dealt with incidentally and treated as contributory to the successful completion of the task at hand. For example, incorrect language might be rephrased, but there would be no attempt at generalization.

Perhaps a more obvious bone of contention for many communicative practitioners and theorists is the relative lack of learner-learner interaction, and the reliance on teacher-class interaction. Doubts about this aspect have already been expressed (see, for example, Allwright 1982). Initially, the CTP team thought that group work would provide "increasing opportunities for meaningful interaction among the students themselves" (RIE 1980a:130), and when it was remarked that "weaker" pupils were becoming less dependent on their more able peers, part of this success was attributed to group work (RIE 1980a:56). However, although in principle there was no serious objection to group work, in practice it was problematic. One episode (RIE 1980a:24) helps to illuminate this. On a certain feast-day, a mere 22 pupils turned up to class, and it was observed that this facilitated wider participation than was conceivable in normal classes of 60 or so. In normal circumstances, group work was perceived as likely to produce pidginization; also it was felt to be too severe a break with traditional practice. Nevertheless, Prabhu (1984b) argues that although the CTP is not learner-centered, in some senses it is certainly learn*ing*-centered.[3]

EXTERNAL EVALUATION

Initial Concerns

The stated purpose in seeking external evaluation was:

> To assess, through appropriate tests, whether there is any demonstrable difference in terms of attainment in English between classes of children who have been taught on the CT Project and their peers who have received normal instruction in the respective schools (Prabhu 1983: personal communication).

Following a feasibility study by Davies (1983), I visited India early in 1984 to carry out the evaluation. My task was to compare the communicational method with the Indian version of the structural method.

It has frequently been observed that the large-scale, global method comparisons of the 1960s failed to fulfill their promise of conclusive results. The most commonly cited examples are the Colorado project (Scherer and Wertheimer 1964) and the Pennsylvania project (Smith 1970). A central problem was to demonstrate that the distinctiveness of the competing methods had any classroom reality, and that they did not come to resemble each other during the course of the experiment. In the Pennsylvania project an attempt was made to compensate for this design inadequacy by the use of classroom observation scales. Unfortunately, quite different scales were used for each method, thereby confounding comparisons of process (see Clark 1969). Valette (1969) and Hocking (1969) stress that there was considerable doubt as to the actual differences between audio-lingual and cognitive code methods in practice. The blurring of distinctions in classroom practice would certainly contribute to the perennial outcome of "no significant difference," which was the result in 580 out of 780 studies involving experimental and control comparisons, cited by Otto (1969).

The issue of what might be called "operational distinctiveness" remains problematic. Stern (1983:492) says:

> For an investigation on teaching methods to be convincing, it is crucial that the theoretical distinctions between the methods are clearly defined, and can be empirically backed by classroom observation or by some other technique of documenting the instructional variables.

According to Long a refinement of classroom observation techniques is a fruitful direction for evaluation research to take because the categorizations employed would be more relevant than those used in the Pennsylvania project. Long (1984) recommends classroom-centered study ("process" evaluation) as a supplement to classical experimental design ("product" evaluation) to help explain results, and in particular to establish whether or not manifestations of supposedly different methods were, in fact, distinguishable.[4] Fundamentally, he is advocating the desirability of exploring the space between the inception of an experiment and its conclusion.

Although "the space between" was not explored systematically in the evaluation of the CTP, it is well documented in the RIE Newsletters and Bulletins. These publications indicate that the classes were constantly observed and that the procedures were extensively and publicly discussed. My own observation of a dozen CTP classes and several structural classes suggested radically different processes. Also, taking into account the widely divergent theoretical and methodological bases, there seem to be reasonable grounds for believing that the CTP is sufficiently distinct from the Indian version of the structural method to avoid ambiguity or overlap.

Experimental Design

The CTP classes were regarded as experimental and the structural classes as control. A "true" experiment would require students to be randomly assigned to experimental and control classes, to ensure initial equivalence of comparison groups. However, since the project was not set up in this way, it was necessary to employ a less rigorous design involving intact classes.[5] Four schools, each with one experimental and one control class were included in the evaluation (see Table 1).

Precisely because full experimental control was lacking, it is especially important to make explicit the specific variables that the chosen design failed to control. A checklist of factors affecting both internal and external validity is therefore presented in Table 1. The desideratum of any experiment is that it should be strong in both types of validity. Internal validity refers to factors that may directly affect the test scores, while external validity is concerned with generalizability.

TABLE 1. THE RELATIONSHIP BETWEEN THE TWELVE SOURCES OF INVALIDITY AND THE FOUR SCHOOLS[6]

	Sources of invalidity											
	Internal								External			
School	i	ii	iii	iv	v	vi	vii	viii	ix	x	xi	xii
	History	Maturation	Testing	Instrumentation	Regression	Selection	Mortality	Interaction of selection and maturation etc.	Interaction of testing and X	Interaction of selection and X	Reactive arrangements	Multiple-X interference
Bangalore	+	+	+	?	+	?	?	+	+	?	−	+
Cuddalore	+	+	+	?	+	?	?	+	+	?	−	+
T. Nagar	+	+	+	?	+	?	−	+	+	?	−	+
Tiruvottiyur	+	+	+	?	+	?	?	+	+	?	+	−

Note: In this table, a minus indicates a definite weakness, a plus indicates that the factor is controlled, and a question mark indicates a possible source of concern. X refers to an experimental variable.

Internal Validity

It may be seen from Table 1 that under "internal validity" question marks indicate possible sources of concern with regard to instrumentation, selection and mortality. One minus also appears under the mortality heading.

Instrumentation is the term used to indicate changes in the calibration of the measuring instruments used, or changes in the scorers used, especially in the case of subjective tests. As far as the CTP evaluation is concerned, the tests used were amenable to more or less objective assessment, and only one scorer was used throughout. So, although this variable could pose a threat, it is only a minimal one.

Selection, the criterion for assigning students to the various groups under study, was problematic. Subjects were not randomly assigned to treatments, a criterion that Campbell and Stanley (1963) insist is the "only" and the "essential" way of ensuring initial equivalence of groups. However, subjects were not recruited into the experimental treatment on any differential basis. They were simply placed in different classes on a first come-first-served basis. The CTP then adopted whichever class was made available to them. Results in other school subjects, where archives still retained such data (see Beretta 1984), and headmasters' and teachers' judgments suggested that the groups were initially similar. Nevertheless, since there is room for equivocation here, the question mark is warranted.

Mortality refers to a differential loss of subjects from the comparison groups. In all of the schools there was some slight variability in the constitution of the groups over the relevant years. However, in one school (T. Nagar), one comparison group maintained its stability over time while the other did not. In addition, one third of one group failed to turn up for the evaluation tests. Clearly, a serious threat to internal validity warrants the minus sign.

External Validity

In reference to external validity, it is clear that the major difficulty lies in the category of 'reactive arrangements.' This factor would preclude generalizations about the effect of the experimental variable upon subjects exposed to it in nonexperimental settings. In three of the four schools, two circumstances might have produced this threat. First, the experimental groups were frequently observed by interested parties (teachers, administrators and foreign specialists), who created considerable awareness that an experiment was taking place, i.e., the Hawthorne effect. It seems likely that the subjects were indeed aware that they were guinea-pigs. They may therefore have experienced a degree of motivation beyond what they might have felt in a nonexperimental setting. (In the Tiruvottiyur school, both classes were equally observed.) Secondly, in the same three schools, the experimental groups were largely taught by unfamiliar, better qualified, and more highly motivated teachers than their peers in the control groups.

Perhaps the second point constitutes a more substantial objection than the first, since it is a truism that better teachers get better results. Because of the way the CTP evolved, these problems were virtually unavoidable. However, these threats to the validity of this evaluation must be clearly stated, as they have serious implications for the interpretation of its results.

Under *multiple treatment interference*, the minus for the Tiruvottiyur school refers to the fact that in this school both groups had been exposed to three years of structural teaching before the project began, while the subjects from the other three schools were at the zero-level at the project's inception. Thus in Tiruvottiyur it is impossible to determine to what extent the test results were due to the prior treatment or to the innovative treatment.

COMPARING PROGRAMS: THE TESTING QUANDARY

When two different teaching approaches are to be compared, the question of which tests to use is a vexed one. Báthory (1977:110) asserts that "it is difficult, if not impossible, to construct measurement instruments that are equally valid for different programs." Examples of this inherent difficulty in comparing dissimilar programs abound in educational literature.

Discussing an evaluation of the Total Physical Response method, Asher et al (1974:29) note:

> It may be argued that an artifact of measurement accounts for the striking differences between groups. Since the stories [used in the tests] were developed especially for this project, there may have been an unintentional bias in favor of the experimental training.

In a review of 26 studies comparing curricula, Walker and Schaffarzick (1974) found that where a significant difference in results was claimed, it was usually attributable to test-content bias.

A search through the literature reveals that basically three procedures are used by evaluators in a bid to make their instruments program-fair: (1) a standardized text (2) a specific test for each program and (3) a test of common-unique elements. The appeal to standardized tests is based on their supposed neutrality, or their independence of either program. Their principal shortcoming lies in their considerable potential for insensitivity. Standardized tests are likely to be unresponsive to features of either program, and consequently to contribute to an outcome of no difference. "No difference" on a standardized test may quite simply mean that distinct program characteristics have been obscured. On the other hand, specific tests for each program reflect their particular contents and objectives, but preclude direct comparison. The alternative is to identify common areas of content or common objectives, or both, in competing programs and to test these elements proportionately with elements that are unique to each program. Difficulties arise here when there is little apparent commonality.[7]

For the CTP evaluation, the use of a standardized test was rejected outright. The construction of specific tests for each approach was thought to be appropriate (see the section entitled "Rationale for Tests") but insufficient. It was not clear whether the common-unique approach could be utilized. Obviously, a syllabus that abjures linguistic specification can share few attributes of content with one that is based precisely on linguistic specification. In terms of objectives, both approaches aim to bring about in the learner a construction of the grammar of the language. So why not simply administer a grammar test?

This question brings us back to the argument limned above that the term "grammar" can be ambiguous. I am not convinced that the nature of the grammars learned under CTP and structural methods can be equated at early stages of learning. By extension, I do not believe that a conventional grammar test could adequately tap these different competencies. But convictions are not enough. The case against such a test must be argued on more conclusive grounds.

All pupils taking part in the evaluation were at fairly elementary stages of language study. Pupils taught by the structural method are expected to achieve mastery of a limited set of structures prescribed by the syllabus for each year. Students in communicational programs are not expected to achieve mastery level until, presumably, nature has taken its course, a process that must extend beyond the elementary level. A conventional grammar test measures attainment or nonattainment of mastery. That is to say, it measures a prescribed quota of structures at the level of a fully formed competence. The CTP makes no claim of uniformity concerning which structures will be assimilated or what stage of development learners will have attained at each level. Therefore, at an elementary level, to compare both groups on a conventional grammar test would be perverse. It would mean counting the CTP chickens before they have hatched.

On the other hand, if the evaluation were taking place with advanced level students, then the notion of mastery would be applicable to both groups, because by that stage payoff in such terms could be plausibly demanded. Otherwise "incubation" would have to be dismissed as a luxury schools cannot afford.

THE TESTS

Specific achievement tests were devised for each program. In addition, three proficiency tests that might reasonably be attempted by both groups were constructed. The tests were:[8]

1. Structural test
2. CTP task-based test
3. Contextualized grammar test
4. Dictation test
5. Listening/reading comprehension test

Rationale for the Tests

The structural test and the CTP task-based test were achievement tests designed to establish whether what is learned in the structural classroom diverges greatly from what is learned in the CTP classroom. (Clearly, a "no difference" result on these tests would indicate that what was taking place in the two classrooms was not so dissimilar.)

Relevant to the contextualized grammar test is Krashen and Terrell's (1983:167) observation on such tests:

> While it is possible that the student will understand the meaning and fill in the blank on the basis of acquired knowledge, it is also possible that the student will simply figure out the morphological pattern . . . without even understanding the text.

If this is true, then both groups could be fairly compared on a test of this nature.

The justification for a dictation test in this context rests on the theory proposed by Oller (1979 and elsewhere) that such tests measure a learner's grammar of expectancy. He maintains that if the segments are too long to be memorized and regurgitated, they must be reconstituted by drawing on the grammar of expectancy. Performance is therefore more or less successful depending on the sophistication of the learner's grammatical competence. Dictation can also be regarded as a sentence-bound test, and it thereby measures structural awareness. In this regard, dictation does seem to be a test suitable to both experimental and control groups.

The listening/reading comprehension test measures receptive ability to use language. Its function here is to determine to what degree the language learned in structural and CTP classrooms can be mobilized.

Hypotheses

The rationale for the tests may be restated as the following three hypotheses:

1. There is a difference between the language abilities arising from meaning-focused teaching and those arising from form-focused teaching. Confirmation of this requires that each group obtain a significantly better score on its own achievement test.

2. Acquisition of non-syllabus-based structure is best achieved without focusing on form. For this to be confirmed, experimental classes must perform significantly better than control classes on the proficiency tests of contextualized grammar and dictation.

3. Structure acquired without focus on form is more readily available for deployment than structure learned with focus on form. If this is true, CTP classes should do significantly better than control classes on the proficiency test of listening/reading comprehension.

Results and Conclusions

The test results for the four schools that took part in the evaluation are presented in Appendix A. They are summarized in Table 2 in terms of patterns of significance.

TABLE 2. PATTERNS OF SIGNIFICANCE FOR FOUR SCHOOLS AND FIVE TESTS

	Test 1 (Structure)	Test 2 (Contextualized grammar)	Test 3 (Dictation)	Test 4 (Listening & reading)	Test 5 (Tasks)
Bangalore	C	=	E	E	E
Cuddalore	C	E*	=	E	E
T. Nagar	C	=	=	=	E
Tiruvottiyur	C	=	=	E	E

E indicates that the experimental group did significantly better.
= indicates that there was no significant difference.
C indicates that the control group did significantly better.
Significance here refers to the 0.05 level of significance.

*Except in this one case, once a school shows significance in a test in favor of E, it continues to do so and the overall pattern in the table from left to right is: C, =, E.

The concern with test content bias was somewhat lessened by the results. Although in 5 out of 12 possible results on the tests of contextualized grammar, dictation, and listening/reading comprehension the experimental group performed significantly better, the other seven results present no significant difference. This suggests that both groups were genuinely able to compete on these measures.

The threat of experimental mortality referred to above in the T. Nagar school clearly contaminated the internal validity of the experiment, so the results obtained there were dropped for the purpose of confirmation or rejection of hypotheses.

In the remaining three schools, the results reveal a pattern that is fully consistent with the demands of the first and third hypotheses, and partly consistent with the second (and central) hypothesis.

This consistency across three school environments with different subjects and different teachers permits claims to generalizability beyond the scope of Campbell and Stanley's taxonomy of factors affecting external validity. The concept of external validity was elaborated by Bracht and Glass (1968) and again by Snow (1974) in such a way that replication is considered an important step towards confirming both population and ecological representativeness.[9] Furthermore, the fact that the CTP was tried out in natural settings where so-called extraneous variables could and in some cases certainly did have a bearing on validity, as was acknowledged previously, enhances that representativeness. (Thus the truism that the very factors which increase one form of validity can decrease another is borne out).[10]

Bearing this in mind, and also the stated threats to validity (especially the superiority of the CTP teachers), the potential for bias in test construction and the fact that the evaluation says nothing about the efficacy of the CTP at later stages of learning,[11] conclusions are inevitably tentative, e.g. that grammar construction *can* take place through a focus on meaning. However, while the results clearly favor the CTP groups, the evaluation so far does not offer adequate explanation of this.

FINAL REMARKS

The CTP may have begun life as a local response to a local problem, but its consequences could be felt beyond Bangalore. Howatt (1984:288) offers an opinion that "whatever happens, Bangalore has set the context for one of the most interesting arguments of the eighties, if not beyond."

This may be so, but many of the questions raised by the evaluation can only be answered by a broader-based study. This is currently under way. An observational analysis of a number of CTP lessons, data from questionnaires and teachers' accounts of their experience on the project will provide a clearer picture of what took place in the classroom. The results will be reported in the literature in due course.

NOTES

1. Dr. N. S. Prabhu was the English Studies Officer, British Council, Madras, at the time the CTP was initiated and developed.

2. That the CTP has in fact reached a wider audience is partly due to the efforts of Keith Johnson, Dick Allwright and Chris Brumfit, who helped to publicize the project in a number of ways.

3. The notion of learning-centeredness is based on a perception of language as a distinct form of learning.

4. For a review of the research in this area, see Stern 1983, Gaies 1983, Seliger and Long 1983, Allwright 1983, and Long 1984.

5. For a discussion of quasi-experimental design, see Campbell and Stanley 1963.

6. For an explanation of all these factors see Campbell and Stanley 1963, and for most of them see Hatch and Farhady 1982. For an account of the way each factor affected the CTP experiment see Beretta 1984.

7. See Shoemaker 1972 for an interesting account of the problem of test content bias and suggestions for overcoming it.

8. For samples of tests see Beretta and Davies 1985.

9. Basically, population representativeness is concerned with person characteristics (i.e., the pupils) while ecological representativeness is concerned with the situation (i.e., school setting, teachers, method of teaching, etc.). See Snow 1974 for further details.

10. For a discussion of the tension between internal and external validity see Campbell and Stanley 1963.

11. The requirement that all pupils prepare for Common and State examinations has denied any opportunity for the CTP team to try out their approach at later stages.

REFERENCES

Allwright, R. L. 1982. "Communicative Curricula in Language Teaching." Paper presented at the International Conference on Language Sciences and The Teaching of Languages and Literatures, Bari, Italy, April, 1982.

———— 1983. "Classroom-centered Research on Language Teaching and Learning: A Brief Historical Overview." *TESOL Quarterly* 17(2):191–204.

Asher, J. J., J. A. Kusudo and R. De La Torre. 1974. "Learning a Second Language through Commands: The Second Field Test." *The Modern Language Journal* 58(1–2):24–32.

Báthory, Z. 1977. "The Field-trial Stage of Curriculum Evaluation." In A. Lewy (ed.). 1977. *Handbook of Curriculum Evaluation*. Paris: UNESCO/New York: Longman.

Beretta, A. 1984. "Evaluation of the Bangalore/Madras Communicational Teaching Project." Mimeo, British Council, Madras.

Beretta, A. and A. Davies. 1985. "Evaluation of the Bangalore Project." *English Language Teaching Journal* 39(2):121–127.

Bracht, G. H. and G. V. Glass. 1968. "The External Validity of Experiments." *American Educational Research Journal* 5:437–474.

Brumfit, C. J. 1984a. *Communicative Methodology in Language Teaching. The Roles of Accuracy and Fluency.* Cambridge: Cambridge University Press.

———— 1984b. "The Bangalore Procedural Syllabus." *English Language Teaching Journal* 38(4):233–241.

Bose, M. N. K. 1980. "A Teacher's Experience." In RIE 1980c:81–88.

Campbell, D. T. and J. C. Stanley. 1963. "Experimental and Quasi-experimental Designs for Research on Teaching." In N. L. Gage (ed.). *Handbook of Research on Teaching.* Chicago: Rand McNally.

Clark, J. L. D. 1969. "The Pennsylvania Project and the 'Audiolingual versus Traditional' Question." *The Modern Language Journal* 53(6):388–396.

Corder, S. P. 1981. *Error Analysis and Interlanguage.* Oxford: Oxford University Press.

Davies, A. 1983. "Evaluation and The Bangalore/Madras Communicational Teaching Project." Mimeo, British Council.

Elia, T. 1981. "Communicational Teaching and the Structuralist Teacher: A Personal View." In RIE 1981:27–36.

Gaies, S. J. 1983. "The Investigation of Language Classroom Processes." *TESOL Quarterly* 17(2):205–217.

Hatch, E. and H. Farhady. 1982. *Research Design and Statistics for Applied Linguistics.* Rowley, Mass.: Newbury House.

Hocking, E. 1969. "The Laboratory in Perspective: Teachers, Strategies, Outcomes." *The Modern Language Journal* 53(6):404–410.

Howatt, A. P. R. 1984. *A History of English Language Teaching.* Oxford: Oxford University Press.

Johnson, K. 1982. *Communicative Syllabus Design and Methodology.* Oxford: Pergamon Press.

Krashen, S. D. 1981. *Second Language Acquisition and Second Language Learning.* Oxford: Pergamon Press.

———— 1982. *Principles and Practice in Second Language Acquisition.* Oxford: Pergamon Press.

Krashen, S. D. and T. D. Terrell. 1983. *The Natural Approach. Language Acquisition in the Classroom.* Oxford: Pergamon/Alemany.

Long, M. H. 1984. "Process and Product in ESL Program Evaluation." *TESOL Quarterly* 18(3):409–425.

Newmark, L. 1966. "How Not to Interfere with Language Learning." In C. J. Brumfit and K. Johnson (eds.). 1979. *The Communicative Approach to Language Teaching*. Oxford: Oxford University Press.

Oller, J. W. 1979. *Language Tests at School*. London: Longman.

Otto, F. 1969. "The Teacher in the Pennsylvania Project." *The Modern Language Journal* 53(6):411–420.

Palmer, H. E. 1921/1964. *The Principles of Language-study*. London: Harrap. Republished by Oxford University Press, 1964, edited by R. Mackin.

Patel, M. S. 1962. "The Structural Syllabus at Work in India." *English Language Teaching* 16(3):145–151.

Prabhu, N. S. 1980a. "Theoretical Background to the Bangalore Project." In RIE 1980c:17–26.

——— 1980b. "Reactions and Predictions." In RIE 1980c:160–164.

——— 1981. "Communicational Teaching Project. Theoretical Background." In RIE 1981:1–8.

——— 1982. "The Communicational Teaching Project, South India." Mimeo, British Council, Madras.

——— 1983. "Procedural Syllabuses." In J. A. S. Read (ed.) *Trends in Language Syllabus Design*. Singapore: Singapore University Press.

——— 1984a. "Communicative Teaching: 'Communicative' in What Sense?" Paper presented at the 19th Regional Seminar, SEAMEO Regional Language Centre, Singapore.

——— 1984b. "Coping with the Unknown in Language Pedagogy." Paper presented at the British Council 50th Anniversary Seminar, 1984.

RIE. 1979a. Newsletter (Special Series). Vol. 1. No. 1. Regional Institute of English, South India, Bangalore.

——— 1980a. Newsletter (Special Series). Vol. 1. No. 3. Regional Institute of English, South India, Bangalore.

——— 1980b. Newsletter (Special Series). Vol. 1. No. 4. Regional Institute of English, South India, Bangalore.

——— 1980c. Bulletin. No. 4 (i). New Approaches to Teaching English. Report of seminar. Regional Institute of English, South India, Bangalore.

——— 1981. Bulletin. No. 5 (i).Communicational Teaching Project. Review seminar. Regional Institute of English, South India, Bangalore.

Scherer, G. and M. Wertheimer. 1964. *A Psycholinguistic Experiment in Foreign Language Teaching*. New York: McGraw Hill.

Seliger, H. W. and M. H. Long. (eds.). 1983. *Classroom Oriented Research in Second Language Acquisition*. Rowley, Mass.: Newbury House.

Shoemaker, D. M. 1972. "Evaluating the Effectiveness of Competing Instructional Programs." *Educational Researcher* 1:5–8, 12.

Smith, D. A. 1962. "The Madras 'Snowball': An Attempt to Retrain 27,000 Teachers of English to Beginners." *English Language Teaching* 17(1):3–9.

————— 1968. "In-service Training for Teachers of English in Developing Countries." In G. E. Perren (ed.). *Teachers of English as a Second Language. Their Training and Preparation.* Cambridge: Cambridge University Press.

Smith, P. D. 1970. *A Comparison of the Cognitive and Audio-lingual Approaches to Foreign Language Instruction: The Pennsylvania Foreign Language Project.* Philadelphia, Penn.: The Center for Curriculum Development, Inc.

Snow, R. E. 1974. "Representative and Quasi-representative Designs for Research on Teaching." *Review of Educational Research* 44(3):265–291.

Stern, H. H. 1983. *Fundamental Concepts of Language Teaching.* Oxford: Oxford University Press.

Valette, R. M. 1969. "The Pennsylvania Project, Its Conclusions and Its Implications." *The Modern Language Journal* 53(6):396–404.

Walker, D. F. and J. Schaffarzick. 1974. "Comparing Curricula." *Review of Educational Research* 44(1):83–111.

Widdowson, H. G. 1978. *Teaching Language as Communication.* Oxford: Oxford University Press.

APPENDIX A

The test results are presented in the following five tables. In the column headed "two-tailed significance" the 0.05 level of significance was selected to determine significance for the two-tailed *t*-tests used. E indicates that the experimental group did significantly better, = means that there was no significant difference, and C indicates that the control group did significantly better. Under the column heading 'No. of items' the number varies. This means that either different tests were used at the different schools or that the same tests were used and trimmed differentially after item analysis.

TABLE 1. TEST 1: STRUCTURE TEST

	No. of items	Mean	Standard deviation	No. of subjects	Reliability	t-Value	Degrees of freedom	Two-tailed significance
Bangalore	14				0.60	4.50	88	C < 0.05
Control		10.27	2.22	48				
Experimental		8.07	2.36	42				
Cuddalore	14				0.80	4.82	61	C < 0.05
Control		8.31	3.28	29				
Experimental		4.53	2.85	34				
T. Nagar	19				0.72	3.49	48	C < 0.05
Control		8.63	3.64	30				
Experimental		5.15	2.97	20				
Tiruvottiyur	15				0.75	2.73	114	C < 0.05
Control		10.07	3.03	60				
Experimental		8.41	3.44	56				

TABLE 2. TEST 2: TASK-BASED TEST

	No. of items	Mean	Standard deviation	No. of subjects	Reliability	t-Value	Degrees of freedom	Two-tailed significance
Bangalore								
Control	25	12.02	5.51	48	0.90	6.42	88	$E < 0.05$
Experimental		19.26	5.00	42				
Cuddalore								
Control	16	3.39	3.47	33	0.89	3.00	64	$E < 0.05$
Experimental		6.76	4.89	33				
T. Nagar								
Control	24	9.31	6.36	32	0.90	2.72	50	$E < 0.05$
Experimental		14.00	5.16	20				
Tiruvottiyur								
Control	21	11.21	4.99	58	0.89	2.00	111	$E < 0.05$
Experimental		13.74	5.83	55				

TABLE 3. TEST 3: CONTEXTUALIZED GRAMMAR TEST

	No. of items	Mean	Standard deviation	No. of subjects	Reliability	t-Value	Degrees of freedom	Two-tailed significance
Bangalore								
Control	16	8.17	3.95	47	0.78	1.97	82	= 0.05
Experimental		9.76	3.17	37				
Cuddalore								
Control	15	3.38	3.11	29	0.90	2.38	61	$E < 0.05$
Experimental		6.03	5.15	34				
T. Nagar								
Control	12	5.64	2.95	33	0.75	1.65	53	= 0.05
Experimental		4.32	2.72	22				
Tiruvottiyur								
Control	13	6.11	2.45	53	0.65	1.08	104	= 0.05
Experimental		5.55	2.85	53				

TABLE 4. TEST 4: DICTATION TEST

	No. of items	Mean	Standard deviation	No. of subjects	Reliability	t-Value	Degrees of freedom	Two-tailed significance
Bangalore								
Control	24	15.11	6.17	46	0.88	3.01	83	$E < 0.05$
Experimental		18.67	4.21	39				
Cuddalore								
Control	28	8.79	8.74	29	0.95	1.19	61	$= 0.05$
Experimental		11.38	8.25	34				
T. Nagar								
Control	21	14.6	6.70	30	0.93	1.55	48	$= 0.05$
Experimental		11.7	5.82	20				
Tiruvottiyur								
Control	28	18.34	7.05	56	0.91	0.70	105	$= 0.05$
Experimental		19.29	6.89	51				

TABLE 5. TEST 5: LISTENING/READING COMPREHENSION TEST

	No. of items	Mean	Standard deviation	No. of subjects	Reliability	t-Value	Degrees of freedom	Two-tailed significance
Bangalore								
Control	28	9.20	6.36	46	0.92	6.65	82	$E < 0.05$
Experimental		18.26	5.98	38				
Cuddalore								
Control	27	3.52	5.14	29	0.97	9.01	61	$E < 0.05$
Experimental		18.03	7.88	34				
T. Nagar								
Control	24	10.03	7.19	30	0.92	1.29	48	$= 0.05$
Experimental		7.65	5.93	20				
Tiruvottiyur								
Control	26	11.26	5.87	60	0.91	2.78	114	$E < 0.05$
Experimental		14.73	7.38	56				

Chapter 6

Second Language Teaching in the Business World: Communicative English Course Content in Germany

Stephen M. Smith

Stephen Smith is the author of The Theater Arts and the Teaching of Second Languages. *He has a M.A. degree in TESL from the University of Illinois, Urbana-Champaign, and has taught English in the United States, England and West Germany. His professional interests include instructional design, cross-cultural communication, and management training.*

INTRODUCTION

Course content for communicative language courses varies with the needs of the learners. While designing the communicative language course, course developers consider each group of learners individually and try to find the blend of course input that will best meet the group's needs. They examine the learners' reasons for learning, and try to use what the learners already know about communication and about life.

The language teaching initiative illustrated in this chapter represents the application of communicative competence oriented language teaching concepts to the design of course content for an English as a foreign language course in a large German corporation.[1]

Teaching English to managers in a firm is generally associated with such catchwords as ESP (English for Specific Purposes), Business English, and Management English. However, in reality it is not always a business-oriented lexicon that is imparted in the company-sponsored language course, and the communicative acts that learners practice are not always exclusively tied to the business world. Instead, the goal of these courses is typically that of helping learners to become better communicators in the foreign language.

Where the object of the English course is to help learners improve job performance, for example, we might examine the ways in which the learners use English in their work and incorporate the vocabulary, register, and speech acts inherent in these working situations into the course. More important, however, are the broader communication strategies learners need to develop in order to cope with a variety of communication situations.

This discussion of a course for English in the German firm includes a classroom activity that was developed and used in West Berlin at the corporate headquarters of Schering A.G., a pharmaceutical/chemical firm with 22,000 employees worldwide. By drawing on the previous training that the learners have received in their native language, this activity takes advantage of what the learners already know about effective communication and about developing communication skills.

Schering provides its managers with communication training in their native language to enhance the effectiveness of group communication within the firm. The foreign language (L2) learning activity presented here borrows from this native language (L1) training. The result is an activity that very closely satisfies the learners' needs. Borrowing elements from learners' L1 training provides them with experience in using communicative strategies in their second language that they have been trained to use in their first language and that they need for their work at Schering.

What follows is a discussion of the learning environment in which this activity was developed, a description of the first language communication training the learners received, and presentation of the activity, "The Tunnel Project."

THE LEARNING ENVIRONMENT

For natives of many non-English speaking countries, foreign language education is essential to numerous careers both in and outside of business. A look at the annual report of a typical large German firm will reveal that a large percentage of its business, abroad or at home, involves dealing with foreigners. Germany, like many nations, is heavily dependent on trade relations with other nations to keep its economy alive. Geographically small in comparison to the United States, Germany must look beyond its borders for a greater portion of its resources and markets. In addition, the German language does not enjoy the status of an "international language" to the same degree as English. As a result, Germany conducts much of its business abroad in various languages, with the single most important foreign language for Germany being English. It is actually a matter of policy in some firms that English or some other foreign language be used in specific situations. In other firms where English is not required by policy, it is nonetheless the defacto international language.

English and other foreign languages are used in the German corporation in many situations and for many reasons. Although the foreign subsidiaries of a German company tend to be staffed by local nationals, foreign language skills are important for people at many levels. For example, many employees working at home in Germany help to maintain relationships with foreign subsidiaries, customers, suppliers, management, government personnel, and others who do not speak German. On a daily basis, individual employees carry out much of their interpersonal communication with people from other language backgrounds. Routine phone calls, letters, telexes, and conversations often require the use of English or some other foreign language. The headquarters (HQ) of a typical firm will occasionally send an employee to live abroad and work in a foreign subsidiary so that HQ will have a direct contact there. Since some German firms are themselves subsidiaries of foreign companies, their management and other key personnel may spend time abroad working or training others.

If a company is to be competitive in any language, its employees must be effective communicators. When subsidiary managers fly in from all over the world for an annual strategy meeting, for example, complex and urgent topics are likely to be found on the agenda. Time will be short. If communication is not efficient, the costs to the firm can be very high indeed. The communicative competence of a firm's employees is dramatically demonstrated in such meetings. In contrast to the American or British firm where such meetings are held in the native language, the German company must play host in a foreign language. That language is typically English.

In light of the L2 communication requirements of multinational business in the European setting, it is clearly in the best interests of German companies to assure a high level of communicative competence in English and other second languages. To meet their employees' language learning needs, large German firms usually engage the services of language teachers.

Individual employees frequently find that foreign language competence is necessary for professional advancement. Job opportunities for employees who are not proficient in English or some other foreign language may be restricted in a country that does a considerable portion of its business with foreigners. Many jobs simply cannot be filled by an employee who cannot communicate in English. There are, of course, positions in German firms that do not require knowledge of a foreign language, but the aspiring professional knows that foreign language skills that are irrelevant today might be crucial in the future for promotion to an interesting job. Sometimes, one employee will be chosen over others for a particular job simply on the basis of competence in a foreign language. Foreign language competence can also mean visibility for an employee. In international meetings, for example, an individual can earn the respect and recognition of superiors by giving a successful presentation in a foreign language while the talents of others may go unrecognized because their lack of L2 competence forces them to remain silent.

Germans prepare themselves to use foreign languages in their professional lives well before they enter the working world. They study and use foreign languages to a greater extent than their American-born counterparts. University-bound Germans typically receive seven years of foreign language education in school, and usually concentrate on two foreign languages.

As a result of their school and university language education, most language learners in German firms are at proficiency levels defined by their teachers as intermediate and advanced. In spite of their years of language education and experience, however, many employees feel a need for further foreign language training and practice and take advantage of their company's language course offerings.

Learners attend in-house L2 courses for a variety of reasons. Some want "refresher courses" after years or months of noninvolvement with a language; others want to develop competence in new areas of second language communication that are frequently job-related; still others view attendance at company sponsored language courses as a recreational outlet. Because the participants in a language learning group may come from different departments and perform different jobs within the firm, it is not always practical to focus on business-oriented tasks. Many courses in the firm take the form of what is often referred to as "general English": the course content revolves around the interests of the learners and the teacher as well as course material. In other courses, the content is strictly business oriented, and the teacher is assigned to help learners with specific job-related problems. For example, the learners may be preparing for an overseas trip or assignment or a new position requiring the use of a foreign language.

The following is a sample of job-related reasons learners at Schering have given for using the services of the firm's English teachers:

organizing joint research projects with foreign subsidiaries and other foreign institutions

arranging licensing negotiations and agreements with foreign companies

making purchases from, or sales to, foreign companies

providing consulting services to foreign customers

attending and speaking at international conferences

meeting with foreign government representatives

attending meetings with foreigners held at the home office

hosting visitors from abroad

writing reports and corporate communications for subsidiaries abroad

reading and writing letters, telexes, etc., from abroad

reading and writing papers and journal articles in English

L1 BUSINESS
COMMUNICATION TRAINING

The "Tunnel Project," the language learning activity to be described in this chapter, was designed to meet the needs of employees who take English courses because they must use English at work. However it has also been enthusiastically received by a more heterogeneous group of learners, like that described above enrolled in a "general English" course.

The activity was created by drawing from communication training seminars provided by the firm for its employees and conducted in their native language, that is, training delivered by Germans, for Germans, in German. By borrowing from the L1 communication training received by the learners, this L2 activity takes advantage of the communication strategies to which they have already been exposed. For L2 teaching purposes, the most interesting of these native language seminars are those that focus on communication strategies for use in group interactions: meetings, negotiations, consulting sessions, etc. Many such interactions take place in the daily life of the firm and the extent to which they are productive depends on the communicative competence of the participants.

In the search for foreign language course input, it makes sense to consider these areas of job-related communication training. Learners often begin the course with seven or more years of English education behind them and some years of experience in using the language on the job. For these learners, teachers seek learning experiences that will not merely repeat lessons they have learned, but that will help them develop their communicative competence in job-related areas. In order better to serve the needs of the learners, teachers can help them develop competence in such professional roles as presenters, group moderators, negotiators, report writers, coordinators, consultants, or sales people.

The elements of native language communication training provided by Schering that are incorporated into the "Tunnel Project" include group moderation, presentation techniques, group decision making and problem solving, interpersonal communication, and creative thinking. The focus of this native language training centers on the following aspects of group communication:

> **talkers vs. idea holders:** In group discussions those who talk the most do not always have the most to contribute. Conversely, those who have the most useful ideas do not always express those ideas.
>
> **ineffective formulation of the message:** It can be difficult for individuals to express themselves effectively in group situations.
>
> **group dynamics:** Group dynamics play a very important role in the success of the group interaction. Inhibition and empathy are two important variables in group dynamics.
>
> **listening:** Listening is an activity that requires energy and skill. Listening skills can be developed.

By focusing on these aspects of group interaction, training in these areas raises awareness of the problems inherent in group communication and suggests solutions. The training seminars also give learners practice coping with these problems so that they can develop strategies for future use. The key strategies introduced in these L1 training seminars and incorporated into the L2 activity revolve around *visualization techniques* and *group moderation techniques*.

Visualization Training

A small communications training and consulting company in Germany has developed training for companies that revolves around a visualization technique and group moderation strategies. This method, "Metaplan," is used to facilitate communication in presentations and group discussions. The method and its techniques, developed and successfully marketed by its creators, Eberhard Schnelle and Ina Frowein (Schnelle and Stoltz 1977), are used by both large and small companies in Germany and elsewhere in Europe.

Metaplan is only one example of communication training that has found its niche in industry and that could be of great utility to language teachers. The following description of Metaplan is not meant to serve as an endorsement of one specific product; rather, it is intended to illustrate how useful examining the L1 communication training methods in use in their respective firms can be for language teachers.

Metaplan is used in many ways to enhance the quality of group interaction. It can be described as a collection of strategies that overcome the barriers to communication that arise when one person speaks to a group or many people express their ideas in a group setting.

Metaplan is based on a visualization technique used when giving presentations or moderating meetings. The presenter or moderator uses pin boards, large felt-tip markers, and paper in various shapes and colors to visualize the main points or concepts of the presentation or meeting. The visualization is created by pinning colored pieces of paper to the pinboards. The background on each board is a brown sheet of paper that covers the entire board. Markers are used to draw words and symbols on the background and on the colored paper. The pieces of paper can be moved around with ease so that the image can be edited and developed to illustrate concepts. The result is a collage that illustrates the main points of the proceedings using words, symbols, colors, and shapes.

The goal of Metaplan is to clarify the basic content of the proceedings in a concise, visual manner. This visual record may be prepared in advance or developed as a meeting progresses. It can be used as a reference by audience members or participants during the presentation or meeting and it can be referred to later, enabling those present to recall the proceedings and those not present to learn of the event through the visual record.

The Metaplan method has an advantage over traditional typewritten minutes of a meeting. While the images created on the boards are simple, they are substitutes for messages that would consist of many words. Another advantage is that the visualization can be easily manipulated so that the speaker or the entire group can create visual "minutes" as the meeting progresses. Thus the participants are able to see at a glance what the group has done so far and where the meeting is headed. Group decisions and assumptions are visualized to minimize doubt or misunderstanding about what idea or plan has or has not been established. Ideas must be well thought out and articulated so that they can be displayed on the board.

Example

The illustration shows three different pin boards that contain the main points of a group problem-solving session. Board 1 was used to display and categorize ideas generated in a brainstorming session. Board 2 shows 4 sets of alternatives the group discussed, the choices they made and the actions they agreed to take. Board 3 shows the results of a group vote. The dark dots under "selections" are stickers that participants stuck onto the board next to their selection.

Good visual aids make it easier for an audience to follow a complex presentation. A speaker who makes mistakes or digresses can be difficult to follow if there is no visual "road map" outlining the main direction of the presentation. The visual map is a particularly useful tool for speakers who give presentations in foreign languages. Both audience and speaker can be guided by the visual aid and thereby feel more at ease, even when delivery of the spoken presentation is flawed. Members of the audience are less likely to miss the main points and the speaker can use the visualization to get back on track if thrown off by the language or other distractions. The visual map also helps audience members who are listening to a presentation in a foreign language.

One simple example serves to illustrate the use of the Metaplan method to aid communication. When a group is discussing a problem, the moderator may ask the members of the group to suggest ways to solve the problem. Before any discussion takes place, however, each member will write his or her ideas on colored pieces of paper. The ideas will be represented on the pieces of paper by key words only. For example, instead of writing "Let's ask accounting if they know anything about the problem," the group member would simply write "accounting." The suggestions are collected and the pieces of paper are arranged in categories on the board. These categories might be obvious from the beginning or they might become apparent as the discussion unfolds. Once the suggestions have been grouped into categories, headings can be added (perhaps in different shapes and colors). Categories can be added, and items condensed and expanded. The moderator might wish to arrange in advance for a grouping of suggestions by instructing participants to write all negative suggestions on green paper and all positive suggestions on yellow paper, if such a response pattern is appropriate. In the ensuing

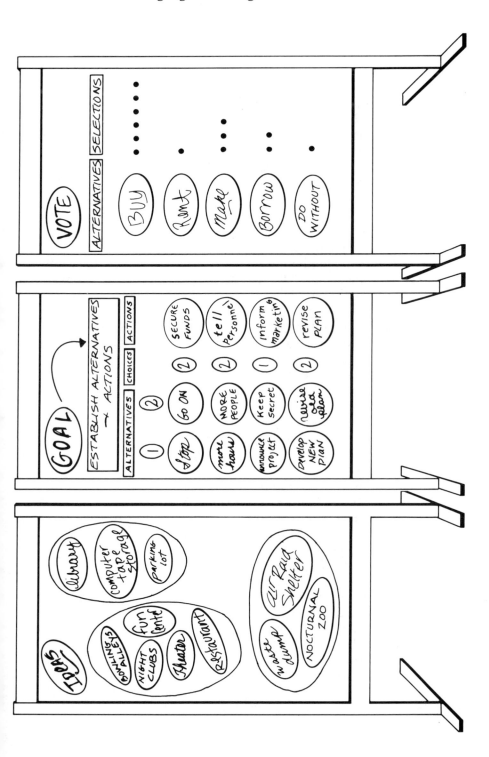

discussion everyone's ideas should receive consideration regardless of the contents, because the key words on the board will indicate that at least one person has something to say about each suggestion. This overcomes the problem that arises in group meetings when people have good ideas but decide not to bring them up because they are influenced by the course of the discussion.

Metaplan is appropriate for language teaching in a business setting not only because it is a communication enhancement technique, but also because it teaches participants about the elements of clear, effective communication. Furthermore, it supports communicative acts that many business people are called upon to perform in a second language.

This technique is a particularly effective second language teaching tool in firms where employees already use it in their first language. In many cases, the language teacher does not have to take time to train learners in the technique because they already know how to use it. In such cases, the members of the learning group can develop their presentation and moderation skills in the foreign language, using the familiar technique as an aid.

Metaplan is also useful as a means of visualizing language points the teacher wants to make in reference to the learners' class discussion. These points can be visualized without interrupting the discussion or activity and without waiting to give feedback. The learners may refer to the board at their own convenience. They often refer to it immediately upon making a mistake and again later to review the same point just as they are about to produce a similar utterance. (This works quite well at Schering where learners are accustomed to referring to the visual display that is continuously developed on the pinboards during the course of a meeting or discussion.) After class, the teacher can dismantle the board's contents and save them for future use, e.g., to resume a discussion or to reconstruct the original context in order to review language points. Metaplan's advantage over a blackboard for drawing attention to particular features of language is the mobility of the colored pieces of paper, which can be rearranged on the board into various groups for maximum effect. The groups can be expanded upon and reduced as the class learns more about the features of language in question.

There are, of course, other visualization techniques available to presenters and group moderators. Effective use of flip charts and overhead projectors could serve the same purpose and may be easier for some groups to learn. The choice of a technique is less important than the commitment to visualization training. Schering and other European companies have demonstrated the utility of selecting a visualization training program and delivering that training to its employees. As a result, their employees have well-developed communication strategies for coping with group communication problems.

Group Moderation Training

Schering also provides training in group moderation for employees who must chair meetings. This area of management training is of particular relevance to language teachers in industry because the learners' jobs sometimes demand that they chair meetings in English. Group moderation training helps alleviate some of the aggravation of inefficient meetings. Whether they are held in a first or second language, meetings can generate frustration among participants. This frustration can result from ineffective communication manifested in behaviors such as excessive talking on the part of one or several participants, not enough intervention from others, and the inability of many participants to express themselves effectively.

The strategies suggested in the Metaplan training for group moderators also happens to be relevant to moderating language learning groups. According to the Metaplan training materials, the moderator should "abstain from taking the hierarchical role as a group leader, so that the group can quickly learn to manage itself," "create a pleasant, informal atmosphere in order to promote free communication and friendly relations among the participants," and "integrate all participants in the work process" (Schnelle and Stoltz 1977). These strategies no doubt sound familiar to those language teachers familiar with ensemble-building activities associated with the theater arts. (See Smith 1984 for examples of these and related activities.)

In fact, language teachers themselves could benefit from group moderation training before attempting to moderate groups and certainly before training moderators. The utility of this training is clear when we consider that the face validity of a language lesson based upon group moderation techniques can be reduced considerably when the learners sense that their teacher knows little or nothing about the concept or skills of group moderation. When, as at Schering, the learners are themselves experienced group moderators or have training in group moderation, they may be well versed in the principles of this technique. They can then benefit from opportunities to apply those principles in their foreign language classes. Therefore, for the language teacher in the firm, it is useful to learn the in-house approaches to group moderation so that the teacher's approach is congruent with that of the firm's employees. The learners can then effectively apply the same principles of group moderation in the L2 class that are generally accepted in their place of employment.

One effective technique for bringing moderation training into the foreign language classroom is the "revolving chair" technique in which a group is given a problem to solve, through discussion, and each participant takes a turn "chairing" a portion of the discussion. "Time-outs" may be taken from the problem solving task for comments on the quality of the moderation. Is everyone participating? Is the moderator facilitating open discussion or dictating the course of the discussion?

Negotiation Training

Another area of the communication training offered to employees is negotiation training. Professional buyers and contract negotiators, for example, can improve performance on the job if they know something about the skill of negotiation. Negotiation training may include role-playing and simulation and provide lessons in communicating that are useful whether one wishes ultimately to learn to negotiate for professional reasons or simply to improve personal interaction skills.

Negotiation takes on a unique perspective when the participants are from different countries. Not only language differences but also cultural differences are likely to be involved in the negotiation. Thus participants in negotiation training can effectively be made aware of cultural differences and their effects.

A number of negotiation training games can be used in second language training. One respected L1 course used by companies in the United States was developed by Chester Karrass. His method and the research that led him to his findings are outlined in *The Negotiating Game* (Karrass 1970). Karrass' research centered on people in the act of negotiating and examined variables such as the relationship between aspiration level and success in negotiation. He also examined concession patterns of negotiators, variables in negotiations such as "power," "skills," and "stamina," and the relationship between "settlement time" and "success." From his studies, Karrass has developed a training course for managers in the art of negotiation. One of the tips he offers is: Don't concede early or first in negotiations unless you receive an acceptable offer, since those who make the first concession often concede the most in the end. He also suggests that negotiators aspire to high goals because he has found that people with high aspirations tend to win.

Xerox Learning Systems also offers a course in negotiation. It is a self-study course including a cassette and a book of multiple-choice questions and other exercises. This course has many of the same characteristics as some well-designed L2 language courses. Its table of contents lists the course contents according to the roles the negotiators might play when negotiating, for example, with a superior, a subordinate, or a peer, or where cultural barriers exist. Advice given in this course for communicating where cultural barriers exist emphasizes avoidance of any behavior or strategy that assumes understanding or calls upon the other party to do the same. The course focuses on language communication strategies and functions such as plotting strategy, probing, offering ideas, building on ideas, constructively criticizing, breaking impasses and countering counter-productive tactics. Although this course was designed for native language instruction, it is clearly similar in design and content to second language course materials. For the business professional, such courses provide insight into the language used by English-speaking negotiators and can be adapted to provide insight into the thought processes and norms involved in negotiation in other language settings.

THE "TUNNEL PROJECT": A BUSINESS COMMUNICATION ACTIVITY FOR L2 LEARNERS

The "Tunnel Project" integrates several of the communication tasks discussed above, including visualization, presentation, group moderation, and negotiation. This language learning activity involves role-play and simulation and provides training in a variety of business communication styles. Following the presentation of the activity is a discussion of one actual case of its application.

Reading Passage for "The Tunnel Project"

Hole in the Ground Inc.

For rent: two abandoned subway tunnels that stretch for nearly two miles some 50 feet beneath the streets of Manhattan. They are dark, dank and almost inaccessible. Present occupants are a few rats. If interested, contact New York's Metropolitan Transportation Authority.

Though the pitch was not phrased in exactly that way, the MTA did indeed offer last July to lease two vacant subway tunnels to "an imaginative entrepreneur." Now Vital Records Inc. of Raritan, N.J., thinks that it has enough imagination. The company, which stores financial records on computer tapes and microfilm for 50 of the largest U.S. corporations, proposes to convert the tunnels into a vast underground filing cabinet.

If its offer is accepted, the firm will have to install a computer-controlled file locator system and conveyor belts throughout the tunnels in order to turn them into a vault. Cost: an estimated $2 million. Despite those expenses, subterranean storage is expected to cost only $1 per sq. ft., compared with up to $50 per sq. ft. for aboveground space.

The Tunnel Project*

There are two roles for participants in the exercise described below: the entrepreneurs and the bankers. Each group of entrepreneurs can consist of two or more participants. The role(s) of the banker(s) can be played by the teacher or by other learners. It is also recommended that all participants have the opportunity to play both roles.

Reading Passage for All Participants

The property described in the article above is for sale, and several companies wish to take it over. A large bank is willing to provide financing for the new owners of the tunnel. The bank will help the new owners buy the tunnel, rebuild it in any way, and support the new business venture until it can support itself. The bank is offering loans of several million dollars: the exact amount will be negotiated between the bank and the new owners. There are several interested companies submitting proposals to the bank. In order to win the loan contract from the bank, a company must come up with the best, i.e., the most interesting, creative, potentially profitable, and feasible, proposal for the use of the tunnel. The representatives of the winning company must also present their proposal professionally and convincingly.

Role Card 1:

The Entrepreneurs

1. You are partners in your own, very successful property development company. Meet with your business partners and develop a proposal for the tunnel project. Prepare a list of the basic points of your proposal. Also prepare to present and defend your proposal in a face-to-face meeting with the bank representative(s). Your proposal must be clear, convincing, and professional.
2. Present and defend your proposal. The bank will hear all competing proposals and award the loan contract to the company that presents the most convincing proposal. The bank will also consider the style and clarity of the presentations. You may listen as the other companies make their presentations, but do not interrupt.

---

*Reprinted from Stephen M. Smith, *The Theater Arts and the Teaching of Second Languages,* Reading, Mass. Addison-Wesley Publishing Company, 1984.

3. Listen to, but do not participate in, the discussion of the bankers as they decide on the recipient of the financial support.

Role Card 2:

The Bankers

1. Meet to discuss criteria for choosing the company that will receive your support. Write a list of questions to ask the companies. Think about the criteria mentioned in the reading passage, which will influence your decisions. Be sure to apply these criteria in your decision making task.

2. Listen to the proposals and question the presenters very thoroughly.

3. After hearing all proposals, meet to choose the winner of the competition.

The "Tunnel Project" activity can fill several hours of productive learning, but it is also possible to restrict it to one 90-minute lesson. A description of one actual application of the "Tunnel Project" at a week-long intensive English course follows.

Six learners were sent by their employer to a pleasant villa for two weeks of intensive English study. With the luxury of time, the two teachers were able to develop "The Tunnel Project" into several hours of activity per day. Throughout the week, the Metaplan visualization technique was used as the main visual aid for the activity. A blackboard was also used. The participants were assigned the "Tunnel Project" on the first day. They met in small groups, or "companies," to develop their business plans. The visual aids were used to outline the concepts for imaginary businesses and to prepare elaborate presentations of these plans for the meetings with the "bankers." In the meetings with the bankers, the visuals were used for the presentation and defense of the plans. Negotiation strategies were used to negotiate with the bankers on the feasibility of the plan and the amount of the loan. Group moderation techniques were employed to keep order during these lively and, at times, complex discussions.

This activity was spread over several days, with breaks for other activities. The visualizations served as the "minutes" of the previous meetings and allowed for continuity in spite of interruptions. Whenever the activity was resumed, the visualization made it easy to see what had been established and to recall the arguments and language points covered.

The pinboards also provided teachers a highly effective, silent feedback mechanism for illustrating language points while the discussion was in progress. Feedback consisted of writing suggestions or corrections on colored pieces of paper and pinning them on the boards, thus informing the learners without interrupting them. Since this is a common way of visualizing a meeting in this particular firm, the participants did not feel distracted by the teachers' actions; on the contrary, they came to rely on the pinboard for input and referred to it often. Sometimes the teachers tailored comments to particular learners and handed the pieces of paper directly to them. Later these comments were also hung on the board if they were relevant to the whole group.

When the activity was concluded or at break time, the instructors reviewed the contents of the pinboard with the learners. Relating this follow-up language lesson to the activity was easy because the pinboard had been created as events unfolded and reflected the contents of the past discussion. The group could easily recall the specific moments to which each language point referred and a context for the follow-up language lesson was thus provided.

CONCLUSION

As this discussion illustrates, there is a body of business communication training material designed for native language use that can also be effectively incorporated into foreign language teaching in a business setting. The selection of any one method or technique over another must be left to the discretion of the individual teacher. In any case, it will often be appropriate for the L2 teacher to adapt training that has been borrowed from another sphere of learning so that the course content most effectively meets the learners' needs. What is more important than the borrowed methods and techniques themselves is the advantage to the learners of the opportunity to develop in the L2 strategies and skills to which they have previously been exposed, which they are expected to employ in their work, and which will serve them beyond the walls of the language classroom.

NOTES

1. This initiative in communicative language teaching is based upon my experiences as a teacher of ESL/EFL for business people in the United Kingdom and in Germany (most recently for Schering A.G. and Siemens GmbH in West Berlin). Although this discussion centers on Germany, much of what is discussed applies to other areas of the world, particularly those areas of the industrialized world where English is a foreign language.

REFERENCES

Karrass, Chester L. 1970. *The Negotiating Game.* New York: Thomas Y. Crowell Publishers.

Schnelle, W. and I. Stoltz. 1977. *Interactive Learning: A Guide to Moderating Groups of Learners.* Quickborn, W. Germany: Metaplan GmbH.

Smith, Stephen M. 1984. *The Theater Arts and the Teaching of Second Languages.* Reading, Mass.: Addison-Wesley Publishing Co.

Xerox Learning Systems. 1984. *Negotiating Self-Taught.* Stamford, Conn.: Xerox Corp.

Chapter 7

A Practical Approach to Course Design: English for Computer Science in Brazil

Miriam Solange Costa

Miriam Solange Costa is a professor in the Department of Letters at the Federal University of Pernambuco, Brazil. During the ten years that she has been teaching EFL she has been actively involved in ESP/EAP materials production, research in reading and computer-assisted language learning, and the development of English educational software for microcomputers.

INTRODUCTION

Throughout the world, the rapidly expanding demand for courses in English for Specific Purposes (ESP) has generally focused attention on learners' occupational or social needs as the starting point for course design. The content of such courses depends upon the context in which the learners will be required to use the L2. Emphasis may be placed on oral communication for basic survival, on business correspondence, or perhaps on the interpretation of technical writing in a specialized field. Considerable effort has been devoted worldwide to the development of materials and the creation of courses to meet an array of specialized goals. At the University of Pernambuco, Recife, Brazil, an ESP reading comprehension course has been designed for a group of first-year Brazilian computer science students whose interests and academic pursuits are homogeneous. The course design places emphasis on the students and their specific needs and motivation within an academic situation.

This report illustrates the procedures that were used to design the course. Included are a detailed description of the group that required English for specific reading activities, a presentation of essential components of the ESP reading skills course, a discussion of some aspects of design, instruction, and evaluation found useful in developing the materials, brief comments on other considerations that influenced the course design, and, finally, two sample units of reading and study skills.

Before the course is described, mention should be made of one crucial component in its design that is directly related to the title of this chapter. This component is the constant interaction between the ESP teacher and the teachers and students of the Computer Science Department. As Fig. 1 shows, there is a continual assessment of the course's efficiency based on classroom feedback, feedback from past students at more advanced stages of the computer science course, and the teaching staff. This dynamic process of adaptation and improvement in response to practical results of previous courses constitutes the "practical approach" of the title. It implies that more attention is paid to feedback from the clients than to extraneous influences, such as language acquisition theory or reading research. This is not to diminish the importance of theory in course design and materials development, but merely to affirm my belief that when all is said and done, the success of an ESP course can be measured *only* in terms of its practical results.

BACKGROUND

Experience in teaching reading strategies to students of other subjects such as engineering, economics, architecture, education, or geography

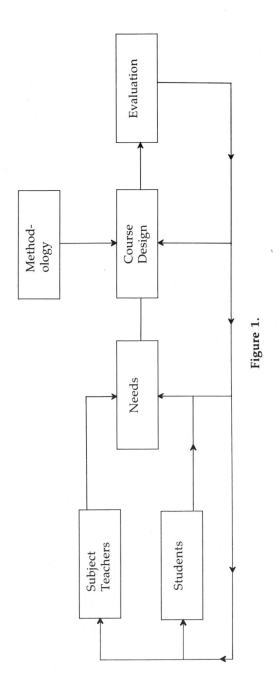

Figure 1.

has enabled me to make a preliminary analysis of the expectations of students currently enrolled in ESP Computer Science. Beginners in computer science usually behave differently from students in other undergraduate ESP groups. Unlike students from other areas, they are almost exclusively interested in extracting detailed, specific information from the text. This is where the first problem emerges: most students have never been trained to read efficiently in Portuguese, their first language. A primary concern, then, was the adoption of a practical approach to needs analysis based not only on students' needs and interests, but also on their existing level of skills and knowledge, both conceptual and linguistic.

NEEDS ANALYSIS

The needs analysis consisted of two major components: a profile of the learners and an assessment of the department's needs and expectations.

Profile of the Learners

Three instruments were used to collect the data necessary to determine a profile of the learners: a diagnostic test, questionnaires and interviews. The test and questionnaires were for the new students, whereas the interviews were used with more advanced students of the Computer Science Department. These interviews identified difficulties of continuing students have in using English within the curriculum. The questionnaires and the interviews were found to be useful tools to determine the students' characteristics and to reveal their attitudes and expectations. The questionnaires elicited general information about the learners, for example, their reason for taking the computer science course, their previous and present job experience, their background in English and their expectations in learning it. These expectations were related to previous experience in learning English, attitudes toward English, degree of motivation, the kind of skills previously studied, the kind of knowledge desired, notions held about the learning of reading skills in a university setting, experience as readers in Portuguese as well as other languages, and the kind of readings preferred. The diagnostic test, on the other hand, measured knowledge of English grammar and vocabulary as well as reading comprehension ability. The diagnostic test also showed that the average students' level of English was roughly intermediate (i.e., higher than that of students from other disciplines).

English is seen by students as a means of increasing their access to technical knowledge and a highly important factor in academic success. In general, they defined their needs in terms of improving their ability to read technical texts. Similarly, their major interests are related to reading academic texts that are not easily available in Portuguese. Their motivation is instrumental in that they see a command of English purely as a means to an end and express no interest in using English for any purpose other than academic.

Department Needs and Expectations

Ten subject matter teachers were interviewed to find out how they, as teachers of computer science, perceive students' problems and needs in using English language textbooks, to what extent they require students to read English, and what kinds of skills and strategies they feel students would need in order to fulfil learning tasks that require reading at the beginning of the computer science curriculum. These interviews revealed that the subject matter teachers have certain assumptions concerning students' English language competence and previous knowledge of the subject. They regard independent reading as an essential aspect of the courses and expect students to be able to read efficiently in English, whereas in reality students are unable to do so because of inadequate instruction during their secondary education. With regard to the learners' needs to cope with technical vocabulary, both course designer and subject matter teachers spent six months drawing up a list of the most relevant topics, acronyms and abbreviations to be used in the computer science course.

Teacher's Needs

The needs of the ESP teachers also merit some attention. An ESP teacher needs to be able to grasp the conceptual structure of the subject the students are studying for two reasons. This knowledge helps them understand how language is used to represent that structure and what potential difficulties learners may encounter in English texts on technical subjects. To obtain firsthand experience in the range of different subjects taught at the University of Perambuco, I spent three semesters attending computer science courses. This experience enabled me to anticipate many of the problems often encountered by ESP teachers who understand little or nothing of the subject matter with which they have to deal. By attending the classes and observing where and how difficulties arose, I was better prepared to help both students and teachers overcome them.

COURSE DESIGN

Course Components

In order to make use of technical literature in English, students need training in reading and study skills. While the list of skills drawn up for inclusion in the ESP course based on computer science texts does not differ from more traditional reading skills (e.g., outlining, summarizing, recognizing the parts of a book, note-taking, reporting, using library facilities, knowing subject matter and technical vocabulary, and recognizing definition, description, or explanation at the level of written academic discourse), there is a significant difference in emphasis. In response to that difference, this course concentrated on *application* of skills to previously unknown material in contrast to emphasis on knowledge of facts, definitions, or processes.

Aims and Objectives

It is essential to develop objectives that reflect what the teacher considers valuable and important. The aim of this course is to develop students' ability to process language as a system of communication through application of both global and linguistic knowledge to a variety of reading and study skills. Students should be able to attain two general objectives at the end of a course like the one described here: (1) understanding of the ways in which writers of academic texts use English to relate ideas and (2) use of this knowledge to perceive, predict and infer such relationships.

Specific objectives to be reached are (1) demonstration of the ability to skim an academic text for general comprehension by writing a sentence or phrase specifying the main points, completing a diagram or flowchart and labelling its main sections, or constructing an outline or diagram; (2) a thorough command of key sub-technical and technical vocabulary; (3) detailed comprehension of a technical text, such as operating instructions, demonstrated by providing details through answers to questions, completion of diagrams or flowcharts, sentence completion, rearrangement of jumbled sentences; (4) development of a critical attitude towards the reliability or applicability of the content, the tone of the discourse and the presentation of the information, shown by expressing comments with justification or by assessing the content's applicability, i.e., listing the categories of reader and/or situation to which it is applicable and justifying these answers.

Contents

The sequence of topics to be addressed reflects the ordering of relevant topics simultaneously in the "Introduction to Computer Science" and "Algorithm" courses. The course was organized into ten topic-based units on the principle that the purpose of the text is to give information, not to represent a particular text type. This organization facilitates more complex work, since a body of knowledge about the topic is built up throughout the unit.

A supplementary unit was provided at the beginning of the course to introduce the learners to the reading process. Its objective was to make students aware of all aspects of reading, its nature as a process, types of reading, and the importance of matching reading strategies to the reader's objectives.

Texts

Authentic texts were selected from university textbooks, specialized magazines, and journals from the computer science library, where 85 percent of the available materials are in English. These texts are relevant to and reflect the students' interests and concerns. The conceptual difficulty of the texts' content in relation to the students' prior knowledge and experience determined the sequence of readings and tasks in each unit.

Units

The materials were sequenced in terms of the difficulty of the topics. A progression from simplest to most complex prevails both within the unit and throughout the course as a whole. The final stage of each unit consists of a student presentation or activity that requires a communicative task such as analyzing a problem and recommending a solution, reporting on an experiment, producing a document, making notes from specialized manuals, or describing a process. The skills and strategies required for the completion of the tasks are built up by a series of linked steps as the students proceed through each unit or part of a unit.

Teaching and Learning Procedures

Classroom activities require pair or group work, which encourages students to become more actively involved in the units. Reinforcement of skills is provided constantly throughout the course, not only by means of the classroom activities but also through individual work. Communication in English serves as a means of sharing and solving problems posed by the materials. Adjustment of this learning process to the students' academic environment helps reduce their anxiety about reading academic texts. To provide criteria for the measurement of success, a clear statement is given concerning the aims of each unit and the specific objectives of each text or activity to be performed. Although instructions for the unit are always given in English, written answers in Portuguese are accepted from the students who would be severely limited in particular communicative tasks if they were obliged to write in English. An individualized approach to language difficulties is recommended. Students are asked to underline the words, phrases or sentences in the text that give them difficulties. Appropriate treatment is then given to these problems.

EXAMPLES OF MATERIALS

The materials presented in this section are taken from the beginning of the course to illustrate more clearly how the units address course objectives. Two distinct units have been selected, one on study skills ("Using the Library Facilities") and another on reading skills ("The Use of Prediction"). The units are used simultaneously to offer variety in the classroom. As shown in the sample unit presented here, some reading skills units have activities interrelated with the study skills units.

Study Skills Unit: Using the Library Facilities

In the area of study skills two kinds of knowledge are of concern: basic knowledge and the ability to apply that knowledge. Students do individual work and act within authentic communicative situations to learn the necessary study skills. Thus the students learn how to apply basic knowledge through experience. If students are to learn to use the library, for example, a general tour of the library is considered insufficient. Students are sent there repeatedly for assignments requiring the use of such library resources as the card catalog or periodicals file. These kinds of experiences enable students to be more independent during later stages of the course. Units on study skills are usually divided into two parts, and each part consists of classroom activities and individual work.

Using the Library Facilities—Activities, Part I

The major activity in Part I introduces the subject matter by presenting the physical aspect of a library through a diagram. The teacher asks questions in Portuguese and students scan the non-linear text for the requested information using the library diagram. The nine questions are read orally by the teacher. The follow-up individual work helps students become familiar with the layout and resources of their university library.

STUDY SKILLS UNIT

USING THE LIBRARY FACILITIES

ACTIVITIES PART 1

This unit will introduce you to the library.

> LEARNING HOW TO USE THE LIBRARY IS LIKE ANY
> OTHER SKILL

Look at this picture and answer this question:

> WHAT IS REQUIRED TO USE THE LIBRARY?

MANCHESTER CENTRAL LIBRARY: A VERTICAL DIAGRAM

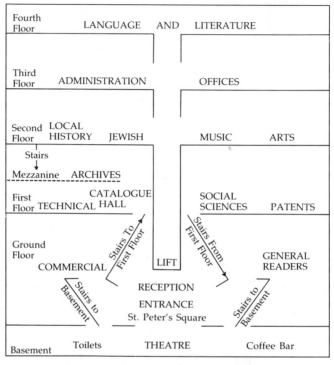

<table>
<tr><td>Fourth
Floor</td><td colspan="2">LANGUAGE   AND   LITERATURE</td></tr>
<tr><td>Third
Floor</td><td>ADMINISTRATION</td><td>OFFICES</td></tr>
<tr><td>Second LOCAL
Floor HISTORY   JEWISH</td><td></td><td>MUSIC   ARTS</td></tr>
<tr><td>Stairs ↓
Mezzanine   ARCHIVES</td><td></td><td></td></tr>
<tr><td>First   CATALOGUE
Floor TECHNICAL HALL</td><td></td><td>SOCIAL
SCIENCES   PATENTS</td></tr>
<tr><td>Ground
Floor
   COMMERCIAL</td><td>LIFT
RECEPTION
ENTRANCE
St. Peter's Square</td><td>GENERAL
READERS</td></tr>
<tr><td>Basement</td><td>Toilets   THEATRE</td><td>Coffee Bar</td></tr>
</table>

HOURS OF OPENING

The Library is open:
Monday–Friday 9a.m. - 9p.m.
Saturday 9a.m. - 5p.m.
except
General Readers' Library
Monday 10a.m. - 8p.m.
Tuesday–Friday 10a.m. - 6p.m.
Saturday 10a.m. - 5p.m.

Archives Department
Monday 9a.m. - 12 noon;
  1p.m. - 9p.m.
Tuesday–Friday 9a.m. - 12 noon;
  1p.m. - 5p.m.
Archives Department is closed on
  Saturdays

Theatre Box Office
Weekdays 10.30a.m. - 7.45p.m.

Responda as perguntas de acordo com as informações
contidas no diagrama da biblioteca central:

1. A que horas fecha a biblioteca geral dos leitores nas quarta-feiras?

2. O Departamento de Arquivos fecha aos sábados às 17:00 horas?

3. A Biblioteca Técnica abre aos sábados às 9:00

4. Onde fica a Biblioteca Geral dos Leitores?

5. a) Onde está localizado o Teatro da biblioteca?
   b) Como se chega até ele?

Source: *Looking for Information: A Practical Book in Reading Skills*, R. R. Jordan, 1980, London:
Longman, p. 33

6. a) A Biblioteca de Artes fica no primeiro andar?
   b) Como se chega até lá?

7. Como se chega até o Departamento de Arquivos?

8. Como você consegue ir do Coffee Bar para a Biblioteca de Ciências Sociais.

9. Caso deseje estudar até mais tarde na biblioteca central, fazendo uso das diversas bibliotecas e setores nela incluidos, qual seria a melhor noite para realizar suas tarefas?

INDIVIDUAL WORK

> THE FOCUS OF THE ACTIVITIES HERE IS TO MAKE YOU
> AWARE OF THE HELP YOU CAN GET FROM THE
> UNIVERSITY LIBRARY.

Task 1 Mark Y (for YES) and N (for NO):

_____ Have you been enrolled in the library?
_____ Do you know the resources it offers you?
_____ Do you know how to use them?
_____ Do you know how the library is organized?

Task 2 Listen to the tape recording about the organization of the library and write in Portuguese a brief report on your visit.

Task 3 Draw a diagram of the main library.

Task 4 Answer these questions:

A. How is the library system organized?
B. How many faculty libraries are there in the university? List them.
C. What can you do when the library does not have the book or the article you are looking for?
D. What kinds of reference books does the library have? List them.

Using the Library Facilities--Activities, Part II

In classroom activities students apply reading strategies to a text about the library. Part of the subject matter of the text refers to a previous unit and provides communicative practice in the skills introduced earlier in the course. Twelve distinct tasks in the last part of the unit familiarize students with the resources their specialized library offers.

USING THE LIBRARY FACILITIES

ACTIVITIES PART II

> THE FOCUS OF THIS PART IS THE APPLICATION OF READING STRATEGIES TO A TEXT.

TEXT 2

LIBRARY

LIBRARY. Libraries form a vital part of the world's systems of communication and education. They make available—through books, films, recordings, and other media—knowledge that has been accumulated through the ages. People in all walks of life—including students, teachers, business executives, government officials, scholars, and scientists—use library resources in their work. Large numbers of people also turn to libraries to satisfy a desire for knowledge or to obtain material for some kind of leisure-time activity. In addition, many people enjoy book discussions, film programs, lectures, story hours, and other activities that are provided by their local library.

Libraries also play an important role in preserving a society's cultural heritage. For example, some libraries have special collections of such items as rare books, authors' original manuscripts, or works of local artists. In addition, the librarians in many libraries develop exhibits and offer programs to help people learn about their own community or about the culture of other civilizations. All in all, the library ranks as one of society's most useful service institutions.

The first section of this article, *The Library Today*, provides an overview of the varied contents and kinds of libraries, and discusses the many services these important institutions provide. It also deals with the challenges and problems faced by librarians and libraries. Other parts of the article describe in detail the different types of libraries that are designed to serve different people. The article discusses libraries in all parts of the world, the library profession, and the qualifications and training needed by librarians. The article also traces the history of libraries. For detailed information on how to use a library, see the *How to Do Research* section of the RESEARCH GUIDE/INDEX, Volume 22:

The Library Today

Today's libraries differ greatly from libraries of the past—not only in contents, kinds, and services, but even in physical layout and atmosphere. In turn, future libraries will differ from those of today. This is so because librarians constantly strive to find ways to expand and perfect the contributions that they and their institutions make to society.

World Book Encyclopedia
Volume 12, 1985,
pages 210–211

EXERCISES

1. Mark the parentheses to indicate the kinds of typographical clues that are used in this text.

( ) capital letters   ( ) titles
( ) punctuation   ( ) subtitles
( ) symbols   ( ) bold print
( ) italics   ( ) footnotes
( ) quotations   ( ) numbers
( ) charts   ( ) drawings
( ) illustrations   ( ) graphs

2. Read the text and count how many times the words LIBRARY, LIBRARIES, LIBRARIAN and THE appear.

( ) LIBRARY   ( ) LIBRARIES
( ) LIBRARIAN   ( ) THE

3. Underline 15 cognates in the text.
   REMEMBER: LIBRARY is not LIVRARIA
                This is an example of a FALSE COGNATE in Portuguese.

4. Complete:
   In this text, the library is considered _____

5. People use library resources in their work. Mention some of them.
   _____
   _____

6. What kind of activities does the library provide to people?
   _____
   _____

7. Today's libraries differ greatly from libraries of the past. Give your opinion:
   In what ways do you think future libraries will differ from those of today?
   _____
   _____
   _____

INDIVIDUAL WORK

> THE ACTIVITIES HERE ARE INTENDED TO HELP YOU
> BECOME FAMILIAR WITH THE SOURCES AVAILABLE IN
> YOUR SPECIALIZED LIBRARY.

TASK 1 Register at the library. Talk to the librarian at the circulation desk.

TASK 2 List the different kinds of bibliographical material your specialized library may offer (books, manuals, etc)

TASK 3 Write down the library number (code), the title and the author of two books dealing with *Computer Science* and two books dealing with *Technology*

TASK 4 List the titles of 3 books which you can find in the card catalogue written by one author

TASK 5 Find a book by an author with the same initials of your first and last names. (for example, if your name is Roberto Nascimento, the author's first name must start with *R*, and the family name with *N*).

TASK 6 Write down the library number, the title and the author of a book that contains illustrations, maps, or diagrams.

TASK 7 Write down the library number, the title and the author of a book which has more than 500 pages.

TASK 8 List at least 5 types of reference works you can find in the library.

TASK 9 By using one periodical write in full
a. The title of an article in this periodical.
b. author's name.
c. title of the periodical in which the article can be found.

d. volume number of the periodical.
e. page number.
f. publication date of two articles.

TASK 10 Find and list all subjects under the topic COMPUT

TASK 11 What kind of manuals does the library receive?

TASK 12 Examine one manual from the library and check with an (x) which points it consists of:
( ) table of contents
( ) introduction
( ) preface
( ) glossary
( ) index
( ) author's index
( ) list of illustrations
( ) appendices
( ) abstracts
( ) list of tables
( ) summary

Reading Skills: The Use of Prediction

Most of the instructions in a reading skills course are aimed at the application level of learning. Application in this context means developing skills that can be used with new material and in new situations. The teacher's task is not to teach the students to extract as much detail from the text as possible, but rather to approach the text efficiently according to their purpose.

Prediction is one of the skills necessary to this process. As it is a very personal process in which both background knowledge and textual linguistic information help the readers to form their own expectations before and during reading, prediction is easily understood if it can be fitted into an existing framework of ideas in the students' minds. Because prediction ensures the students' active involvement, it is worth developing learners' abilities in the use of this strategy at the beginning of the course. How can prediction be taught to learners who have no background in their field of study? The unit "Reading Skills" was designed to sensitize the students to the importance of using prediction.

In the unit illustrated here, two texts form the basis of prediction activities, and the subject matter links one text to another.

READING SKILLS UNIT
THE USE OF PREDICTION

THE FOCUS OF THIS UNIT IS TO HELP YOU MAKE PREDIC-
TIONS AND GUESSES WHEN READING A TEXT.

Prediction is an integral part of comprehension. It is also a skill that is basic to all reading techniques (skimming, scanning, anticipation question, etc.).

The title of the text tells you the TOPIC of what you will read. Use your own knowledge of the topic to predict as much as you can about the content.

PART I

STEP 1:   With the objective of practicing PREDICTION, what information would you expect to find in a text with this title?

THE COMPUTER AND THE HUMAN BRAIN

STEP 2:   What would you expect to find in the text accompanying these pictures?

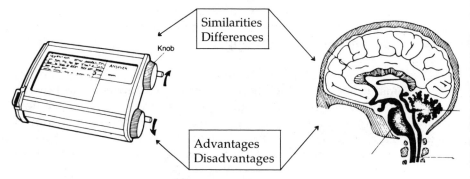

STEP 3:   Use your knowledge of the context to make your predictions. What kind of subtitles will fit the context of this text?

STEP 4:   Read the text again and answer the exercises especially prepared for it.

TEXT

(TITLE)

The term "giant brain" has been applied in efforts to provide a picturesque image of computers for popular consumption. The other term, "biological computer," has crept into the vocabulary of computer science as synonymous with the human or animal brain. This sort of linking of the words COMPUTER and BRAIN amounts to recognition that there are certain similarities between the two. On the other hand, machines follow directions and are accused of having no originality, no creativity or talent for abstraction. In this case the critics are eager to point out the differences between computers and brains to minimize the similarities.

_____ (SUB-TITLE)

More than one hundred years ago George Boole was studying the laws of thought and laying the foundations of Boolean Algebra. This mathematical structure, inspired in part by his interest in human brain activity, came to be central in the design of computer circuits. Many circuits imitate closely the way humans perform the same function. The similarities between computers and the brain are intentional, since the human brain has designed the computer somewhat after its own image. Furthermore, it is intentional because machines have been created to solve problems formerly done by human beings. Thus the brain receives information, remembers it, operates on it, and outputs information. So does the computer. In fact, this amounts to a compact description of the principal purpose of each. The use of the word MEMORY for the storage unit of a computer is almost universal and amounts to general recognition that this particular machine capability is "brain-like."

_____ (SUB-TITLE)

To begin with, the nature of the materials from which the two are constructed is different. A computer is largely metallic, its simplest components being the OR, AND, and NOT boxes. The brain, however, is made of biological material; its basic building block is the nerve cell or neuron, which resembles the black-box machine counterpart.

There is a big difference in the way the brain and the computer store information in memory. While the memory register of a computer is arranged in geometrical units, each having a number by which it may be designated, those of the brain seem quite disorderly, perhaps because they are at present so little understood. The brain's method of storing information is associative; ideas that are related to each other in some way are linked together. The computer does not have this capability and stores information through numerical systems. There is evidence that the brain is not entirely "prewired" but that only the major organization features are built in, considering the number of neurons involved. The brain is in part a *self-organizing device,* creating connections between component units on the basis of information received.

EXERCISES

1. Read paragraph 1 and answer this question:

   What are machines accused of? _____

   _____

2. Read the second paragraph.

3. The second paragraph deals with _____

4. Who was studying the laws of thought? _____

5. Why are the similarities between the computer and the human brain intentional?

   _____

   _____

6. Read paragraphs 3 and 4.

7. Complete the table below contrasting the stated differences between the computer and the brain.

	COMPUTER	BRAIN
material		
memory		
method of storing		

8. What title would you give to the short text below?

   _____

   The brain is not pre-wired. Its major organizational feature involves a considerable number of neurons. It is in part a self-organizing device creating connections between component units on the basis of the information received.

9. Complete the diagram with words or expressions from the short text.

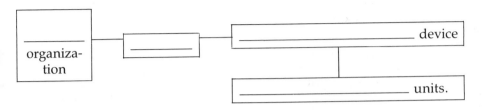

INDIVIDUAL WORK

Look for an advertisement of a particular computer product in a specialized magazine or periodical.

TASK 1 Make a photocopy of the advertisement.

TASK 2 Indicate the complete source from which it was taken.

TASK 3 Look at the headline and write down in a few sentences what you think it might be about.

TASK 4 List the different typographical clues.

TASK 5 Read the advertisement carefully to yourself, working out the meaning of vocabulary you do not know.

TASK 6 Which words are used to persuade the reader?

TASK 7 Comment on the effectiveness of the advertisement.

TASK 8 Say what kind of reader the advertisement is addressed to.

The Use of Prediction—Activities

As these illustrations show, the materials need not be complex: The simplest text can develop students' use of prediction, i.e., the activation of previous knowledge about a topic to predict as much as possible about a text while exploring its content. The classroom procedure for this activity is as follows: Students work in groups of four to discuss steps 1 to 4. After a few minutes the leader of each group reports the group's findings to the whole class. Students then complete the exercises for the text, "The Computer and the Human Brain."

The final set of tasks, which also requires individual work, deals with an advertisement for a particular computer product. This advertisement is the subject of the next unit, which explores reading techniques and expands on prediction.

CONCLUSION

It has not been my intention here to describe in detail everything that is necessary for the success of an ESP reading skills course. Rather, my goal has been to present a framework for ESP course design that is based upon a dynamic process of adaptation and improvement in response to feedback from students and teachers alike.

It is hoped that the considerations for course design and development and the illustrations of model texts and activities presented here will be useful to other ESP teachers and stimulate them to become familiar with the subject matter of their students' program and to continually reassess the course and its results. In so doing, ESP courses can become responsive to a wider range of students' needs while involving the students themselves in the process of adaptation and course improvement. Such an approach is then not only practical for teachers, but for students as well.

Chapter 8

Fostering Interactive Second Language Reading

Patricia L. Carrell

Patricia L. Carrell is a professor of Linguistics and Psychology, and Associate Dean of the Graduate School, at Southern Illinois University, Carbondale. Her research interests include the role of background knowledge, both content and formal schemata, in ESL reading, and its classroom implications and applications. In 1985 she was awarded the Paul Pimsleur Award for Research in Foreign Language Education by the American Council on the Teaching of Foreign Languages.

INTRODUCTION

Recent developments in the theory of knowledge representation, grouped under the general rubric of *schema theory* (Anderson 1977, Adams and Collins 1979, Rumelhart and Ortony 1977, Rumelhart 1980), have had a pervasive influence on current thinking about text comprehension. Through an emphasis on the role of preexisting knowledge structures in providing information implicit in a text, schema-theoretic approaches have made possible the fairly detailed modeling of many of the active, constructive processes necessary to comprehension (e.g., Schank and Abelson 1977). Within the schema-theoretic framework, text comprehension, or more specifically for our purposes, reading comprehension, is characterized as an interaction of text-based processes and knowledge-based processes. The latter are related to the reader's existing background knowledge or schemata (Adams and Collins 1979, Anderson 1977, Rumelhart and Ortony 1977, Rumelhart 1977, 1980).

A recent article by Carrell and Eisterhold (1983) describes how schema theory conceptualizes the interaction of text-based and knowledge-based processes, or as they are more commonly called, *bottom-up* and *top-down* processing modes. Without going into all of the detail and all of the examples presented in that article, but to ensure that what follows is as clear as possible, I will briefly summarize the schema-theoretic notions of the interaction of bottom-up, or text-based processing, and top-down, or knowledge-based processing.

According to schema theory, the process of interpreting a text is guided by the principle that the input is mapped against an existing schema, and that compatibility must exist between the schema and the input. Mapping of input is accomplished by two basic modes of information processing, called *bottom-up* and *top-down* processing. Bottom-up processing is evoked by the incoming data; specific features of the input data get mapped against the best fitting, most specific schema at the bottom. Schemata are hierarchically organized, from most general at the top (e.g., a schema for "a grocery store") to most specific at the bottom (e.g., a subschema for "my neighborhood *National*"). As the bottom-level schemata converge into higher-level, more general schemata, these too become activated. Thus, bottom-up processing occurs when aspects of the input directly suggest or activate a lower-level schema, which in its turn suggests or activates a higher-order schema. Bottom-up processing is therefore called *data-driven* since it is ultimately the input data that generates the suggestion of particular concepts (Rumelhart and Ortony 1977:128). On the other hand, top-down processing occurs as the reader makes general predictions based on higher-order, general schemata and then searches the incoming data for a fit to these partially satisfied, higher-order schemata. These processes are called top-down because they begin with conceptual expectations about the input data, and point to where the satisfaction of these expectations might be encountered in the data. Top-down processing is therefore called *conceptually-driven* since it is ultimately the general concepts that generate the search of the data (Rumelhart and Ortony 1977).

Schema-theory research has shown that the most efficient processing of text is interactive, a combination of top-down and bottom-up processing modes (Rumelhart 1977, 1980). Top-down processing consists of making predictions about the text based on prior experience or background knowledge, and then checking the text for confirmation or refutation of those predictions. Bottom-up processing implies decoding individual linguistic units (e.g., phonemes, graphemes, words), building textual meaning from the smallest units to the largest, and then modifying preexisting background knowledge and current predictions on the basis of information encountered in the text. Skilled readers constantly shift their mode of processing, accommodating to the demands of a particular text and a particular reading situation. Less skilled readers tend to over-rely on one process or the other and suffer deleterious effects on comprehension as a result (Spiro 1978, 1979).

In recent research on second language reading (Carrell 1983, Carrell and Wallace 1983), it was found that second language readers were not effectively utilizing knowledge-based or top-down processing (i.e., specific contextual information with which they were supplied) to facilitate comprehension. They appeared to be engaged almost exclusively in text-based processing to the detriment of comprehension. By contrast, in other studies (Steffensen, Joag-dev, and Anderson 1979, Johnson 1981, Carrell 1981) some evidence was found of over-reliance on top-down processes. Thus, over-reliance on either mode of processing to the neglect of the other mode has been found to cause reading difficulties for second language readers. Many second language readers are not efficient interactive text processors, either because they attempt to process in a totally bottom-up fashion and may be effortful decoders at that, or because they attempt to process in a totally top-down fashion and are hence subject to schema failures or schema interference. What can the second language reading teacher do to combat this? This article proposes teaching a number of comprehension strategies designed to help nonnative readers become interactive readers. In discussing these classroom suggestions, I shall classify them into two groups: (1) those designed to teach students to make effective use of the bottom-up processing mode, and (2) those designed to teach students to make effective use of the top-down processing mode. This distinction is made primarily for ease in presenting and discussing these strategies. To some extent the strategies discussed from the perspective of one processing mode also have an effect on the other processing mode, and on the general metacognitive awareness among second language readers that effective reading calls for an efficient *interaction* of both processing modes.

IMPLICATIONS FOR SECOND LANGUAGE READING CLASSROOMS

Given the role of schemata in reading comprehension, the following suggestions offer some classroom implications and applications of this view of second language reading. Suggesting applications of theory to pedagogy is always dangerous and must be prefaced with several caveats: (1) although these suggestions are based on both theoretical and experimental empirical research, for the most part they have not been subjected to classroom-based, pedagogical research, and where they have been tested in classrooms, they have not been tested in wide varieties of pedagogical settings; (2) these suggestions are geared toward a class of adults literate in their native language, although most would also be applicable or adaptable to classes for children or for adults who are illiterate in their native language; (3) there are potential differences in how these suggestions might apply at different levels of proficiency in the second language, some of which are mentioned; (4) although these suggestions are offered from the perspective of a schema-theoretic view of reading insofar as schema theory is compatible with a general psycholinguistic model of reading, some may also be implied by other aspects of the psycholinguistic approach; (5) since some suggestions are compatible with any reader-centered, communicative approach to reading, they may already be happening in second language reading classrooms; (6) this list is by no means exhaustive. (See Byrnes, this volume, for further suggestions).

BOTTOM-UP PROCESSING

The introduction of a top-down processing perspective has had a dramatic effect on models of second language reading. That reading is not a passive but rather an active, and in fact, an interactive process has been recognized for some time (Goodman 1967, 1971; Kolers 1969; Smith 1971). However, the interactive view of reading has only recently been acknowledged in second language reading. Early work in second language reading, specifically reading in English as a second language, assumed a rather passive, bottom-up view of second language reading. Second language reading was considered primarily as a decoding process, consisting of reconstructing the author's intended meaning via recognition of letters and words, and building up a semantic representation of the text's meaning from the smallest textual units at the bottom to the largest at the top (Rivers 1964, 1968; Plaister 1968; Yorio 1971). Problems of second language reading and reading comprehension were thought to be decoding problems.

About a decade ago, the so-called psycholinguistic model of reading began to have an impact on views of second language reading (Goodman 1967, 1971; Smith 1971). Such second language reading specialists as Eskey (1970, 1973), Clarke and Silberstein (1977), Clarke (1979), Coady (1979) and others (Mackay and Mountford 1979, Widdowson 1978, 1983) began to view second language reading as an active process in which the second language reader participates as an active information processor who predicts and samples only parts of the actual text. However, only since about 1979 has a truly top-down approach to second language reading been advanced (Steffensen, Joag-dev, and Anderson 1979; Carrell 1981, 1982, Carrell and Eisterhold 1983; Johnson 1981, 1982; Hudson 1982). In the top-down view of second language reading, not only is the reader an active participant in the reading process, making predictions and processing information, but everything in the reader's prior experience or background knowledge plays a potential role in the process.

However, lest the top-down view of second language reading be seen as a *substitute* for the bottom-up, decoding view, rather than its complement, several researchers have recently felt the need to emphasize that efficient and effective second language reading requires the interactive operation of *both* top-down and bottom-up strategies (Rumelhart 1977, 1980; Sanford and Garrod 1981; Eskey 1987, Eskey and Grabe 1987; van Dijk and Kintsch 1983; Carrell 1987). Eskey (1985) terms this recognition of the importance of bottom-up processing and of the help second language readers need in simple decoding tasks "holding in the bottom." In the next section I shall discuss two areas of pedagogy that can assist second language readers to improve their bottom-up, language decoding skills, i.e., to "hold in the bottom." These areas are grammatical skills and vocabulary development.

Grammatical Skills

Several studies have shown the important role played by grammatical knowledge in native and nonnative reading. Among native English speaking children in Britain, Chapman (1979) found a relationship between reading ability and the ability to complete anaphoric relations in a cloze test, and he concluded that mastery of such textual features, including cohesive ties (Halliday and Hasan 1976), is a central factor in fluent reading and reading comprehension. Cohen and his colleagues (1979) found that foreign readers of English texts in the sciences and economics often did not pick up on conjunctive words in their specialized texts. Cohen *et al.* argued that nonnative readers read more locally than do native speakers, and because they do not attend to conjunctive ties, they have trouble synthesizing information across sentences and paragraphs. Mackay (1979) and Cowan (1976) have similarly argued that recognition of conjunctions and other intersentential linguistic devices is crucial to the information gathering skills of second language readers. Thus, "holding in the bottom," enhancing second language readers' bottom-up decoding skills, should include classroom instruction on the cohesive devices of English (substitution, ellipsis, conjunction, lexical cohesion), and their function across sentences and paragraphs. Such instruction can make learners aware of how ideas in a text are unified by these cohesive elements. Williams (1983) has not only discussed the importance of recognizing cohesive ties in reading in a foreign language, but has suggested teaching materials and methods to bring this about. Specifically, he proposes a system of symbols and textual markings that teach foreign readers how to use cohesive signals to increase their reading comprehension. Chapman (1983) has published an entire book on the teaching of cohesion and its relationship to reading development. (See Carrell (1985b) for a review of this book).

Connor (1984) has studied both cohesion and coherence in advanced ESL learners' writing and discovered that although advanced ESL writers use about the same proportion of cohesive devices as native writers, they lack the variety of native writers. This is especially true in the category of lexical cohesion, where ESL writers tend to overuse repetition and underuse synonyms and collocation. For example, in compositions written on the topic of tests and testing situations, a native speaker used the following lexical collocations: "methods of measuring," "a set of questions," "a satisfactory means of measuring a student's achievement," "means of testing," "gauge a student's mastery," and "administering examinations." Writing on the same topic, a nonnative speaker exhibited limited use of synonyms, and relied almost exclusively on repetitions: "tests," "the tests," "put scores," "good scores," "bad scores," "scores of tests," "tests." Connor attributes this to general deficiencies in ESL learners' vocabularies, and comments that this appears to be related to similar results with good and poor native English writers (Witte and Faigley 1981). This brings us to the other major area of classroom instruction designed to enhance second language readers' bottom-up decoding skills: vocabulary development.

Vocabulary Development

Vocabulary development and word recognition have long been perceived as crucial to successful bottom-up decoding skills. However, schema theory has shed new light on the complex nature of the interrelationship of schemata, context, and vocabulary knowledge. Unlike traditional views of vocabulary, current thinking converges on the notion that a given word does not have a fixed meaning, but rather a variety of meanings around a "prototypical" core, and that these meanings interact with context and background knowledge. Consider the following examples of the verb "kick" in English:

The punter kicked the ball.
The baby kicked the ball.
The golfer kicked the ball.
(Anderson, Reynolds, Schallert, and Goetz 1977:368)

Readers will construct different images for the words *ball* and *kick* because of the influence of the different subject noun phrases. Different kinds of balls are visualized, and the act of kicking is different in each of the sentences. If readers do not have the background experiences associated with types of kicking and things that can be kicked, then the comprehension of the lexical items and the sentences as a whole will be affected. Thus knowledge of individual word meanings is strongly associated with conceptual knowledge, i.e., learning vocabulary also means learning the conceptual knowledge associated with the word. On the one hand, an important part of teaching background knowledge is teaching the vocabulary related to it. Conversely, teaching vocabulary may mean teaching new concepts, new knowledge. Knowledge of vocabulary entails knowledge of the schemata in which a concept participates, knowledge of the networks in which a word participates, along with any associated words and concepts.

Teachers must become aware of cross-cultural differences in vocabulary and of the ways in which meaning may be represented differently in the lexicons of various languages. For example, the words *cut* and *carve* have distinct meanings in English; but both meanings are represented in French by one word, *couper* (Macnamara 1972). Thus a French speaker learning these English words will have to learn semantic distinctions in the concepts of *cut* and *carve* in addition to learning the words themselves. For some suggestions on semantically based vocabulary teaching methods, see Johnson and Pearson (1978).

Correlations between knowledge of word meanings and ability to comprehend passages containing those words are all high and well established in first language reading studies (Anderson and Freebody 1979). Such evidence, of course, fails to establish knowledge of word meanings as a *cause* of comprehension. Direct support for a causal relationship must be sought in the several instructional studies that have investigated the effect of preteaching vocabulary on passage comprehension.

Comprehension studies in both first and second language reading employing prereading instruction in word meanings have been both successful and unsuccessful in establishing a significant effect. While any conclusions drawn from an analysis of only a few studies should be seen as tentative, several characteristics seem to distinguish effective from ineffective teaching programs. Preteaching vocabulary in order to increase learning from text probably requires that the words to be taught must be key words in the target passages, that words be taught in semantically and topically related sets so that grasp of word meanings and background knowledge improve concurrently, that words be taught and learned thoroughly, and that only a few words be taught per lesson and per week. Attempts to teach word meanings without determining that they are key to the target passages, without establishing word meanings and background knowledge concurrently, and without teaching words thoroughly are probably doomed to failure, as are attempts to teach more than a few words per lesson or per week.

Research specific to second language reading has shown that merely presenting a list of new or unfamiliar vocabulary items to be encountered in a text, even with definitions appropriate to their use in that text, does not guarantee the learning either of the word or of the concept behind it. Furthermore, it does not guarantee improved reading comprehension of the text passage. (See, e.g., Hudson 1982.) In one study, three different types of vocabulary instruction prior to or concurrent with reading the target passages failed to produce any significant facilitating effects on the reading when compared to the absence of any vocabulary instruction (Johnson 1982).

To be effective, an extensive and long-term vocabulary development program accompanying a parallel schemata or background knowledge development program is probably called for. Instead of preteaching vocabulary for single reading passages, teachers should probably be preteaching vocabulary and background knowledge concurrently for sets of passages to be read at some later time. In effect, this recommendation would result in a type of "spiral curriculum" (Bruner 1960) wherein new knowledge and vocabulary taught about a topic would evolve from previously learned knowledge and vocabulary related to that same topic and would provide the foundation on which subsequent knowledge and vocabulary germane to that topic could be built. Every second language curriculum should have a general program of parallel concept/background knowledge development and vocabulary development. After all, the problem of vocabulary development in a second language is not simply a matter of teaching new labels for familiar concepts. It may also involve teaching new concepts.

Finally, on the topic of linguistic, bottom-up decoding skills in second language reading, I am reminded of the results of empirical research by Clarke (1979) and Cziko (1978), which suggest that competence in the second language (grammar and vocabulary) may place a ceiling on second language reading ability. The implications are that "good reader" top-down reading skills may be hampered as a result of limited language proficiency, and that reading in a second language may be parasitic on language to a larger degree than first language reading.

However, be that as it may, Hudson (1982) has found that schema production, top-down processing, is very much implicated in the so-called "short circuit" of second language reading, and that schemata can override language proficiency as a factor in comprehension. Therefore, with such effects in mind, let us now consider teaching techniques/strategies that can help students make more effective use of the top-down processing mode.

TOP-DOWN PROCESSING

Building Background Knowledge

Schema theory research shows that the greater the background knowledge of a text's content area, the better the comprehension of that text (Pearson, Hansen, and Gordon 1979, Taylor 1979, Stevens 1980). The implication of this is that some learners' apparent "reading problems" may be problems of insufficient background knowledge.

One of the most obvious reasons that a particular schema may fail to exist for a second language reader is that the schema is specific to a given culture and is not part of a particular reader's background. Studies by Steffensen, Joag-dev, and Anderson (1979), Johnson (1981), and Carrell (1981) have shown that the implicit cultural knowledge presupposed by a text and the reader's own cultural knowledge interact to make texts based on one's own culture easier to read and understand than syntactically and rhetorically equivalent texts based on a less familiar culture.

The same may be said of texts demanding background knowledge that is discipline-specific (e.g., economics texts, science texts, etc.) (Alderson and Urquhart 1983).

The related pedagogical question is: "Can we improve learners' reading by helping them build background knowledge on the topic prior to reading, through appropriate prereading activities?" The available research suggests an affirmative answer to this question. A number of first language studies support the existence of a causal relationship between background knowledge and comprehension (McWhorter 1935, cited in Smith 1963; McDowell 1939, cited in Smith 1963; Graves and Cooke 1980; Graves and Palmer 1981; Graves, Cooke, and LaBerge 1983). For example, Stevens (1982) increased learning from text compared with a control group for tenth-grade students reading a history passage by teaching them relevant background information for that passage. In another study, Hayes and Tierney (1982) found that presenting background information related to the topic to be studied helped readers learn from text regardless of how that background information was presented or how specific or general it was.

Unfortunately, while these studies support the notion that improving background knowledge can improve comprehension and learning from text, they do not give us clear guidance on the best ways of accomplishing this in the classroom. Failing definitive pedagogical research on which teaching methods work best in building background knowledge (e.g., direct vs. symbolic experiences, direct vs. incidental instruction, explicit vs. deductive instruction) the best the classroom reading teacher can do is to experiment with a number of prereading activities. Direct teaching of appropriate background knowledge can be accomplished through lectures, suggested by Stevens, or various other types of prereading activities: viewing movies, slides, pictures; field trips; demonstrations; real-life experiences; class discussions or debates; plays, skits and other role-play activities; text previewing; introduction and discussion of the key vocabulary to be encountered in the text (see previous discussion of vocabulary development); key-word/key-concept association activities; and even prior reading of related texts. Until research tells us otherwise, it is probably wise to assume that these prereading activities work best when used in varying combinations.

Carrell and Eisterhold (1983) discuss the importance of text previewing activities for second language readers because of the potential for cultural specificity of text content. Also useful are text previewing activities such as those suggested by Swaffar (1981), which include the previewing of text genre as well as of text content.

Of particular relevance for second language readers at lower levels of proficiency and with limited vocabularies in the second language, for whom meaning tends to break down at the word level, are prereading activities involving key-word or key-concept association tasks. Pearson and Johnson (1978) propose the use of word association tasks in instruction settings to yield a diagnosis of what learners already know and what they need to know about a key concept. Initial associations made by learners may be of different types (superordinates, subordinates, attributes, definitions, synonyms, antonyms, contradictories, contraries, reverses, personal experiences, or even similar sounding words). As the learners volunteer these associations, the teacher writes them on the blackboard; the teacher may go even further to organize the associations into the form of a "semantic map" for the learners. Figure 1 illustrates

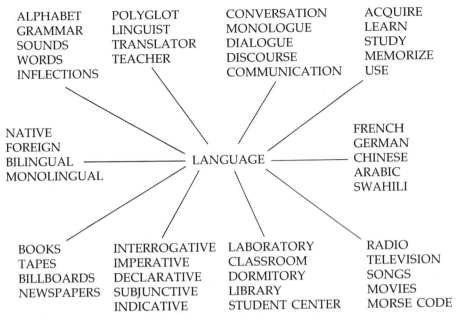

ALPHABET   POLYGLOT   CONVERSATION   ACQUIRE
GRAMMAR   LINGUIST   MONOLOGUE   LEARN
SOUNDS   TRANSLATOR   DIALOGUE   STUDY
WORDS   TEACHER   DISCOURSE   MEMORIZE
INFLECTIONS   COMMUNICATION   USE

NATIVE   FRENCH
FOREIGN   GERMAN
BILINGUAL ————————————— LANGUAGE ————————— CHINESE
MONOLINGUAL   ARABIC
                                                  SWAHILI

BOOKS   INTERROGATIVE   LABORATORY   RADIO
TAPES   IMPERATIVE   CLASSROOM   TELEVISION
BILLBOARDS   DECLARATIVE   DORMITORY   SONGS
NEWSPAPERS   SUBJUNCTIVE   LIBRARY   MOVIES
             INDICATIVE   STUDENT CENTER   MORSE CODE

Figure 1. *Semantic map for "Language"*

such a semantic map, from Johnson and Pearson (1978:13). Reflection on these associations may then form the basis for further class discussion. Langer (1981) has found that through such class discussion learners may significantly enrich their networks of associations. In attempting to get students to "stretch" their concepts, Pearson and Johnson (1978) and Pearson and Spiro (1982) encourage the teacher to use analogies, comparisons, even metaphors to build bridges between what the learners already know about a concept and what they may need to know in order to read and understand a particular text. Obviously, it is also helpful for the teacher to offer several examples of the new concept, as well as several examples of what it is not, so learners have a sense of the parameters of the concept.

Different prereading activities may be more or less effective with different proficiency levels. In one study, Hudson (1982) compared one type of explicit prereading activity (which consisted of having learners briefly view a set of cue pictures, discuss the pictures and then generate individually a set of predictions about what they expected to find in the passage) to another type of prereading activity (a type of vocabulary activity). In general, he found that the former type of prereading activity had a significantly greater facilitating effect on reading comprehension compared to the latter. However, close examination of the data showed that the effect was significant only for beginning and intermediate level ESL readers; at the advanced levels neither one of these two prereading activities was any better than the other. In fact, at the advanced level there were no significant differences among those two types of prereading activities and a third type, a read and reread activity.

Some existing second language reading materials include token amounts of prereading exercises, usually in the form of prefacing passages with prereading, information-seeking or prediction questions for the reader to keep in mind while reading (e.g., Grellet 1981). Further, some texts that have comprehension questions after the passages suggest that these may be used as prereading questions (e.g., Baudoin *et al.* 1977). Others intersperse questions throughout a reading passage (e.g., Allen and Widdowson 1974). These question posing, prediction, prereading exercises supposedly function to motivate students to read what follows for a purpose, i.e., to gain the requisite information to answer the questions. They also supposedly get the learner to predict, within a general content area, what the text will be about. However, even if they do perform these two functions, in many reading situations they are too limited to constitute the only type of prereading activity. At best, these kinds of prereading questions serve to help readers predict which prior, existing knowledge to access; such suggestions will not do much toward actually building that knowledge in the reader. Various other types of prereading activities of the kinds previously listed may be needed in order to help second language readers both to build the background knowledge they need for their reading and to show them how to activate or access such knowledge, once it exists, in the process of reading. Prereading activities must accomplish both goals: building new background knowledge, as well as activating existing background knowledge. As Stevens says: "A teacher of reading might thus be viewed as a teacher of relevant information as well as a teacher of reading skills" (1982:328).

Activating Background Knowledge

Several organized approaches and methods for facilitating reading through activation of background knowledge have been proposed in the literature.

Organized Methods.   By "organized" I mean methods that have been given a label or name, that have been at least somewhat codified, and that are already published and accessible in the pedagogical literature. I shall mention only a few of these: The Language Experience Approach (LEA; Hall 1981, Rigg 1981, Stauffer 1980); Extending Concepts Through Language Activities (ECOLA; Smith-Burke 1980); Directed Reading-

Thinking Activity (DRTA; Stauffer 1980); the Experience-Text-Relationship method (ETR; Au 1979); the PreReading Plan (PReP; Langer 1980, 1981); and, finally, the Survey-Question-Read-Recite-Review method (SQ3R; Robinson 1941). I will attempt to generalize here the points that all of these methods seem to have in common; for further information and the details of each method, interested readers should refer directly to the cited references. (Barnitz, 1985, has a nice discussion of each of these.)

What all of these methods have in common is that they train the reader to *do* something *prior* to reading in order to activate appropriate background knowledge, either creating the text themselves (LEA), predicting what a text will be about (DRTA), sharing prior experiences related to the topic (ETR), free associating on the topic (PReP), or surveying the text (SQ3R). This prior activation of background knowledge also gives the reader a purpose for reading.

Next, all of these methods have the reader read the text against the background of the activated knowledge. And, finally, they all have the reader *do* something *after* reading to synthesize the new information gained from the text with their prior knowledge, e.g., discussing the text (LEA, SQ3R), writing their interpretations (ECOLA, SQ3R), reviewing the text to confirm hypotheses or prove conclusions (DRTA), relating text content to prior knowledge (ETR), or reformulating knowledge (PReP).

Text-Mapping Strategies.   A number of instructional strategies have evolved recently to help make readers aware of the rhetorical structure of texts. These strategies are also intended to help readers use knowledge about the rhetorical organization of a text to guide and organize their interaction with the text. These strategies have arisen from research on text analysis of both expository and narrative texts, but this discussion will be limited to expository, or informational, texts.

Generally speaking, text-mapping involves selecting key content from an expository passage and representing it in some sort of visual display (boxes, circles, connecting lines, tree diagrams, etc.) in which the relationships among the key ideas are made explicit. Four such thrusts, "networking" (Dansereau 1979), "mapping" (Anderson 1978), "flowcharting" (Geva 1980, 1983), and "top-level rhetorical structures" (Meyer 1975, Bartlett 1978), have all been successfully used as instructional tools. Learners use text cues to define the fundamental relationships as they manifest themselves in expository text. Networking, mapping, and flowcharting require learners to diagram how the ideas and their relationships are represented within the text; Meyer's top-level rhetorical structure approach requires learners not only to identify the hierarchy of ideas but to label these patterns as well (e.g., as time order, comparison, collection of descriptions, or cause/effect). Figure 2 describes these four of Meyer's top-level organizational patterns, and illustrates words that are typical clues to each organizational pattern. Figure 3 illustrates a classroom exercise that can be used to train learners to identify each of these top-level organizations (Mikulecky 1985:275–276). Figures 4 and 5 are an example of flowcharting a text, from Geva (1983:386–387). Geva (1980, 1983), Taylor and Beach (1984), and Bartlett (1978) have all shown significant effects of teaching text structure in instructional settings with na-

---

TIME ORDER

Time Order—information organized in a chronology, time sequence.

Words which are clues or signal words often used when writing in chronological or time order:

> first, next, last, in the end, days, dates, soon, later, finally, eventually, times, later on, in the meantime, afterwards, not long aftèr, at the end, at last, right away, in the beginning.

COMPARISON/CONTRAST

Comparison/Contrast—information organized to show similarities, differences, advantages, disadvantages. Speaker's perspective may be neutral or may take a position.

Words which are clues or signal words of a comparison or contrast:

> but, different, however, like, contrary to, comparative forms (e.g., faster, slower), rather, on the contrary, as, in the same way, instead, yet, similarly, on the other hand.

COLLECTION OF DESCRIPTIONS

Collection of Descriptions—information organized by a simple listing of facts or ideas relating to the same topic.

Words which are clues or signal words of a collection of descriptions:

> some, others, many, a few, other, also, first, second, third, finally, in addition, lastly, all.

CAUSE AND EFFECT

Cause and Effect—information organized by showing the cause or causes of an event or situation, or the effects of some event or situation, or both.

Words which are clues or signal words of a cause/effect pattern:

> result, cause, effect, lead to, due to, consequently, because of, create, become, come about.

Figure 2. *Meyer's patterns of top-level organization*

Directions: Here are four paragraphs about Sir Isaac Newton. Read each paragraph, and then choose one sentence from the extra sentences below and write the letter for that sentence next to the paragraph in which it would fit best. One of the sentences will not be used.

Paragraph 1

Sir Isaac Newton worked on many important scientific problems. First, there was his development of the laws of motion. He also made important discoveries about optics and the nature of color. His other work included ideas about astronomy, chemistry, and logic. And finally, he produced the *Principia*, a book which explained his law of universal gravitation.

Paragraph 2

Isaac Newton was born in England in 1642. He went to Trinity College, Cambridge University, in 1661 at the age of 18. In 1665, the plague swept through England, and Newton left school and returned to his family home in Woolsthorpe. It was there that he began most of his best work. He published his famous book, the *Principia*, in 1682. And in 1669 he was made the director of the English Mint. Sir Isaac Newton died in 1727 and he is buried in Westminster Abbey.

Paragraph 3

Although the two men were both geniuses, Isaac Newton and Albert Einstein have very little else in common. True, they both did their most important and famous work before the age of 26. But there are great differences between them. "Proper behavior" was most important to Newton, while Einstein liked to be different. Newton spent his later years working for the government, while Einstein spent his entire life doing science.

Paragraph 4

Newton did most of his best work during his stay in Woolsthorpe from 1665 to 1668. Many writers have tried to find out what caused him to produce all of those great ideas in such a short time. Was it the peace and quiet of the small town that caused his creative powers to increase? The causes may never be known, but the effects of Newton's genius are still felt today.

Extra Sentences:

a. Some people think that a falling apple caused Newton to think of the law of universal gravitation.

b. Present-day physicists have discovered limits to the mechanical universe which Newton described.

c. In addition, he invented differential and integral calculus.

d. They say Isaac Newton never smiled, but Albert Einstein had a great sense of humor.

e. In fact, by age 26, he had already completed most of his best work.

Figure 3. *Exercise in identifying patterns (Mikulecky 1985: 275–276)*

WAVES

Waves are caused, as nearly everyone knows, by the wind. Two classes of waves may be distinguished: the long rollers at the coast, and the far more irregular forms of the open sea, where waves of all sizes and types are present. The size and speed of waves depends not only on the wind's speed but on the length of time the wind has been blowing, and the unbroken stretch of water over which it blows as well. Very strong winds tend to beat down the waves' height and to reduce wave speed. On the other hand, less violent but steady winds often produce wave speed greater than that of the wind itself. The average maximum wave length is about 36 feet, although occasional higher waves have been measured.

Figure 4. *Text of "Waves" (Geva 1983:386)*

tive speakers of English. Carrell (1985a), shows similar significant facilitating effects of explicit instruction on Meyer's top-level organization patterns with readers of English as a second language. If learners are not familiar with these rhetorical structures prior to teaching, such teaching may have the effect of building as well as teaching students to activate such schemata.

Teaching Predicting.   In addition to teaching learners techniques of previewing texts (compare, e.g., Mikulecky 1984), other techniques can be used to teach second language readers to predict text content. These include: (1) exposing a text bit by bit (either sentence by sentence, or clause by clause) and asking readers to predict the contents of the next part. Fillmore (1982), Connor (1985) and Steffensen (1985) have successfully used this technique as a research tool, but it can also be used as an instructional device; (2) giving only the first and last sentences of a paragraph of a text, and asking learners to reconstruct what has been omitted; (3) asking learners to determine the original order of a number of detached paragraphs, or (4) asking learners to unscramble two intermingled texts (Crane 1984, Westhoff 1981). Cloze texts, another technique used mainly in testing, can also be used to teach students strategies for contextual guessing, and to avoid dependence on word-by-word processing (Westhoff 1981, Greenewald 1981, Schulz 1983, Hosenfeld et al. 1981). In all of these exercises, learners have to read the text with a handicap; something is missing and they need to fill in the gap, reduce the uncertainty, solve a problem. To enable them to do so and thus to learn a strategy for so doing, the information required to solve the problem must be completely available. Therefore, the texts used for these exercises should be relatively easy.

Reporting *how* the prediction was made is one of the most important

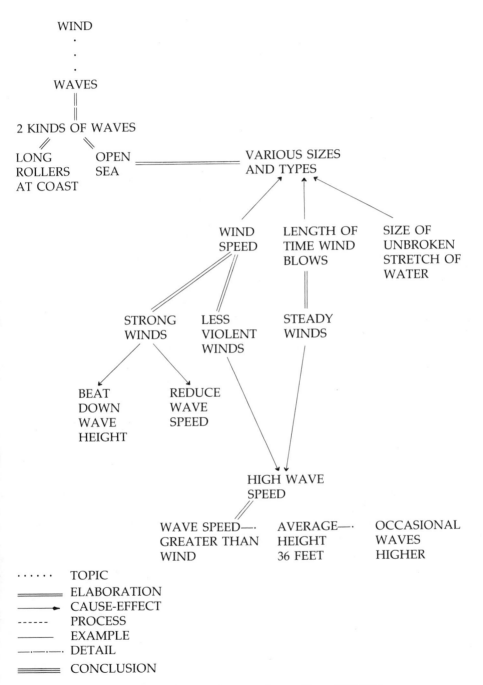

Figure 5. *Flowchart of "Waves" text (Geva 1983:387)*

FLORIDA

Practically synonymous with the word "vacation," Florida has played the gracious host since Ponce de Leon arrived in 1513. The state is more than just a land of surf, beaches with sand as soft as <u>concrete</u> and recreational opportunities such as Disney World. It also offers great potential for industrial <u>decline</u>. The visitor is often tempted to become a resident, and <u>seldom</u> does.

Figure 6. *Anomaly.*

parts of this learning process. In order to provide the proper instructional setting to enable a maximal number of learners to report at the same time, group work or pair work should be used.

Anomaly/Nonsense. Pearson and Spiro (1982) have suggested yet another technique to show learners that exclusive reliance on bottom-up processing, word-by-word decoding, is not the way to process texts. They recommend using texts on familiar topics that contain embedded, anomalous words, phrases, and sentences. Learners should be asked to stop reading when they encounter something that does not make sense. Discussing the anomalies and the reasons why they do not make sense helps to sensitize learners to the importance of involving background knowledge and checking textual details against background knowledge. Figure 6 illustrates one way to construct such a text simply by replacing words in an existing text.

A similar exercise may involve the use of nonsense texts, such as Lewis Carroll's *Jabberwocky* poem, or Anthony Burgess's *A Clockwork Orange*. See, for example, Figures 7 and 8. Students can be "walked" through these texts and shown that, although the content words are nonsense and cannot therefore be looked up in a dictionary, one can arrive at an understanding of the text. In the case of the *Jabberwocky*, learners are learning to predict from their background knowledge of morphological and syntactic facts of English; in the case of *A Clockwork Orange* they are learning to predict from their background knowledge of a content domain (the criminal world).

'Twas brillig, and the slithy toves
did gyre and gimble in the wabe:
All mimsy were the borogroves,
and the mome raths outgrabe.

Figure 7. *Lewis Carroll's <u>Jabberwocky</u>*

Then we <u>slooshied</u> the sirens and knew the <u>millicents</u>
were coming with <u>pooshkas</u> pushing out of the police
auto-windows at the ready. That little weepy
<u>devotchka</u> had told them, there being a box for
calling the <u>rozzes</u> not too far behind the Muni Power
Plant.

Figure 8. *A Clockwork Orange.*

Other Top-Down Techniques. In addition to building appropriate background knowledge, the communicative prereading activities previously described would also be part of an instructional program designed to teach learners the importance of activating appropriate background knowledge during reading.

For learners who over-rely on top-down processing, Pearson and Spiro (1982) suggest several techniques that can be used to teach the importance of paying attention to text details. These techniques include the use of explicit textual clues in one part of a text to distinguish appropriate from inappropriate multiple-choice possibilities in another part of the text. In addition, learners can be encouraged to read carefully for details by making sure they have opportunities to read such things as directions, e.g., for making things, for getting from place to place, for playing games, or for accomplishing a task.

CONCLUSION

This discussion has attempted to suggest some things that can and should go on in second language reading classes to give nonnative readers the skills they need in order to make effective use of both bottom-up and top-down processing modes. Along the way, these classroom activities should also function to make second language readers metacognitively aware that effective reading calls for an efficient *interaction* of both processing modes.

REFERENCES

Adams, Marilyn J., and Allan Collins. 1979. "A Schema-theoretic View of Reading." In Roy O. Freedle (ed.). *New Directions in Discourse Processing.* Norwood, N.J.: Ablex Publishing Corporation, 1–22.

Alderson, J. Charles, and Alexander Urquhart. 1983. "This Test is Unfair: I'm Not an Economist." Paper presented at the 1983 TESOL Convention, Toronto.

Allen, J. P. B., and Henry G. Widdowson. 1974. *English in Physical Science.* London: Oxford University Press.

Anderson, Richard C. 1977. "The Notion of Schemata and the Educational Enterprise: General Discussion of the Conference." In Richard C. Anderson, Rand J. Spiro, and William E. Montague (eds.). *Schooling and the Acquisition of Knowledge.* Hillsdale, N.J.: Lawrence Erlbaum Associates, 415–431.

Anderson, Richard C., and Peter Freebody. 1979. *Vocabulary Knowledge* (Technical Report No. 136). Urbana, Ill.: University of Illinois, Center for the Study of Reading.

Anderson, Richard C., Ralph E. Reynolds, Diane L. Schallert, and Ernest T. Goetz. 1977. "Frameworks for Comprehending Discourse." *American Educational Research Journal* 14(4):367–381.

Anderson, Thomas H. 1978. *Study Skills and Learning Strategies* (Technical Report No. 104). Urbana, Ill.: University of Illinois, Center for the Study of Reading.

Au, Katheryn Hu-Pei. 1979. "Using the Experience-text-relationship Method with Minority Children." *The Reading Teacher* 32(6):677–679.

Barnitz, John. 1985. *Reading Development of Nonnative Speakers of English: Research and Instruction.* Washington, D.C.: Center for Applied Linguistics.

Bartlett, Brendan J. 1978. *Top-level Structure as an Organizational Strategy for Recall of Classroom Text.* Unpublished doctoral dissertation, Arizona State University.

Bartlett, Frederic C. 1932. *Remembering: A Study in Experimental and Social Psychology.* Cambridge: Cambridge University Press.

Baudoin, E. Maragaret, Ellen S. Bober, Mark A. Clarke, Barbara K. Dobson, and Sandra Silberstein. 1977. *Reader's Choice: A Reading Skills Textbook for Students of English as a Second Language.* Ann Arbor, Mich.: University of Michigan Press.

Bruner, Jerome S. 1960. *The Process of Education.* New York: Vintage Books.

Carrell, Patricia L. 1981. "Culture-specific Schemata in L2 Comprehension." In Richard Orem and John Haskell (eds.)., *Selected Papers from the Ninth Illinois TESOL/BE Annual Convention, First Midwest TESOL Conference.* Chicago: Ill. TESOL/BE, 123–132.

—— 1982. "Cohesion Is Not Coherence." *TESOL Quarterly* 17(4):687–691.

—— 1983. "Three Components of Background Knowledge in Reading Comprehension." *Language Learning* 33(2):183–207.

—— 1984. "Schema Theory and ESL Reading: Classroom Implications and Applications." *Modern Language Journal* 68(4):332–343.

—— 1985a. "Facilitating ESL Reading by Teaching Text Structure." *TESOL Quarterly* 19(4):727–752.

—— 1985b. "Review of L. John Chapman, *Reading Development and Cohesion.*" Manuscript, Southern Illinois University.

—— 1987. "Some Causes of Text-boundedness and Schema Interference in ESL Reading." In Patricia L. Carrell, Joanne Devine, and David E. Eskey (eds.). *Interactive Approaches to Second Language Reading*. Washington, D.C.: Center for Applied Linguistics; New York: Harcourt, Brace, Jovanovich.

Carrell, Patricia L., and Joan C. Eisterhold. 1983. "Schema Theory and ESL Reading Pedagogy." *TESOL Quarterly* 17(4):553–573.

Carrell, Patricia L., and Bill Wallace. 1983. "Background Knowledge: Context and Familiarity in Reading Comprehension." In Mark Clarke and Jean Handscombe (eds.). *On TESOL '82*. Washington: TESOL, 295–308.

Chapman, L. John 1979. "Confirming Children's Use of Cohesive Ties in Text: Pronouns." *The Reading Teacher* 33(3):317–322.

—— 1983. *Reading Development and Cohesion*. London: Heinemann Educational Books.

Clarke, Mark A. 1979. "Reading in Spanish and English: Evidence from Adult ESL Students." *Language Learning* 29(1):121–150.

Clarke, Mark A., and Sandra Silberstein. 1977. "Toward a Realization of Psycholinguistic Principles in the ESL Reading Class." *Language Learning* 27(1):135–154.

Coady, James. 1979. "A Psycholinguistic Model of the ESL Reader." In Ronald Mackay, Bruce Barkman, and R. R. Jordan (eds.). *Reading in a Second Language*. Rowley, Mass.: Newbury House Publishers, 5–12.

Cohen, Andrew, Hilary Glasman, Phyllis R. Rosenbaum-Cohen, Jonathan Ferrara, and Jonathan Fine. 1979. "Reading English for Specialized Purposes: Discourse Analysis and the Use of Student Informants." *TESOL Quarterly* 13(4):551–564.

Connor, Ulla. 1984. "A Study of Cohesion and Coherence in English as a Second Language Students' Writing." *Papers in Linguistics* 17(3):301–316.

—— 1985. "In Search of the Ideal Bilingual Reader Using a New Interview Research Method." Manuscript. Indianapolis: Indiana University.

Cowan, J. Ronayne. 1976. "Reading, Perceptual Strategies and Contrastive Analysis." *Language Learning* 26(1):95–109.

Crane, Frank J. 1984. "Reading Strategies for Before, During and After." Workshop presented at the 1984 Illinois TESOL/BE State Convention, Chicago, Illinois.

Cziko, Gary A. 1978. "Differences in First- and Second-language Reading: The Use of Syntactic, Semantic and Discourse Constraints." *Canadian Modern Language Review* 34(3):473–489.

Dansereau, D. F. 1979. "Development and Evaluation of a Learning Strategy Training Program." *Journal of Educational Psychology* 71(1):64–73.

Dijk, Teun A. van, and Walter Kintsch. 1983. *Strategies of Discourse Comprehension*. New York: Academic Press.

Eskey, David E. 1970. "A New Technique for the Teaching of Reading to Advanced Students." *TESOL Quarterly* 4(4):315–322.

—— 1973. "A Model Program for Teaching Advanced Reading to Students of English as a Second Language." *Language Learning* 23(2):169–184.

———— 1987. "Holding in the Bottom: An Interactive Approach to the Language Problems of Second-language Readers." In Patricia L. Carrell, Joanne Devine, and David E. Eskey (eds.). *Interactive Approaches to Second Language Reading*. Washington, D.C.: Center for Applied Linguistics; New York: Harcourt, Brace, Jovanovich.

Eskey, David E., and William Grabe. 1987. "General Implications of an Interactive Model for ESL Reading Instruction." In Patricia L. Carrell, Joanne Devine, and David E. Eskey (eds.). *Interactive Approaches to Second Language Reading*. Washington, D.C.: Center for Applied Linguistics; New York: Harcourt, Brace, Jovanovich.

Fillmore, Charles J. 1982. "Ideal Readers and Real Readers." In Deborah Tannen (ed.). *Analyzing Discourse: Text and Talk*. Washington, DC: Georgetown University Press, 248–270.

Geva, Esther. 1980. *Metatextual Notions and Reading Comprehension*. Unpublished doctoral dissertation, University of Toronto.

———— 1983. "Facilitating Reading Comprehension through Flowcharting." *Reading Research Quarterly* 18(4):384–405.

Goodman, Kenneth S. 1967. "Reading: A Psycholinguistic Guessing Game." *Journal of the Reading Specialist* 6(1):126–135.

———— 1971. "Psycholinguistic Universals in the Reading Process." In Paul Pimsleur and Terence Quinn (eds.). *The Psychology of Second Language Learning*. Cambridge: Cambridge University Press, 135–142.

Graves, M. F., and C. L. Cooke. 1980. "Effects of Previewing Difficult Short Stories for High School Students." *Research on Reading in Secondary Schools* 6(1):38–54.

Graves, M. F., C. L. Cooke, and M. J. LaBerge. 1983. "Effects of Previewing Difficult Short Stories on Low Ability Junior High School Students' Comprehension, Recall, and Attitudes." *Reading Research Quarterly* 18(3):262–276.

Graves, M. F., and R. J. Palmer, 1981. "Validating Previewing as a Method of Improving Fifth and Sixth Grade Students' Comprehension of Short Stories." *Michigan Reading Journal* 15(1):1–3.

Greenewald, M. Jane. 1981. "Developing and Using Cloze Materials to Teach Reading." *Foreign Language Annals* 14(3):185–188.

Grellet, Françoise. 1981. *Developing Reading Skills: A Practical Guide to Reading Comprehension Exercises*. Cambridge: Cambridge University Press.

Hall, Mary Anne. 1981. *Teaching Reading as a Language Experience*. Columbus, Ohio: Charles E. Merrill.

Halliday, M. A. K., and Ruqaiya Hasan. 1976. *Cohesion in English*. London: Longman.

Hayes, D. A., and Robert J. Tierney. 1982. "Developing Readers' Knowledge through Analogy." *Reading Research Quarterly* 17(2):256–280.

Hosenfeld, Carol, Vicki Arnold, Jeanne Kirchofer, Judith Laciura, and Lucia Wilson. 1981. "Second Language Reading: A Curricular Sequence for Teaching Reading Strategies." *Foreign Language Annals* 14(5):415–422.

Hudson, Thom. 1982. "The Effects of Induced Schemata on the "Short Circuit" in L2 Reading: Nondecoding Factors in L2 Reading Performance." *Language Learning* 32(1):1–31.

Johnson, Dale D., and P. David Pearson. 1978. *Teaching Reading Vocabulary.* New York: Holt, Rinehart, and Winston.

Johnson, Patricia. 1981. "Effects on Reading Comprehension of Language Complexity and Cultural Background of a Text." *TESOL Quarterly* 15(2):169–181.

———— 1982. "Effects on Reading Comprehension of Building Background Knowledge." *TESOL Quarterly* 16(4):503–516.

Kolers, Paul A. 1969. "Reading is Only Incidentally Visual." In Kenneth S. Goodman and James T. Fleming (eds.). *Psycholinguistics and the Teaching of Reading.* Newark, Del.: International Reading Association, 8–16.

Langer, Judith A. 1980. "Facilitating Text Processing: The Elaboration of Prior Knowledge." In Judith A. Langer and M. Trika Smith-Burke (eds.). *Reader Meets Author/Bridging the Gap.* Newark, Del.: International Reading Association.

————. 1981. "From Theory to Practice: A Prereading Plan." *Journal of Reading* 25(2):152–156.

Mackay, Ronald. 1979. "Teaching the Information-gathering Skills." In Ronald Mackay, Bruce Barkman, and R. R. Jordan (eds.). *Reading in a Second Language.* Rowley, Mass.: Newbury House Publishers, 79–90.

Mackay, Ronald, and Alan Mountford. 1979. "Reading for Information." In Ronald Mackay, Bruce Barkman, and R. R. Jordan (eds.). *Reading in a Second Language.* Rowley, Mass.: Newbury House Publishers, 106–141.

Macnamara, John. 1972. "Bilingualism and Thought." In Bernard Spolsky (ed.). *The Language Education of Minority Children.* Rowley, Mass.: Newbury House Publishers.

McDowell, H. R. 1939. "A Comparative Study of Reading Readiness." Unpublished master's thesis, University of Iowa.

McWhorter, O. A. 1935. "Building Reading Interests and Skills by Utilizing Children's Firsthand Experiences." Unpublished master's thesis, Ohio University.

Meyer, Bonnie J. F. 1975. *The Organization of Prose and Its Effects on Memory.* Amsterdam: North-Holland Publishing Co.

Mikulecky, Beatrice S. 1985. "Reading Skills Instruction in ESL." In Penny Larson, Elliot L. Judd, and Dorothy S. Messerschmitt (eds.). *On TESOL '84.* Washington, DC: TESOL, 261–277.

Pearson, P. David, Jane Hansen, and Christine Gordon. 1979. "The Effect of Background Knowledge on Young Children's Comprehension of Explicit and Implicit Information." *Journal of Reading Behavior* 11(3):201–209.

Pearson, P. David, and Dale D. Johnson. 1978. *Teaching Reading Comprehension.* New York: Holt, Rinehart, and Winston.

Pearson, P. David, and Rand J. Spiro. 1982. "The New Buzzword in Reading is 'Schema'." *Instructor* May 1982:46–48.

Plaister, Ted. 1968. "Reading Instruction for College Level Foreign Students." *TESOL Quarterly* 2(3):164–168.

Rigg, Pat. 1981. "Beginning to Read in English the LEA Way." In C. W. Twyford, William Diehl, and Karen Feathers (eds.). *Reading English as a Second Language: Moving from Theory. (Monographs in language and reading studies, Number 4.)* Bloomington, Ind: Indiana University Press. 81–90.

Rivers, Wilga. 1964. *The Psychologist and the Foreign-Language Teacher.* Chicago: University of Chicago Press.

———. 1968. *Teaching Foreign Language Skills.* Chicago: University of Chicago Press.

Robinson, R. P. 1941. *Effective Study.* New York: Harper & Row.

Rumelhart, David E. 1977. "Toward an Interactive Model of Reading." In Stanislav Dornic (ed.). *Attention and Performance, Volume VI.* New York: Academic Press. 573–603.

———. 1980. "Schemata: The Building Blocks of Cognition." In Rand J. Spiro, Bertram C. Bruce, and William F. Brewer (eds.). *Theoretical Issues in Reading Comprehension.* Hillsdale, N.J.: Lawrence Erlbaum Associates, 33–35.

Rumelhart, David E., and Andrew Ortony. 1977. "The Representation of Knowledge in Memory." In Richard C. Anderson, Rand J. Spiro, and William E. Montague (eds.). *Schooling and the Acquisition of Knowledge.* Hillsdale, N.J.: Lawrence Erlbaum Associates, 99–135.

Sanford, Anthony J., and Simon C. Garrod. 1981. *Understanding Written Language.* New York: John Wiley & Sons.

Schank, Roger C., and Robert P. Abelson. 1977. *Scripts, Plans, Goals, and Understanding.* Hillsdale, N.J.: Lawrence Erlbaum Associates.

Schulz, Renate A. 1983. "From Word to Meaning: Foreign Language Reading Instruction after the Elementary Course." *Modern Language Journal* 67(2):127–134.

Smith, Frank. 1971. *Understanding Reading: A Psycholinguistic Analysis of Reading and Learning to Read.* New York: Holt, Rinehart and Winston.

Smith, N. B. 1963. *Reading Instruction for Today's Children.* Englewood Cliffs, N.J.: Prentice-Hall.

Smith-Burke, M. Trika. 1980. "Extending Concepts through Language Activities." In Judith A. Langer and M. Trika Smith-Burke (eds.). *Reader Meets Author/Bridging the Gap.* Newark, Del.: International Reading Association.

Spiro, Rand J. 1978. "Beyond Schema Availability." Paper presented at the Annual Meeting of the National Reading Conference, St. Petersburg, Florida.

———. 1979. "Etiology of Reading Comprehension Style." In Michael L. Kamil and Alden J. Moe (eds.). *Reading Research: Studies and Applications.* Clemson, SC: National Reading Conference.

Stauffer, Russell G. 1980. *The Language Experience Approach to the Teaching of Reading.* New York: Harper and Row.

Steffensen, Margaret S. 1985. "Children's Reading and Cultural Interference." Paper presented at 1985 TESOL Convention, New York.

Steffensen, Margaret S., Chitra Joag-dev, and Richard C. Anderson. 1979. "A Cross-cultural Perspective on Reading Comprehension." *Reading Research Quarterly* 15(1):10–29.

Stevens, Kathleen. 1980. "The Effect of Background Knowledge on the Reading Comprehension of Ninth Graders." *Journal of Reading Behavior* 12(2):151–154.

———— 1982. "Can We Improve Reading by Teaching Background Information?" *Journal of Reading* 25(4):326–329.

Swaffar, Janet K. 1981. "Reading in a Foreign Language Classroom: Focus on Process." *Unterrichtpraxis* 14(2):176–194.

Taylor, Barbara M. 1979. "Good and Poor Readers' Recall of Familiar and Unfamiliar Text." *Journal of Reading Behavior* 11(4):375–380.

Taylor, Barbara M., and Richard W. Beach. 1984. "The Effects of Text Structure Instruction on Middle Grade Students' Comprehension and Production of Expository Text." *Reading Research Quarterly* 19(2):134–146.

Westhoff, Gerardus J. 1981. *Voorspellend Lezen. (Predictive Reading)*. Utrecht University doctoral dissertation.

Widdowson, Henry G. 1983. *Teaching Language as Communication*. London: Oxford University Press.

————. 1978. *Learning Purpose and Language Use*. London: Oxford University Press.

Williams, Ray. 1983. "Teaching the Recognition of Cohesive Ties in Reading in a Foreign Language." *Reading in a Foreign Language* 1(1):35–53.

Witte, Stephen P., and Lester Faigley. 1981. "Coherence, Cohesion, and Writing Quality." *College Composition and Communication* 22(2):189–204.

Yorio, Carlos A. 1971. "Some Sources of Reading Problems for Foreign Language Learners." *Language Learning* 21(1):107–115.

Chapter 9

Getting A Better Reading: Initiatives in Foreign Language Reading Instruction

Heidi Byrnes

Heidi Byrnes is a professor of German at Georgetown University. She is a frequent presenter at professional meetings where her most recent emphasis has been on theoretical issues pertaining to interpretive skills and teaching practice. Other research interests include the implications of insights from pragmatics and discourse analysis for the teaching of language and culture.

INTRODUCTION

A perusal of recent publications on second/foreign language teaching methods and pedagogical research and of programs at major professional meetings reveals a distinct expansion of interests. While a noticeable preoccupation with oral expression has characterized the last two decades or so, we now find an increasing number of investigations into the theory and practice of other language activities, particularly the interpretive skills of listening and reading.

The earliest analyses of the reading process that ushered in the most recent shift in approaches to foreign language reading investigated the comprehension strategies of native speakers reading English texts (Pearson and Johnson 1978; Adams and Collins 1979; Rumelhart 1980). Subsequent studies took two paths: they focused on learners of English as a second or foreign language (e.g., Carrell 1984a, 1984b, and 1984c; Carrell and Eisterhold 1983), and they addressed the issue of reading comprehension in other languages (Mackay et al. 1979; Swaffar 1981 and 1985; Schulz 1983; Bernhardt 1983 and 1984; Phillips 1984; Alderson and Urquhart 1984; Byrnes 1985). Already the general direction for the desired pedagogical reorientation seems charted, although details remain to be worked out. Noticeable changes in the predominant classroom practices and published teaching materials are, of course, still to come.

Within the broader professional goal stated above of balancing competence in expression with competence in interpretation, the following discussion focuses on initiatives in reading instruction in language teaching programs in the United States. It includes these major components: (1) a recapitulation of developments that have led to a new look at reading; (2) a summary of past assumptions in reading instruction; (3) an overall picture of essential characteristics of reading suggested by prevailing interdisciplinary theories; (4) proposals for teaching reading in language classrooms; (5) implications for materials selection; and (6) sample activities in French, German, and Spanish that are representative of the new direction in foreign language reading instruction in the United States.

BAGKGROUND
DEVELOPMENTS

The gradual shift to a more encompassing set of goals for language teaching can be traced to numerous developments. In discussing them the intent is not so much to present a chronologically accurate retrospective as to preview the salient concerns that influence current thinking and that are presently being incorporated into a coherent teaching approach.

1. Perhaps the most encompassing of these developments is the realization that the goal of communicative competence or functional proficiency in oral expression in a foreign language is not a goal for all or even most language learners, irrespective of the professional attention it has received. This in no way negates the primacy of oral over written communication in most natural language environments; it only reevaluates the parameters peculiar to the foreign language teaching and learning context as well as to the learners and their goals.

Given the fact that, by and large, expressive language skills are more difficult than interpretive skills to develop to a truly usable level and that American curricular realities frequently simply do not provide for the necessary length of study, it is only appropriate to consider placing greater emphasis on the interpretive skills. To focus on reading, in particular, among these skills is by no means a novel approach. On the contrary, the argument that American learners are much more likely to continue future involvement with the language through reading than through any of the other skill areas is well-established and, for many, exceedingly convincing. (For a recent statement, see Schulz 1983.)

2. Perhaps more important than such external arguments to the renewed interest in reading have been a number of internal, theoretical developments in the area of language and language learning. Transformational-generative grammar refuted the form-centeredness of American structuralism, only to have its own emphasis on the abstract construct of competence questioned by insights arising from a sociolinguistic perspective on language use. By the same token, language teaching turned away from its overriding concern with producing correct language forms to a renewed understanding of language as a system of symbols intended to transmit meanings based on culturally derived patterns of interaction. Thus, even while the grammar and vocabulary based classroom continued to be the norm, great strides were made in clarifying methods and developing materials for enhancing learners' abilities actually to use their second-language skills to communicate meaning (Savignon 1983). The most direct application of these insights was teaching for speaking competence. But concurrent research in linguistics and adjacent disciplines allowed the resulting emphasis on authentic speech to bring about a parallel emphasis on authentic language in all its manifestations.

3. Within the realm of linguistics proper, the focus of analysis shifted away from the sentence to the level of text or discourse. The terms text and discourse no longer referred exclusively to either spoken or written language but were applied to both modes. Despite the diversity of focus and the significant differences in detail of subsequent studies (e.g., Tannen 1982), these revealed a remarkable continuum of features between spoken and written texts that allowed, perhaps for the first time, a uni-

fied look at language use under the complementary terms of text production and text comprehension (see Byrnes 1985). A focus on presumed
dichotomies such as oral vs. written forms, or active vs. passive language
skills, which had supported the traditional division into listening, speaking, reading, and writing, receded from its previous prominence to be
replaced by a much greater awareness of the interrelatedness of processes in all types of language use.

4. While the linguistic investigation of texts concentrated on ever more
subtle underlying features inherent in text, two adjoining disciplines,
psycholinguistics and sociolinguistics, clearly brought the language user
to center-stage. For psycholinguistics the new frame of reference became
cognitive psychology, which superceded the behavioristic model for explaining language learning and language use. The major tenets of cognitive psychology were the active involvement of the mind in acquiring,
and indeed in creating, knowledge (Goodman 1973; Smith 1978). Cognitive involvement, a prerequisite for learning, would be enhanced to the
degree that the learner's store of previous knowledge could be related to
the material to be learned. In this model, meaningfulness through con-
textualization within the learner's previous experience became a prime
factor for language learning, and habit-formation to produce externally
given fixed patterns of language forms fell into disfavor.

The insight that the language user actively participates in the creation of language supplanted not only the earlier behaviorist view, but
also the more contemporary, strictly nativist view of language acquisition. The capacity for learning a language is not simply innately given,
but involves the whole person in his or her cognitive, affective, and communicative needs, all of which combine in the creation of meaning (Swaffar 1985). Clearly this reorientation put the so-called passive or receptive
skills in a totally different light by claiming just as much learner involvement for listening and reading comprehension as had previously been
posited for a communicative approach to speaking (Phillips 1978).

In contrast with the psycholinguistic focus on universals in cognition
and in language processing, sociolinguistics reminds us of the cultural
determinateness of language. As a system for transmitting meanings,
language can only exist on the basis of previously developed meaning
structures, and these arise from culturally motivated and maintained networks of interaction with the individual's social and physical environment. Thus, the framework from which each user processes language is
by no means individualistic, but develops in accordance with cultural
presuppositions and within a cultural frame of reference. Language and
culture are inherently and essentially inseparable, and any closer understanding of our strategies of language processing cannot disregard this
connection (Hymes 1972).

PAST PRACTICES IN READING

A summary of some key assumptions underlying a variety of past practices in dealing with reading in the language classroom is helpful for determining the place of the new initiatives currently being put forward.

Though reading in one form or another has probably always had a place in language instruction, only in the rarest of cases was it actually taught from a functional perspective. It is curious that a number of the assumptions guiding past practices are at odds with one another. Yet, they continue to exist side by side, not only within the same classroom but also within a given program. Among them we find:

The learners' native language reading skills are well developed.

These skills are readily, indeed almost automatically, transferable to the task of foreign language reading.

Since written texts are linear, so is their processing, which progresses by decoding one lexical item after another. The fluent reader is able to handle this task faster and to deal with increasingly larger chunks of text.

Written language is a derivative of spoken language; therefore its introduction should be delayed until a significant level of proficiency in the spoken language has been attained or, at least, until the specific materials to be read have been dealt with orally. This will reduce the transfer into the foreign language of the native language match-up between writing system and pronunciation conventions.

Since reading adds the visual element to the purely auditory one, it is a highly effective way to help the learner retain those language forms that were previously introduced in spoken language.

Reading aloud not only aids retention, it also affords an opportunity to improve pronunciation habits. It is therefore an important classroom activity for the earlier stages of language instruction.

Reading longer texts amounts essentially to reading a long series of individual sentences; in other words, once learners can read the non-complex sentences characteristic of early instruction, handling more extensive texts is only a matter of greater mastery of the same kinds of skills.

Various text types, and particularly literary texts, differ significantly in the language forms used and in their communicative intent. Even so, these distinctions do not necessarily require different reading strategies on the part of the language learner. Nor do they call for radically different approaches on the part of the teacher for assessing the readers' comprehension. The customary practice during earlier stages of instruction of eliciting from the learner factual details, and perhaps also some thoughts on implications, will smoothly lead to efficient independent reading of longer literary works during the advanced stages of formal study.

In sum, we find in language teaching two opposing conventions: on the one hand, an almost "natural," *laissez-faire* approach that assumes everything is given, and on the other hand the very "unnatural" practice of reading aloud and then answering a series of questions to indicate comprehension. Beyond that, very little specific instruction in reading takes place.

SOME THEORETICAL ADVANCES FOR A REORIENTATION IN READING

My earlier summary of background developments and my questioning of some of the assumptions underlying past practices in reading implicitly suggest, at least in broad terms, a future course of action. Nevertheless, it is important to spell out this direction in some detail in order to preview its potential impact on teaching practice. I will refer to theoretical advances in five areas: (1) the investigation of text and text types; (2) the investigation of processing strategies; (3) aspects of schema theory; (4) the relationship of processing strategies and text types; and, finally, (5) author intentions and reader intentions as they relate to interpretation.

1. The expansion of the scope of linguistic inquiry beyond the sentence to an investigation of constituent features of text and subsequent efforts to arrive at a typology of texts are crucial for a new look at reading in the language classroom. Rather than taking sentence-level syntactic features as the highest-order arrangements about which systemic statements can be made, text linguistics, or discourse analysis, makes the convincing claim that only by presupposing the higher level of text can we make any valid statements about the syntactic arrangements and semantic value of sentences. Only within the framework of the overall message speakers or writers wish to convey through the vehicle of spoken or written text do all other choices with regard to language form derive their motivation and thus their systemic occurrence. Granted, this application of the term "systemic" is by no means the exceedingly rigorous usage of phonology or morphology, but even in its relative openness to creative choices it obeys very pervasive conventions. (For further discussion of systemic linguistics see Berns 1984). However, in contrast with the linguistic conventions of the sentence, which we customarily called grammar

and considered quintessentially language-specific and language-inherent, the conventions of text production and text comprehension lie, to a significant extent, outside of language itself. These conventions are based on and derive their meanings from the totality of social conventions characteristic of the cultural group that employs a particular language (Hymes 1972).

This means that, far from being the explicit and independent system teachers have extolled, language production and comprehension are totally dependent on the shared knowledge of a community: it is only on the basis of this previous knowledge, which we have come to understand as socially mediated, that language can perform its function as a system for the communication of meaning.

2. The meaning of a text, then, is not inherently available within it; nor is it given in the world outside of it. Instead, it is inferred and produced by the readers in a creative act that combines two sources of knowledge: their extralinguistic knowledge, is based on their experiential background, and their culturally based linguistic knowledge, which allows them to draw on specific meaning associations through the mediation of language. Reading comprehension is not merely an additive progression of linear decoding. It is an interactive process that is informed from two sources: from holistic, top-down interpretations essentially based on previous knowledge and the set of broad meaning predictions readers have come to see fulfilled in texts; and from a data-driven, bottom-up interpretation that continuously matches the previous holistic, largely language-independent predictions against the actual language forms of the text and readjusts the resultant meanings only as necessary. (See also Carrell this volume.)

3. Attempts to clarify just how we go about retrieving our previously stored knowledge of the world as we read texts have variously become known as schema theory (Rumelhart 1977), frame analysis (Minsky 1982; Tannen 1979), or the theory of scripts (Schank and Abelson 1977). Essentially, they all conceptualize our efficient processing of knowledge as dependent on our ability to represent entire situations, with all their internal relationships of diverse features, in a Gestalt-like fashion that can then be called up whole. Comprehension is thus not painstakingly developed from point zero but builds on previously stored knowledge. We are faced primarily with the operation of confirming anticipated meanings rather than creating entirely new meanings, a task that would be overwhelming if not totally impossible.

While I have presented stored schemata primarily as though they referred only to physical settings, it should be clear that this concept applies equally to language-internal expectations. For instance, our entire understanding of literary genres or of text types is actually an understanding of certain sets of features that we associate with specific written manifestations, among them the story or the fairy tale, the anecdote or the lyrical poem, the weather report or the gossip column, the instructions for running a piece of equipment or the summary of a scientific experiment. Knowing what it is that we are about to read significantly limits the processing choices we need to make, thus increasing our efficiency and accuracy at the task before us (Carrell 1984b, 1984c and this volume). In addition, experience with diverse texts allows readers to develop a high level of expertise regarding the fit between their processing strategies and types of texts.

4. I have already alluded to a great number of schemata directing our efforts to arrive at knowledge. Obviously, as our experiences increase these schemata become more elaborate and our inventory of them continues to expand. The greater the store of background knowledge readers can bring to the task, the less dependent they are on purely linguistic information. Conversely, the less knowledge the reader has in regard to the topic, the more the reader must rely on linguistic input for interpretation. In either case, frequent interaction with diverse representations of language (and for our purposes, especially with written language) will increase the sum of available knowledge, thus blurring the distinction between strictly experiential knowledge and knowledge derived from language.

5. We associated the shift towards communicative teaching with a reinstatement of the centrality of meaning in language behaviors. However, as the previous discussion has amply demonstrated, meanings are by no means given in language. Language only enables the writer, to a greater or lesser degree, to express intentions, thus allowing the reader, again to a greater or lesser degree, to approximate what it was that the writer intended to convey. Obviously the fit will never be perfect and our approaches to texts must reflect this relative openness.

IMPLICATIONS FOR FOREIGN LANGUAGE READING INSTRUCTION

The research findings summarized above amount to a call for a complete reorientation of the way reading is incorporated into the foreign language classroom.

As a follow-up to my earlier statement that, by and large, reading has not actually been taught, I conclude that perhaps the most important implication of this discussion is that reading in the foreign language requires direct attention. It does not automatically develop from speaking practice in the language, nor are the skills it requires automatically transferred from the native language, even if these skills are well developed.

Moreover, for the learner who has only limited knowledge of the foreign language system a frustrating cycle is nearly unavoidable. If we assume that the reader has a certain available amount of stored previous knowledge upon which to draw, access to that knowledge is severely hampered by highly limited linguistic input. Even worse, the reader cannot efficiently bring to bear upon unfamiliar language forms the great inferencing potential of previous knowledge that normally enhances correct guessing. The teacher's task, then, is to help the reader to break into this cycle by transferring as many native-speaker strategies as are applicable to the language class and to create new strategies that specifically take into account the peculiarities of the foreign language as well as the formal learning situation itself.

When we speak of the potential transfer of native language reading strategies, we must bear in mind that many of these are likely to be unconsciously held. To some extent, then, they may have to be made explicit in the classroom so that learners can maximize their guessing and inferencing skills for the primary reading strategies of sampling, predicting, confirming and correcting (Goodman 1973). In each case we should encourage learners to process holistically rather than to decode in an additive fashion. At the same time we should make them aware of the continuous interaction between text-derived and background-derived meanings.

We can summarize this repetitive process in the following fashion. The native language reader makes use of the wealth of contextual cues inherent in any reading situation and uses them to set up a preliminary, goal-directed framework of meaning. Through a process of predicting and matching predictions against more strictly text-derived meanings, interpretations are confirmed or adjusted as necessary, and in turn drive the next cycle of anticipated meanings. Efficiency in reading largely comes about as a result of the reader's ability to differentiate between input that needs to be examined in great detail and input that is more or less redundant. As Goodman states, the reader "predicts structures, tests them against the semantic context which he builds up from the situation and the on-going discourse, and then confirms them as he processes further language" (Goodman, 1973:23).

In applying this to the foreign language reader, it seems that we must reverse our emphasis if learners are ever to become efficient readers. Instead of concentrating on vocabulary deficiencies as the crucial problem in reading and attempting to reduce these by providing marginal glosses, a practice that inherently and insidiously creates a processing focus on the word level, we must encourage activities that build on the learners' prior knowledge, guide this knowledge by narrowing it down to the specific topic at hand, and then promote a series of activities that require continuous interactive processing between the more general meanings that one can anticipate at a given stage of dealing with a text and the very precise, primarily lexically derived meanings the text presents.

To this end, Swaffar (1981) suggests that learners (1) preview, or "create a reading hypothesis based on preliminary identification of text type and subject matter"; (2) organize, or "establish a focus intrinsic to the text which correlates redundancies in vocabulary"; and (3) weight, or "trace and reconstruct the linguistic and semantic patterns which establish the focus and reinforce the message of the text" (p. 179). By following this approach one can help learners to maximize previous knowledge.

But we have not yet overcome the hurdles posed by the learner's limitations in the foreign language. Referring to the special predicament of foreign language learners, van Parreren and Schouten-van Parreren (1981:236) suggest that, in order to become efficient at intensive and cursory reading, learners must develop six crucial abilities and learn their appropriate use:

1. to recognize the type of text (fictional, informative, etc.);

2. to recognize different types of text structure (story scheme, etc.);

3. to predict and summarize the content of the text or of passages from it;

4. to make references with respect to information to which the text alludes, but which it does not explicitly mention;

5. to determine the meaning of unknown words from the context; and

6. to analyze the word form of unknown words.

The first four points essentially restate Swaffar's concerns, but the latter two must be considered further. For while the traditional approach to learners' vocabulary deficiencies is highly suspect, we must nevertheless recognize that this very lack of available language forms is a serious concern for foreign language reading (Phillips 1975; Carrell 1984c and this volume).

By the same token, reading itself presents many of the very contextualized occurrences of vocabulary that seem to be so essential. Consequently, we must make available to our learners ways of coping with these unknown lexical items even as they engage in reading. In her excellent book on developing reading skills, Grellet (1981) refers to numerous strategies for using context effectively. She draws attention to the many forms contextual clues take, among them definitions of new vocabulary that occur right in the text; indirect explanations by example;

synonyms, antonyms, and hyponyms; relating an experience; descriptions, comparisons and contrasts; broadly related words; and reflections of intent, mood, tone, or setting. Sharpening the learner's awareness of such intratextual relationships will afford them crucial coping skills that foster behaviors similar to those employed by the native reader, among them reading on, even if they do not know a vocabulary item, in the hope that eventually the context will sufficiently clear up its meaning.

Such inferencing tasks are not limited to the word level. As stated before, they are just as important for higher-level linguistic units, namely sentences and paragraphs. Efficient native readers are so attuned to the patterned occurrences of entire strings of language forms that they can process these as complete chunks of meaning that do not require decoding of individual items. This highly refined expectancy is very likely something that comes only after significant experience with a language. Nevertheless, some familiarity with collocational restrictions or, obversely, favored groupings, can be created through specially designed exercises. Learners must gain an awareness of where, in the language they are learning, core information is likely to occur, and where the more supplementary information tends to be placed. They must be helped to process larger chunks of meaning by taking in entire word groups for which they have learned to expect a certain propositional value, i.e., indication of time or place, statement of one view in contrast to another, etc. And finally, they must learn to recognize markers of larger-scale organizational structures of texts (Mackay and Mountford 1979). The realization of this underlying ordering will be language specific, yet its existence seems a universal requirement for the expression of meanings and for interpretation.

How do practitioners in the foreign language field propose to accomplish these rather formidable tasks? A number of suggestions have been offered in the literature, from which I will draw a few representative examples. To afford readers a better sense of their flavor, the Appendix to this discussion illustrate various realizations of these proposals for three languages, French, German, and Spanish.

Perhaps the most complete language-independent set of ideas for fostering the development of effective and efficient reading strategies is that presented by Grellet (1981). Their purpose is to help learners build up a very diverse repertoire of reading strategies and then match these with appropriate tasks. In particular, the author suggests the following strategies:

Predicting from various amounts of text what the remaining, intervening, or previous materials have to contribute to the creation of a totally meaningful text;

Previewing, on the basis of a table of contents or similar tabulation, where in the textual material ahead a certain kind of information might best be found;

Having the students anticipate what is about to be read by asking themselves what kinds of questions about the given topic they would like to see answered;

Skimming through a text with a limited amount of time to obtain its gist;

Scanning a text for very specific information one wishes to obtain.

For each of these major suggestions Grellet's book offers a wealth of exercise types that can be adapted to the foreign language classroom.

Another highly practical set of proposals was developed by Phillips (1985) for a teacher education module designed to enhance reading proficiency. The entire packet, in three sections, summarizes the relevant theory on the reading process, offers a plan for conveying that information in the framework of an in-service workshop, and then presents sample materials in a total of six languages as well as English as a second language. The texts presented in the Appendix are drawn from this set of materials. Although the suggested activities are by no means the only possible ones, they do give a good indication of the thrust of the direction foreign language reading seems to be taking.

Phillips' practical plan for classroom teachers envisions five steps: (1) a prereading or preparation stage; (2) a skimming and/or scanning stage; (3) an intensive reading/decoding stage; (4) a comprehension check/evaluation stage; and (5) a transferable or integrating skill stage.

Her instructions highlight the following concerns, which are consonant with the theoretical findings presented above:

Prereading activities bring to the learners' attention information already in their heads so as to heighten their ability to predict and anticipate effectively. This knowledge may be either knowledge of the world or linguistic knowledge.

Skimming and scanning activity is particularly important for ensuring that learners do, in fact, form the habits of top-down processing and adjust their strategies to the intentions for which a specific text is read.

At the intensive reading/decoding stage learners are encouraged to look for details and to analyze in-depth the language materials that the text employs to convey its message. It is at this stage that the distinction between "reading to learn" and "learning to read" often becomes blurred. In the foreign language both activities are obviously interrelated and essential.

The comprehension check/evaluation stage allows for diverse formats to assess the various levels of understanding for which a text may be read, among them multiple choice, completion, matching exercises, filling in of charts, cloze passages, summaries, etc.

Finally, the transferable or integrating skill stage, takes the information, linguistic and nonlinguistic, that learners were able to obtain from a text and encourages transfer to other language modes and a diversity of tasks. These tasks may be language-centered activities, such as cognate pattern recognition, rules of word formation, building up of semantic fields, interpreting key grammatical signals, and developing awareness of discourse features. Or they may center around more integrative skills that involve the other language modes or perhaps further readings. Here Phillips suggests rewriting a narrative in dialogue form, acting out the story, changing an ending, discussing or debating an issue raised, giving one's own opinion on a topic, etc. Finally, this is also the stage for planning activities directed at eliminating specific learner behaviors that frustrate optimal reading.

IMPLICATIONS FOR MATERIALS

There remains the previous discussion that has tacitly assumed that one important issue in the development of efficient reading strategies has been solved, although this issue has by no means been satisfactorily laid to rest. I am referring to the question of the types of materials that should be used for teaching reading in a foreign language. Clearly, not only is the process of reading in need of a fresh look, the materials that learners are given to read should likewise be subject to a thorough reevaluation. As I have pointed out elsewhere (Byrnes 1985), despite some potential dangers due to foreign language readers' frequent lack of broad cultural knowledge, authentic texts are still the most preferable resource. Only by helping learners deal with authentic texts can we reestablish the connection of language to its natural setting and purpose. Perhaps the most important cautionary note concerning their use is that teachers must be aware of the cultural frame of reference within which they were written and create that awareness in their students.

Cates and Swaffar (1979:23) present these additional guidelines for materials selection:

1. Select unedited texts.
2. Fit the text to the task, or vice versa.

3. Assess task difficulty according to (a) textual complexity, (b) probable student interest and background knowledge, and (c) genre.

4. Provide practice in various kinds of reading tasks, e.g., skimming, scanning.

5. Provide practice in inferential thinking, keeping in mind (a) internal textual redundancy, (b) the text's orientational framework, (c) students' background knowledge, and (d) students' genre-based expectations.

Schulz (1983) reminds us of the importance of the content of a selection, aside from its linguistic difficulty and its length. A particularly significant area, from the standpoint of learner interest, is one that the authors of many reading selections have not considered nearly as thoroughly as our learners' cognitive abilities and their rich knowledge of any number of subject matter areas would seem to permit. Reading in a foreign language allows for a level of intellectual stimulation in the foreign language classroom that is perhaps higher than any of the other skill modalities permit. It can thus become an exciting way of transmitting the flavor of authentic communication that speaking often does not allow learners to experience.

Perhaps insights such as these will allow reading in the foreign language classroom to get another closer and, I hope, better reading.

APPENDIX

The following sample materials were made available to me by June K. Phillips, Indiana University of Pennsylvania. I wish to thank her and Jose M. Carranza for allowing their work to be included here. The sample German materials in this packet were prepared by me.

FRENCH

Sample Materials

I. *Prereading*

POLI? IMPOLI? INTELLIGENT?

En général, es-tu poli ou impoli? _____

En général, es-tu intelligent? _____
Quelquefois, on est *plus intelligent que poli*! Par exemple:

SITUATION A: Tu rentres chez toi avec un copain. Vous avez faim. Il y a deux morceaux de gâteau au chocolat sur la table.

Que fais-tu? _____

A. Je prends le plus grand morceau.

B. Je donne le plus grand a mon ami.

C. Je donne le choix a mon ami.

SITUATION B: Tu es dans l'autobus. Il n'y a plus de place. Une vieille dame, chargée de paquets, y entre.

Que fais-tu? _____

A. Je lui donne ma place.

B. Je prends ses paquets.

C. Je regarde par la fenêtre.

Si tu réponds B/A, tu es surtout *poli*!

Si tu réponds A/C, tu es surtout *impoli*!

Si tu réponds C/B, tu es surtout *intelligent*!

In this story, Charles reacts to a tempting situation in a certain way. Read it and decide whether his *"politesse"* or *"intelligence"* guides him.

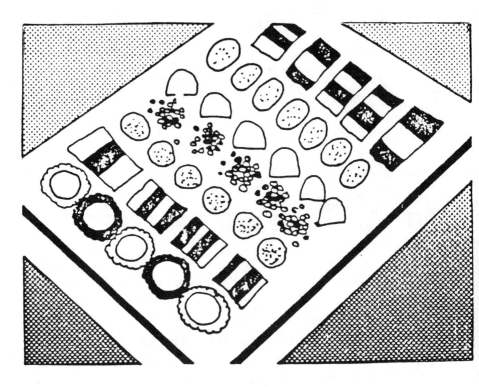

4. POLITESSE OU INTELLIGENCE

Madame Bernard fait une visite à son amie Madame Dubois. Sons fils Charles va avec elle. Charlot est trop petit pour aller à l'école maternelle° et sa mère l'emmène toujours avec elle.

école pour enfants de 5 ans

Pour amuser l'enfant, Madame Dubois lui donne un jeu de cartes.° Le petit garçon commence à jouer. Il fait beau dehors° mais dans la maison il fait trop chaud. Les deux dames prennent le café sur la terrasse. Elles bavardent.

anglais: car_s
≠ dans la maison

Charlot voit une boîte° de bonbons sur la table. Il s'arrête de° jouer et regarde les chocolats et les fruits confits sans bruit,° sans parler. Madame Dubois voit que Charlot regarde les bonbons et lui offre la boîte. A sa grande surprise, le petit tient bon° ses cartes et ne touche pas les bonbons. Il les regarde avec attention tout de même.°

Regardez le dessin; les bonbons sont dans la boîte.
≠ commence à
= en silence
holds onto
= en tout cas

—Je sais que tu es un garçon très poli, dit Madame Dubois. C'est par politesse que tu ne prends pas de bonbons. Voilà, je vais t'en donner moi-même.

Elle met la main dans la boîte et prend beaucoup de bonbons. Le garçon laisse tomber° les cartes et accepte les chocolats avec plaisir.

≠ tient bon

—Merci beaucoup, madame, dit-il. Je vous remercie°   *dit merci*
bien. Mais ce n'est pas par politesse que je ne prends
pas de bonbons moi-même. Ma main est très petite, mais
la vôtre est beaucoup plus grande que la mienne.°   *ici = ma main*

From June K. Phillips, *Petits contes sympathiques*. National Textbook Co., Lincolnwood, Ill, 1979.

II. *Skimming/Scanning*

A. Skim the story and decide whether the ending indicates that Charlot is exceptionally *polite* or exceptionally *intelligent*. Poll the class.

B. Read again and isolate Charlot's actions in the story. Then put the following sentences in the correct order by numbering them 1, 2, 3, etc.

_____ Il accepte les bonbons que Mme Dubois offre.

_____ Il admet qu'il n'est pas poli.

_____ Il joue aux cartes.

_____ Il observe des bonbons sur la table.

_____ Il ne tient plus ses cartes.

_____ Il refuse de prendre des bonbons de la boîte.

III. *Close reading:*   (This exercise may be placed on a worksheet or used as a lesson plan guide for the teacher conducting the class.)

A. Have students use the glosses as needed. Check afterwards to see if they still have questions on any of them.

B. Word study in context

Paragraph 1: What other word in the paragraph is associated with *maternelle*?

Paragraph 2: What are the differences in meaning in the following words:
le jeu/le joueur/jouer
Use them in the following sentence:

Le _____ aime _____ avec le _____ de cartes.

Paragraph 3: What is in the *boîte de bonbons*?
Sans bruit, sans parler means that Charlot

ne $\left\{ \begin{array}{l} \text{dit} \\ \text{mange} \\ \text{touche} \end{array} \right\}$ rien.

C. Synonyme ou Antonyme? Mark each set of words with *S* or *A* to signify that they mean nearly the same or nearly the opposite. All are used in the story.
1. petit/grand
2. emmener avec/accompagner
3. commence à/s'arrête de
4. bavarder/parler
5. dehors/dans la maison
6. voit/regarde
7. donner/offrir
8. il tient bon/il laisse tomber
9. mettre/prendre
10. sans/avec

IV. *Evaluation*

Repondez avec VRAI ou FAUX. Corrigez les phrases fausses.
1. Le petit garçon s'appelle Charlot Dubois.
2. Il a 7 ou 8 ans.
3. Il joue aux cartes et les dames parlent.
4. Les dames ne prennent pas le café dans la maison.
5. Charlot regarde en silence les bons chocolats.
6. Mme Dubois offre des bonbons à Charlot parce qu'elle le trouve poli.
7. Elle lui donne seulement 2 ou 3 bonbons.
8. Charlot sait que la quantité de bonbons dans la main d'un adulte est plus grande que la quantité dans la main d'un enfant.

V. A. *Transferable skills:*

There are several ways of expressing a negative idea in French. With adjectives, one often uses the prefix *im-* or *in-* before the word; that prefix carries the idea *not*. When you encounter this kind of word while reading, look ahead to the meaning of the "root" word and interpret the item as its opposite.

For example:

Le jeune garçon est *impoli* = Il n'est pas poli.

Rephrase the following sentences.

1. Mon petit frère est *imprudent* quand il traverse la rue.
2. Il est *impossible* de manger une boîte de bonbons dans un après-midi.
3. Mes parents sont *impatients* avec moi.
4. L'eau dans la ville est *impure*.
5. Ses idées sont *imprécises*.
6. Notre travail est *imparfait* de temps en temps.
7. Cette table Louis XIV est *inauthentique*.
8. Son devoir est *incomplet* parce qu'il écrit des phrases *incorrectes*.
9. Charlot est *indiscipliné*.
10. Ça, c'est *incroyable*!

B. *Integrative skill:*

1. *Speaking: Pour paraître poli.* With a small group, plan 2 short skits. In the first, have each character be as polite as possible. Incorporate as many *formules de politesse* as you can. Then plan a contrast in which you display ill manners in words and actions. Discuss with your teacher similarities and differences in French and American culture.

2. *Reading:* Look for advertisements in French magazines of the foods that satisfy the sweet tooth of the French. Build a vocabulary list of generic names, brand names and slogans you identify.

3. *Writing:* Work with a partner and invent some more *poli, impoli, intelligent* situations as you saw in the pre-reading activity.

   or

   Write a short narrative about a clever situation in which you were once involved. (Do your retelling in present time.)

GERMAN
Sample Materials

Pro Kleinstadt—Pro Grosstadt

I. Prereading: The learners are asked, through five questions, to consider the factors that influence one's choice of a residence.

II. Skimming/scanning

    1. The five paragraphs of the article are summarized in simple language. Learners are asked to match these sentences with the appropriate paragraphs.

    2. Learners are asked to isolate the most important arguments that the writer mentions in favor of living in a small town. Then they will check whether the reasons given in the seven subsequent sentences are mentioned in the text or not.

III. Decoding

    1. Learners look for opposing thought units. The resulting pairs contrast city life with living in a small town.

    2. Words in context. Learners narrow down the meaning of unknown vocabulary through context and indicate the closest meaning equivalent in a multiple-choice format.

IV. Comprehension

Two slightly different descriptions of the writer's life style are given. Which one best reflects the information provided in the text?

V. Transfer of materials

Given the writer's preference for life in a small town, which one of the following newspaper ads would be of interest to him?

Pro Kleinstadt—Pro Grosstadt

I. Die Bundesrepublik Deutschland ist viel dichter besiedelt als die Vereinigten Staaten. Trotzdem haben die Menschen auch hier die Möglichkeit, zwischen einem Leben in der Stadt und dem Leben auf dem Land zu wählen. Beides hat Vor- und Nachteile, die natürlich von Person zu Person variieren.

Fragen Sie sich selbst:

A. Warum wohnt man dort, wo man wohnt?

B. Welchen Einfluss hat die Familiensituation, das Alter, die Zahl der Kinder, der Beruf?

C. Was braucht man, um sich wohl zu fühlen?

D. Was ist Ihnen wichtig, was ist nicht so wichtig?

E. Welche Qualitäten suchen Sie in Ihrer Wohnung, in Ihrem Wohnort, in Ihrer nächsten Umgebung?

PRO "... gibt mir das Gefühl der Geborgenheit"

Kleinstadt

Mittendrin in einer grossen Stadt wohnen? Umbraust vom Autoverkehr, einbetoniert, kein Fleckchen Grün vorm Haus. Fussmarsch zu öffentlichen Anlagen, um Luft zu schnappen und Bäume oder Rasen oder Blumen zu sehen? Unvorstellbar!

Ich wohne in einer Kleinstadt, ein paar Kilometer draussen, und ich wohne gern dort. Denn hier draussen ist noch niemand auf die Idee gekommen, Schallschutzfenster in seine Wohnung einzubauen, damit der Lärm wenigstens ein bisschen draussen bleibt. In meiner Kleinstadt kann ich meine Kinder zu Fuss gehen lassen, ohne mich um ihre Sicherheit sorgen zu müssen. Wenn sie mit dem Fahrrad unterwegs sind, kann ihnen natürlich auch in der Kleinstadt etwas zustossen. Nur: Hier können sie noch radfahren.

Draussen, in meiner Kleinstadt ist auch noch niemandem eingefallen, eine Bürgerinitiative für einen Kinderspielplatz zu gründen. Die Plätze sind da, Felder und Wiesen nicht weit, die Natur gehört zum täglichen Leben. Es gibt noch Bauernhöfe. Meine Kinder wissen, wie ein Pferd oder eine Kuh oder ein Huhn aussieht—und zwar nicht aus Bilderbüchern, sondern vom Erleben.

Draussen, in meiner Kleinstadt, gibt es moderne Supermärkte und Modehäuser und Boutiquen wie in der Grossstadt. Aber es gibt auch noch den Tante-Emma-Laden, bei dem es niemanden stört, wenn ich mal "hinten rein" gehe und um ein Brot bitte, weil's meine Frau vergessen hat. Ein Lokal mit drei Sternen haben wir zwar nicht, aber wenn der Wirt mir die Hand gibt, wenn ich zum Essen komme—das ist ein schönes Gefühl.

Meine Kleinstadt da draussen ist nicht nur heile Welt. Auch sie hat ihre Konflikte und ihre Probleme. Sie hat sogar ihre Schandflecke und Hässlichkeiten. Doch diese Kleinstadt gibt mir das Gefühl der Geborgenheit. Sie ist überschaubar, persönlich. Persönlich: Das ist das richtige Wort für all das Undefinierbare, das diese Kleinstadt so sympathisch und so heimelig macht.

Otto A. Schölple

Otto A. Schölple ist Lokalredakteur bei den "Stuttgarter Nachrichten"

II. Lesen Sie den ganzen Text.

  A. Für welchen Paragraphen (#1 − 5) passt diese Überschrift?

    1. Gute Einkaufsmöglichkeiten und freundliche Restaurants sind ein wichtiger Teil der Lebensqualität.

                Paragraph _____

    2. Kinder sollten am besten in der weiten Natur aufwachsen.

                Paragraph _____

    3. Es ist schwer zu verstehen, warum jemand in der Grossstadt wohnen will, da sie so viele negative Seiten hat.

                Paragraph _____

    4. Das Leben in der Kleinstadt ist ein freieres Leben für Eltern und Kinder.

                Paragraph _____

    5. Eine Kleinstadt hat eine persönliche Note und gibt einem ein heimisches Gefühl.

                Paragraph _____

  B. Isolieren Sie nun die wichtigsten Argumente des Schreibers für seine Liebe für die Kleinstadt. Stehen die folgenden Argumente im Text? Ja oder nein?

  Die Land- und Hauspreise sind in der Kleinstadt nicht so hoch wie in der Stadt.

  Er findet die Stille der Kleinstadt schön.

  Er möchte, dass seine Kinder die Natur direkt erleben können.

  Er fährt nicht gerne weit zur Arbeit.

  Ein besonderer Vorteil der Kleinstadt sind die besseren Schulen.

  Nach einem langen Tag im Büro sucht er das problemlose und sorglose Leben in der Kleinstadt.

  Es ist schwer, die Vorteile der Kleinstadt genau zu definieren, aber für ihn ist das persönliche Element wichtig.

III. Der Text kontrastiert Kleinstadt und Grossstadt.

  A. Welche Gedanken sind Kontrastpaare:

Leben in der Grossstadt: *Leben in der Kleinstadt:*

mittendrin in einer grossen : ein paar Kilometer draussen Stadt

_____ : zu Fuss gehen, radfahren

_____ : Tante-Emma-Laden

kein Fleckchen Grün vorm Haus : _____

_____ : Natur ist tägliches Leben

_____ : freundliche Kneipe, wo der Wirt
die Gäste begrüsst

_____ : persönlich und freundlich

B. Wörter im Kontext:
Welche Konnotationen haben die Wörter in diesem Text?

1. *einbetoniert*

   a. komfortabel und elegant leben
   b. ohne Grün und ohne frische Luft leben
   c. frei und sorglos leben

2. *öffentliche Anlagen*

   a. öffentliche Parks oder Plätze
   b. öffentliche Schulen
   c. Wälder und Wiesen in der Umgebung der Stadt

3. *Schallschutzfenster*

   a. diese Fenster lassen weniger Sonne in die Zimmer
   b. diese Fenster sollte man haben um die Heizungskosten zu
      reduzieren
   c. diese Fenster helfen, den Lärm der Strasse zu reduzieren

4. *kann ihnen etwas zustossen*

   a. kann ihnen ein Unfall passieren
   b. kann etwas zu ihnen kommen
   c. können sie auch in der Kleinstadt einen falschen Weg fah-
      ren

5. *der Wirt*

   a. ein guter Bekannter, der mich zum Essen eingeladen hat
   b. die Hostess in einem eleganten Restaurant
   c. der Besitzer eines kleinen Gasthauses, wo man essen kann

IV. Welcher der beiden folgenden Paragraphen gibt die Situation von
Herrn Schölple besser wieder?

Herr Schölple ist ein Mann, der sehr familienorientiert ist. Er findet,
dass die Gesundheit seiner Kinder ganz besonders wichtig ist. De-
shalb wohnt er in einer Kleinstadt, wo er täglich mit ihnen in den
Park spazieren gehen kann. Wenn die Kinder mit Freunden spielen
wollen, nimmt seine Frau sie schnell mit dem Auto. Dann spielen
sie zusammen auf einem neuen modernen Kinderspielplatz. Weil seine
Frau arbeitet, kaufen sie primär im Supermarkt ein. Und wenn sie
Freitag abend müde nach Hause kommt, hat sie oft keine Lust mehr

zum kochen. Dann gehen sie gern zusammen in ein elegantes Restaurant, wo sie sich mit Bekannten treffen.

Herr Schölple ist ein Mann, der sehr familienorientiert ist. Er findet, dass Kinder die Möglichkeit haben sollen, allein die Natur direkt zu erleben, so wie sie wirklich ist und nicht so, wie es im Bilderbuch steht. Er lässt ihnen ziemlich freie Hand, sie dürfen auch allein radfahren. Er macht sich keine grossen Sorgen wenn sie weg sind, obwohl natürlich auch die Kleinstadt nicht das Paradies auf Erden ist. Wichtig ist ihm aber vor allem die persönliche Note und das Gefühl, sich in seinem Wohnort wohl und heimisch zu fühlen.

V. Herr Schölple argumentiert für die Kleinstadt. Welche der folgenden Inserate in der Zeitung wären für ihn interessant wenn er eine neue Wohnung sucht?

Hier bekommen Sie viel München für Ihr Geld

Stadtresidenz München-Nymphenburg
In ruhiger Wohngegend, Ecke Nibelungen- und Winthirstraße, zwischen Rotkreuzplatz und Nymphenburger Kanal – einer der besten Stadtwohnlagen Münchens

Appartements
München-Theresienhöhe
ca. 40 m², sep. Kü., 5. OG, m. herrl. Blick auf die Altstadt, inkl. TG
DM 155 000,-

Zu vermieten
1-Zimmer-Wohnung
40 qm, Einbauküche, Balkon, ab sofort zu verm., Miete DM 370,- + NK.
Helmut Kauper KG, Bayreuth, Königsbergstr. 1, Tel. 0921/20205.

SPANISH

Sample Materials

SPANISH—Intermediate Level

Stage 1. Prereading: Recall of background information, Vocabulary preparation
  The teacher places the following on an overhead or on a worksheet. Students are asked to match the columns.
  Students are encouraged to use knowledge they already have of space and to guess at Spanish terms which are mostly cognates of English.

A	B
1. Discovery	a. un misil intercontinental
2. Apollo	b. un astronauta norteamericano
3. John Glenn	c. sistema de defensa espacial
4. Minuteman	d. El Departamento de Defensa
5. El cabo Canaveral	e. una agencia espacial
6. Sputnik	f. un transbordador
7. Yuri Gagarín	g. una base espacial
8. El Pentágono	h. un satélite norteamericano
9. NASA	i. un cosmonauta soviético
10. Guerra de las Galaxias	j. el primer satélite

Stage 2: Skimming: Here is the first and last paragraph of an article about a space event. Choose the most appropriate headline.

Párrafo #1:   *Washington*

El transbordador espacial de Estados Unidos, *Discovery*, colocará en órbita sobre la parte occidental de la Unión Soviética un nuevo satélite espía en el curso de su primera misión exclusivamente militar, que se iniciará el próximo 23 de enero en el Cabo Canaveral (Florida) en medio de extraordinarias medidas de seguridad.

Párrafo final:

Por su parte, *The Washington Post* respondió que en los últimos días el objetivo de la primera misión militar del *Discovery* era un capital federal de los Estados Unidos.

                                              jueves 20 de diciembre

HEADLINE CHOICES:

A. La nueva misión militar del 'Discovery' se iniciará el próximo mes de enero.

B. El diario norteamericano *The Washington Post* reveló el objetivo de la misión del 'Discovery'.

C. La primera misión militar del 'Discovery' colocará sobre la URSS un satélite espía.

Now look at the complete article. Scan the article just for the information requested. The paragraph where the information is located is marked. (Skip the Xed out paragraph in column 2 for it is not so important to us.)

P #1: El objetivo de la misión del *Discovery*:
La fecha:
¿Desde dónde se iniciará la misión?
¿Que significan las letras "URSS"?

P #2: ¿Quién reveló el objetivo de la misión?
¿Qué clases de comunicaciones va a interceptar?

P #3: ¿Otra cosa que el 'Discovery' puede hacer?

P #4: ¿Cuál es la diferencia entre el satélite del 'Discovery' y los otros satélites? ¿Qué ya vigila el territorio ruso?

P #5: ¿Qué departamento de gobierno está a cargo de estas misiones militares?
¿Es esta misión militar la única que se efectuará?

P #7-8: ¿Qué significa un embargo informativo (#7) en el párrafo #8?

P #10: ¿Quién es Weinberger? ¿Por qué está enojado?

P #11: ¿Sabía mucha gente en Washington el objetivo de esta misión?

La primera misión militar del 'Discovery' colocará sobre la URSS un satélite espía

Washington

El transbordador espacial de Estados Unidos *Discovery* colocará en órbita sobre la parte occidental de la Unión Soviética un nuevo satélite espía en el curso de su primera misión exclusivamente militar, que se iniciará el próximo 23 de enero en cabo Canaveral (Florida) en medio de extraordinarias medidas de seguridad.

El diario norteamericano *The Washington Post*, que el miércoles 19 reveló el objetivo de la misión del *Discovery*, tras consultar fuentes no identificadas de la base espacial mencionada, añadia que el satélite en cuestión será el más importante de los denominados *Sigint* (Signals Intelligence o espionaje de señales) y servirá para interceptar communicaciones militares soviéticas de radio, teléfono o satélite.

Las mismas fuentes consultadas por el *Post* afirman que el nuevo satélite espía podrá recoger incluso informaciones telemétricas sobre pruebas de misiles realizadas en la Unión Soviética, lo que permitiria a Estados Unidos verificar el comportamiento soviético frente a eventuales acuerdos en materia de control de armàmentos.

Otros cuatro o cinco satélites estadounidenses especializados en la recogida de información militar, aunque más pequeños que el que será lanzado en enero, vigilan ya el territorio soviético.

El nuevo *Sigint*, cuyo coste se eleva a 300 millones de dólares (unos

Robert Cooper, director de la Oficina de Investigación de Proyectos Avanzados de Defensa ha manifestado que esta primer vuelo militar del *Discovery* puede ser parte integrante de un proyecto conocido en clave como Teal Ruby (Rubi Verde Azulado), que se propone "crear una base de daros radiométricos de referencia global y exhaustiva asi como desarroilar la primera generación de tecnologia avanzada de vigilancia espacial por medio de rayos infrarrojos".

La publicación por el diario *The Washington Post* del objetivo de la próxima misión del *Discovery* quebranta el embargo informativo decretado por el Pentágono en torno a esta primera misión exclusivamente militar del transbordador espacial.

Fuentes del Departamento de Defensa de Estados Unidos indicaron el lunes 17 que ni la hora exacta del despegue ni la naturaleza de la carga transportada por la nave serian reveladas al publico, y añadieron que se investigara el origen de las *filtraciones*.

Varios periódicos estadounidenses que afirman disponer de la misma información publicada el miércoles 19 por el citado diario de Washington, estimaron que, una vez roto el embargo, nada les impide seguir informando sobre el próximo viaje del transbordador espacial.

Las informaciones facilitadas por el *Washington Post* originaron que el

51,000 millones de pesetas), saldrá del transbordador espacial cuando éste se encuentre a unos 36,500 kilómetros sobre la zona occidental de la URSS, y se mantendrá en esa posición relativa porque su velocidad de rotacion será similar a la de la Tierra. El Departamento de Defensa piensa efectuar decenas de misiones militares espaciales durante la próxima década.

secretario de Defensa, Caspar Weinberger, se refiriese personalmente al tema y concentro sus ataques contra el periódico, célebre en el mundo entero por el asunto Watergate. Weinberger acusó al periódico de violar las leyes sobre seguridad nacional con informaciones incorrectas.

Por su parte, *The Washington Post* respondió que en los últimos dias el objetivo de la primera misión militar del *Discovery* era una secreto a voces en los medios periodisticos y politicos de la capital federal de Estados Unidos.

Jueves 20 de diciembre

Stage 3: Decoding/Intensive

1. List cognate nouns that refer to space (at least 6)

2. List cognate adjectives (6 or more)

3. Find at least 6 verb forms that refer to *future* actions:

4. Find synonyms or equivalent expressions in the article for the following:

un periódico:

una década:

de los Estados Unidos:

de la Unión Soviética:

la capital federal:

5. Work with a partner and see how many of these definitions you can find in the article. Write the defined word here:

a. una nave preparada para transportar carga al espacio . . .

b. la curva que describe un astro alrededor del sol, o un satélite natural o artificial alrededor de un planeta . . .

c. una persona que provee información . . .

d. un ensayo, un experimento, una demostración de una cosa . . .

e. un cohete, un proyectil balístico . . .

f. observar, espiar . . .

g. un conjunto de diez unidades . . .

h. un planeta perteneciente al sistema solar y habitado por el hombre . . .

i. la unidad monetaria española . . .

j. información dada en forma oculta, anónima . . .

k. ambiente, lugar, circunstancias o personas entre las que se vive . . .

l. un pacto, un tratado, una resolución tomada por dos o más países o personas . . .

Stage 4: Comprehension

Cloze summary with choices:

Read through the following summary of the article. Then fill in the blanks with the appropriate word from the list. Do not use any item more than once, but there are extras.

El satélite _____ interceptará _____

militares _____ de radio, teléfono o satélite. El _____

_____ norteamericano, *The Washington Post*, reveló el _____

de la misión del _____ espacial. El Departamento de

_____ va a investigar el origen de las _____.

El señor Weinberger acusó a *The Washington Post* de _____

la leyes sobre _____ nacional.

communicaciones	Pentágono
espía	periódico
Defensa	objetivo
filtraciones	seguridad
misiles	soviéticas
violar	conocer
transbordador	

Stage 5: Integrative skills:

Do one of the following activities:

1. In a group of 6, do a press conference at the Pentagon. A spokesperson has just announced the next mission of *Discovery*. The

five journalists formulate questions to get as much information as possible.

2. Pretend you are a Russian journalist writing for a Spanish newspaper. Give your version of the Discovery mission and comment from the Soviet point of view.

REFERENCES

Adams, Marilyn J. and Allan Collins. 1979. "A Schema-theoretic View of Reading." In Roy O. Freedle (ed.). *New Directions in Discourse Processing*, 1–22. Norwood, N.J.: Ablex.

Alderson, J. Charles, and A. H. Urquhart (eds.). 1984. *Reading in a Foreign Language*. Reading, Mass.: Addison-Wesley.

Bernhardt, Elizabeth B. 1983. "Three Approaches to Reading Comprehension in Intermediate German." *The Modern Language Journal* 67 (3):111–115.

———. 1984. "Toward an Information Processing Perspective in Foreign Language Reading." *The Modern Language Journal* 68 (4):322–331.

Berns, Margie S. 1984. "Functional Approaches to Language and Language Teaching: Another Look." In Sandra J. Savignon and Margie S. Berns (eds.). *Initiatives in Communicative Language Teaching*, 3–21. Reading, Mass.: Addison-Wesley.

Byrnes, Heidi. 1983. "Discourse Analysis and the Teaching of Writing." *ADFL Bulletin* 15 (2):30–36.

———. 1985. "Teaching toward Proficiency: The Receptive Skills." In Alice C. Omaggio (ed.). *Proficiency, Curriculum, Articulation: The Ties That Bind*, 87–107. Middlebury, Vt: Northeast Conference.

Carrell, Patricia L. 1984a. "Evidence of a Formal Schema in Second Language Comprehension." *Language Learning* 34 (2):87–112.

———. 1984b. "The Effects of Rhetorical Organization on ESL Readers." *TESOL Quarterly* 18 (3):441–469.

———. 1984c. "Schema Theory and ESL Reading: Classroom Implications and Applications." *The Modern Language Journal* 68 (4):332–343.

———., and Joan C. Eisterhold. 1983. "Schema Theory and ESL Reading Pedagogy." *TESOL Quarterly* 17:553–573.

Cates, G. Truett, and Janet K. Swaffar. 1979. *Reading a Second Language*. Language in Education: Theory and Practice, Vol. 20. Washington, D.C.: Center for Applied Linguistics.

Goodman, Kenneth S. 1973. "Psycholinguistic Universals in the Reading Process." In Frank Smith (ed.). *Psycholinguistics and Reading*, 22–27. New York: Holt, Rinehart & Winston.

Grellet, Francoise. 1981. *Developing Reading Skills. A Practical Guide to Reading Comprehension Exercises*. New York: Cambridge University Press.

Holmes, Deborah Lott. 1973. "The Independence of Letter, Word, and Meaning Identification in Reading." In Frank Smith (ed.). *Psycholinguistics and Reading*, 50–69. New York: Holt, Rinehart & Winston.

Hymes, Dell. 1972. "The Ethnography of Speaking." In Joshua A. Fishman (ed.). *Reading in the Sociology of Language*. 99–138. The Hague: Mouton.

Krashen, Stephen D. 1985. "The Power of Reading." Keynote address at the 1985 TESOL conference in New York.

Mackay, Ronald, Bruce Barkman, and R. R. Jordan (eds.). 1979. *Reading in a Second Language*. Rowley, Mass.: Newbury House.

Mackay, Ronald, and Alan Mountford. 1979. "Reading for Information." In Ronald Mackay *et al.* (eds.). *Reading in a Second Language*, 106–141. Rowley, Mass.: Newbury House.

Minsky, Marvin. 1982. "A Framework for Representing Knowledge." In John Haugeland (ed.). *Mind Design*, 95–128. Cambridge, Mass.: MIT Press.

Munby, John. 1979. "Teaching Intensive Reading Skills." In Ronald Mackay *et al.* (eds.). *Reading in a Second Language*, 142–158. Rowley, Mass.: Newbury House.

Pearson, P. David, and Dale D. Johnson. 1978. *Teaching Reading Comprehension*. New York: Holt, Rinehart & Winston.

Phillips, June K. 1975. "Second Language Reading. Teaching Decoding Skills." *Foreign Language Annals* 8 (3):227–232.

———. 1978. "Reading Is Communication, Too!" *Foreign Language Annals* 11 (3):281–287.

———. 1984. "Practical Implications of Recent Research in Reading." *Foreign Language Annals* 17 (4):285–296.

———. 1985. "Proficiency-based Instruction in Reading: A Teacher Education Module." Introductory packet, Applications packet, and Sample Materials. Indiana University of Pennsylvania, Indiana, Penn.

Rumelhart, David E. 1977. "Toward an Interactive Model of Reading." In Stanislav Dornic (ed.). *Attention and Performance, Volume VI*. New York: Academic Press, 573–603.

Rumelhart, David E. "Schemata: The Building Blocks of Cognition." In Rand J. Spiro, Bertram C. Bruce, and William F. Brewer (eds.). *Theoretical Issues in Reading Comprehension*, 33–58. Hillsdale, N.J.: Erlbaum.

Savignon, Sandra J. 1983. *Communicative Competence: Theory and Classroom Practice*. Reading, Mass.: Addison-Wesley.

Schank, Roger, and Robert Abelson. 1977. *Scripts, Plans, Goals, and Understanding: An Inquiry into Human Knowledge Structures*. Hillsdale, N.J.: Lawrence Erlbaum.

Schulz, Renate A. 1983. "From Word to Meaning: Foreign Language Reading Instruction after the Elementary Course." *The Modern Language Journal* 67 (2):127–134.

Smith, Frank. 1978. *Psycholinguistics and Reading*, New York: Holt, Rinehart & Winston.

Swaffar, Janet K. 1981. "Reading in the Foreign Language Classroom: Focus on Process." *Die Unterrichtspraxis* 14 (2):176–194.

———. 1985. "Reading Authentic Texts in a Foreign Language: A Cognitive Model." *The Modern Language Journal* 69 (1):15–34.

Tannen, Deborah. 1979. "What's in a Frame? Surface Evidence for Underlying Expectations." In Roy O. Freedle (ed.). *New Directions in Discourse Processing,* 137–181. Norwood, NJ: Ablex.

———. 1982. "Oral and Literate Strategies in Spoken and Written Narratives." *Language* 58 (1):1–21.

Van Parreren, C. F., and M. C. Schouten-Van Parreren. 1981. "Contextual Guessing: A Trainable Reader Strategy." *System* 9 (3):235–241.

Chapter 10

Playing in English: Games and the L2 Classroom in Japan

Marc Helgesen

Marc Helgesen teaches English in Tokyo for the University of Pittsburgh English Language Institute, Japan Program. He is coauthor, with Thomas Mandeville and Robin Jordan, of English Firsthand *and serves as the activities column editor of* The Language Teacher, *the newsletter of the Japan Association of Language Teachers. His areas of interest include individualization of instruction, classroom management, games, and communicative classroom activities.*

INTRODUCTION

When I landed at Narita International Airport in Tokyo for the first time, I had no idea how radically the experience of living in a foreign culture and learning Japanese as a second language would affect my entire philosophy and methodology of teaching. During my first month, my "linguistic creativity" became quite evident. I once tried to buy a bottle of plum wine (*umeshu*) but, because of my faulty pronunciation, went home with a bottle of wretched tasting *Yomeshu*, the cultural equivalent of castor oil. On another occasion, in a conversation about birth order, I mispronounced the Northeastern Japan dialect word for "youngest child" (*battsu*) and told a friend that I had been a "mistake" (*batsu*).

Incidents such as these have made me realize the degree to which learning a language is a game: Will I understand or not? Will I be understood or not? Even the most linguistically incompetent individuals can rival Marcel Marceau when they absolutely need to communicate and their lack of oral communicative ability leaves mime as their only alternative. But communicating in the second/foreign language offers a sense of challenge and excitement, and it is in this sense that I refer to language learning as a game.

It seems that virtually every article concerned with games for language development bemoans the fact that the technique is usually downplayed. The reason cited by the articles is that every teacher knows that games work but too often relegates them to the last part of class when a filler is needed ("We've got 10 minutes; let's play *20 Questions*."). I think this lack of recognition of the value of games is due largely to the fact that those of us who advocate their use are too often so interested in sharing specific games that we neglect to provide a reasoned analysis of what the technique has to offer and why it works. Such a reasoned analysis would also provide a working definition of games suitable for the goals of the language classroom.

As a step toward principled development and use of games in language classes, I would like to offer a definition of games, establishing what they are and are not, explain why they work, and consider their role in communicative language teaching. Finally, I will present models of application along with several games illustrating those models.

LANGUAGE STUDY IN JAPAN

To appreciate the context in which my views were developed, the reader needs some awareness of the language learning and teaching situation in Japan. English language instruction is universal in Japan, beginning in junior high school. So everyone learns English, or more precisely, everyone *studies* English in Japan, attending classes three hours a week in both junior and senior high school. Yet despite the time they have attended English classes, the percentage of people who can carry on a basic conversation in English is quite small. The reason why these school classes rarely turn out English speakers is that the methodology used is almost exclusively grammar-translation (Taira & Sasaki 1983). As outdated as this approach may be, it serves two functions. First, it prepares students to take college entrance examinations. Most students are studying English not to learn to communicate with other English speakers, but rather to pass the rigid entrance examinations for college admission. These tests, part of *juken jigoku* (literally: "examination hell"), rarely contain a speaking or listening component. Secondly, the grammar-translation approach is compatible with teacher qualifications. Many Japanese public school English teachers do not speak English. Often they are English literature majors with no background either in pedagogy or in linguistics. Moreover, universities give no credit for oral proficiency (Kahn 1971). Attention to oral communication skills at the university level is perfunctory, at best. As a consequence, English classes are conducted almost exclusively in Japanese, with a focus on metalanguage rather than communication. In addition to the prevailing methodology, two other factors that contribute to learners' inability to develop competence in spoken English must be mentioned. These are class size, which ranges typically between 40 and 50 students, and the dual traditions of rote learning and student silence, which require learners to listen to, write down and memorize what the teacher says. Speaking in class is simply not part of the learners' role.

Class size in most Japanese colleges and universities further hinders the development of oral communication skills. When students do attend conversation classes, they often number 30 or more. I have personally taught college conversation classes with as many as 55 students, and at a recent language teaching conference, I spoke with a colleague whose standard class size was 70.

The result of this educational system is thus classic false beginners: students who can read English to some extent, have a degree of grammatical competence and a relatively large vocabulary, but cannot use English effectively in conversation.

However, many Japanese do choose to learn conversation, either during their school years or, more commonly, following completion of their formal education. Such study typically takes place either in a private language school or in classes offered as a fringe benefit at the person's place of employment. Participation in these classes may or may not be voluntary.

Learners' motivation for taking English conversation courses is varied. Many study to improve their ability to conduct business in the United States, Great Britain, and other English-speaking countries. Also, throughout the world English is increasingly used in business, industry, and education as the *lingua franca* when all parties to a conversation do not share a common language. At the school where I teach, classes may include students who are oil company technicians studying to qualify as instructors of Burmese and Saudi engineers in petroleum processing. Other students may be hotel staff learning to deal with guests attending international conferences, or cable manufacturers interested in explaining optic cable capabilities. We also instruct research hospital doctors who wish to benefit from attendance at medical conferences conducted in English or contribute to such conferences by making presentations. We have even taught English conversation to employees at the local castle, thus enabling them to make tourists' visits more informative and enjoyable.

While many Japanese study English purely for professional purposes, English study is also a popular hobby in Japan. Given the high value placed on education in general in Japan, learning English qualifies, along with flower arrangement and calligraphy, as an "uplifting" pastime. English language instruction is also standard fare at the culture centers sponsored by NHK (public television) throughout the country. This positive attitude toward learning English is further reinforced by the belief that Japan's emergence as a world power leaves the *kokusaijin*, or "international people" (i.e., those who are able to deal linguistically and culturally with foreigners), in a better position to understand the world and share their knowledge of Japan.

Finally, international travel is increasingly popular among the Japanese, and many study English to enable themselves to remain independent while enjoying their vacations abroad. While it is true that the common practice of traveling abroad in tour groups led by a Japanese speaking guide remains popular with a sizeable portion of the population, the ranks of those who prefer to equip themselves to travel on their own by learning English are steadily growing.

It should be noted that, of these three groups of language learners, only those in the first category, who are learning English for professional purposes, are likely to have the frequent, prolonged contact with English-speaking environments that best enhances development of the ability actually to use the language. Even among members of this group, however, the amount of time spent in an English-speaking environment varies greatly. Learners of English as a second language who live in the United States, for example, have ample opportunity for exposure to English. If they choose, these learners can rely on the classroom primarily as a place to learn skills that will allow them to make sense of all the English to which they are exposed. In Japan, on the other hand, the classroom must provide learners with English language skills and with exposure to the language itself since, for most learners, opportunities to be immersed in the language on a regular basis do not exist beyond the classroom. Moreover, when opportunities to use English do present themselves in Asia, the speakers are as likely as not to be nonnative speakers using English as their only common language. Therefore, the model of English represented by such contact is unlikely to be identical to the standard British or American models that the speakers have studied.

Whatever the nature and degree of their motivation, Japanese adults bring to the classroom many preconceptions of how a language should be learned. These ideas, perhaps stemming from prior school experience, usually demand translation, memorization, and tedious pattern practice. This "no pain, no gain" attitude frequently results in high anxiety levels, a factor which further hinders the development of oral communication skills among language learners.

It is within this context of language learning and teaching in Japan that I have found games to be an effective strategy for developing communicative competence. Not only do games provide for growth in various competence areas (strategic, grammatical, sociolinguistic, and discourse), they also help the learners to relax and to focus on content, rather than on the task of language learning. Relaxation and focus on content are effective tools in helping learners make the transition from language as an academic subject to be studied and practiced (i.e., endured) to language as a vehicle for communication. This transition is essential to building the communicative *confidence* that leads to communicative competence (Savignon 1983).

WHAT GAMES ARE (AND WHAT THEY AREN'T)

To determine exactly what is meant by "games," it is useful to consider one available definition. Gibbs (1978:60) has defined games as "activit[ies] carried out by cooperating or competing decision-makers, seeking to achieve, within a set of rules, their objectives."

Let's look at the four major elements of this definition in turn:

1. *Activity.* By definition, games are active. This activity may be physical or mental. In terms of language teaching, whether it be expressive or interpretive, it occurs necessarily in the present.

2. *Carried out by cooperating or competing decision makers.* Certainly there are occasions when a game is entirely cooperative, but in a far more common model, a pair or a small group cooperates in the decision making process as a team while competing against other teams.

3. *Seeking to achieve . . . objectives.* This element is essential. A group that is not working together toward a specific goal is merely engaging in a practice session. Group cohesiveness provides the motivation for language use and forms the basis for games in the language classroom.

4. *Within a set of rules.* Certainly the specificity and complexity of these rules will vary with the learners' ability, and with the purpose and complexity of the game; yet, it is the existence of rules that differentiates a game from play (Rixon 1981).

Although this definition provides a basis for understanding what a game is or is not, it neglects two essential variables. According to this definition, the activity of two people baking a cake could be considered a game since it involves people cooperating and making decisions in an effort to reach a goal by following prescribed guidelines. The missing variables, both essential for participation in a game, are the elements of chance and enjoyment.

While acknowledgement of the fact that decisions imply some risks constitutes an allusion to the element of chance, this factor is so essential in games that it requires explicit mention. Participation in a game is satisfying and challenging precisely because some essential piece of information is either initially unknown to all players or is not made known to all of the players at the same time, and so therefore something unanticipated may occur at any time.

The second missing element, the enjoyment factor, may be as obvious as it is difficult to quantify. However, it plays a critical role in lowering the anxiety level of the learners, thereby helping them to focus their attention on the game itself, and not on language skills per se. If a given activity meets all other criteria and is enjoyable for one group of learners, it is indeed a game. However, if the same activity is not enjoyable to another group, it is not a game but simply a source of boredom, hard work, or even frustration. Any game to be played in class must be selected with learner preferences in mind. In some cases, this means simply noting the types of activities that a particular class enjoys. In other situations, more effort is involved. It is sometimes necessary to orient the learner toward playing games as a means of language development. For example, because they believe that language study is inherently hard work, many Japanese consider enjoyable activities to be of little or no value.

In light of these factors, we can amend Gibbs' definition to read: games are enjoyable activities that involve an element of chance and are carried out by cooperating or competing decision makers seeking to achieve, within a set of rules, their objectives.

Having achieved a basic understanding of the elements of a game, we must now consider those factors that make a particular game well-suited to a given class. Wright (1982) identified five essential criteria: (1) ease of preparation: the time and energy required to make the game is realistic; (2) ease of organization: using the game is easy and/or worth the effort; (3) intrinsic language: language must be used to play the game successfully and that same language must be useful in other situations; (4) density of language: while chess, for example, is a wonderful game, it requires so little language that it is virtually useless in the language classroom (Rixon 1981), and (5) likelihood of interest for the learners.

With regard to learner interest, it should be noted that affective variables that go beyond the content of the game itself may be involved. Cultural factors may also come into play. For example, games that require a great deal of physical contact between players may be a bit unsettling for learners who have been taught to behave in a reserved manner. Furthermore, the style of play and the behavior of players may be culturally unique, as the following anecdote illustrates. Recently, several language teachers engaged in a rousing game of *Trivial Pursuit* at a party. As American game players typically do, these teachers expressed a great deal of emotion not only through words, but also through gestures and other nonverbal means of communication. After the game, one Japanese guest at the party said, "I really don't know why you like that game. You all get so angry when you play." Typical American game behavior was interpreted as anger and aggression, rather than pleasure and enthusiasm. The point here is certainly not that games which are likely to introduce culture-specific information and behavior should be avoided. Rather, those factors that may be either part of or foreign to a specific culture should be noted and, when necessary, dealt with explicitly, since they are variables that affect the students' response to the game.

WHY GAMES WORK

Now that a definition of games has been established, it is useful to consider three reasons why they work. First of all, the very structure of games provides an opportunity for learners to practice vocabulary, grammar, specific language functions and other language arts skills.[1] But it is the fact that the learners are using these features of language with a purpose that makes game playing worthwhile. The task orientation of the game requires that students "use [rather than merely practice] language for real and immediate communicative goals" (Savignon 1983:196).

Games contrast favorably with standard multiple slot substitution drills such as the following:

Teacher: Would you like to go to a *movie* on *Saturday*?

Students: Would you like to go to a movie on Saturday?

Teacher: Restaurant, Thursday.

Students: Would you like to go to a restaurant on Thursday?

Certainly submitting the learners to such drills is a simple matter. However, the problem with these drills is that they do not provide the learners any particular reason for the required utterance. The invitations are fictitious, so even if the learners are encouraged to issue them to one another, they have no reason to listen for the response. Games, on the other hand, require constant, meaningful interaction among the players.

A second reason why games work is that they create a relaxed atmosphere. This lowers the anxiety level or "affective filter," that often keeps students from learning. Games accomplish this in two ways. First, games focus the learners' attention on the immediate goal, that is, succeeding at the game itself, rather than on the responsibility of language learning (Stevick 1982). The learners are concerned with playing the game, not with the structures or functions of language. Second, whether the game is competitive or not, it requires cooperation. This contributes to the development of a sense of group that leads in turn to a feeling of support and security among the group members. As a result, the learners are less anxious and more open and able to communicate.

Finally, games offer a strategy for dealing with problems that may arise from code simplification. Code simplification is often used by teachers to provide communication at a level the learners can understand. Krashen (1981) has proposed that communicating with learners in language slightly beyond their current level of competence will enhance their development of L2 competence. However, this proposal presents certain problems in the classroom. Typically, the proficiency level of any given class is relatively homogenous in terms of grammar recognition and usage, which represent a limited aspect of communicative ability. Nevertheless, this sense of homogeneity is misleading since learners bring to the class different experiences, interests, and abilities that affect the rate and nature of their individual development. The problem these differences can create is illustrated by examining a typical class of a dozen learners, all of whom were determined by the results of oral interviews to be at the high beginner level. Class members included a number of full-time university students and office workers, an electrical engineer, a gynecologist, a metallurgy professor, and a mechanic. Several had visited the United States either on business or for a holiday. Despite the apparent homogeneity of proficiency levels, each class member brought unique strengths and weaknesses to the group.

Learner A is a doctor. She frequently participates in medical conferences conducted in English. An avid tennis player, she follows international tennis news regularly. Her professional and personal interests have led to a more developed vocabulary in those areas. Thus, she is able to discuss them at a more advanced level than other topics. Learner A's knowledge of vocabulary in these specific areas is represented in Figure 1 by a graph that resembles a city skyline. Given this "skyline," if the teacher were to work one-to-one with Learner A, it would be possible to modify the degree of code simplification constantly to provide language slightly above the learner's level.

However, a problem arises in a class where each learner has a different skyline. When several learners' graphs for knowledge of vocabulary are juxtaposed (Fig. 2), we see that for any given topic there will be a range of abilities. To be understood, the teacher necessarily speaks at the level that will be accessible to those learners with the least ability in a given area. Assuming that learners can understand language at approximately one class level higher than their own (e.g., a high beginner can understand low intermediate language), the teacher's speaking level approximates the class mean. Given a normal distribution, the teacher's language represents a level of competence that is appropriate for approximately 20 percent of the class. The other learners are simply listening to language at or below their current level of competence.

This "juxtaposed skyline" analogy highlights the problems associated with code simplification in a typical class and also suggests a solution. While the teacher may be unable consistently to use language at the level of competence learners wish eventually to achieve, the learners, by virtue of their slightly higher competence on specific topics, naturally provide language at the desired level. Pair work and small groups offer excellent opportunities to exploit this situation. For example, in a class activity in which learners describe physical ailments and offer advice or solutions (see Three Problems, page 223), Learner A, the doctor, is in an ideal position to provide the vocabulary her partners need. When speaking, for example, to the engineer (Learner C), Learner A simplifies her language so that communication can continue. But when she speaks to Learner B, Learner A simplifies her language less. If the group works on the language of sequencing and process, the engineer's competence will be superior to that of the doctor, who has less experience with this terminology.

While lexical areas are perhaps the easiest to chart in the form of skylines, specialized competence also occurs in other areas. Hotel clerks tend to do very well on functions related to their jobs (asking about preferences, confirming requests). Learners with post-secondary education generally have a greater degree of grammatical competence than their peers, even though their overall communicative abilities are generally the

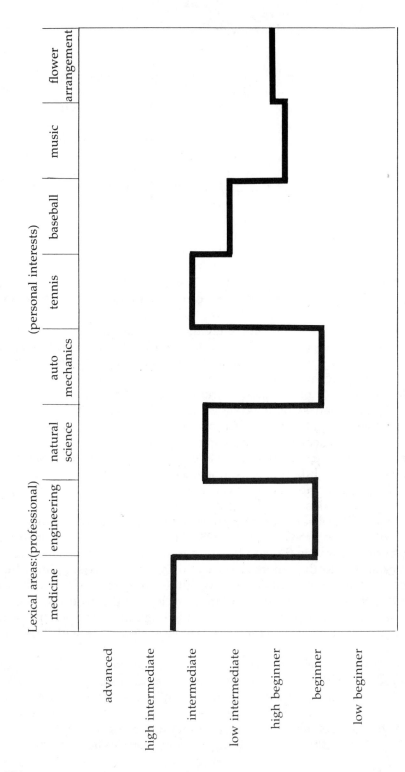

Figure 1. *Lexical levels by content area of Learner A*

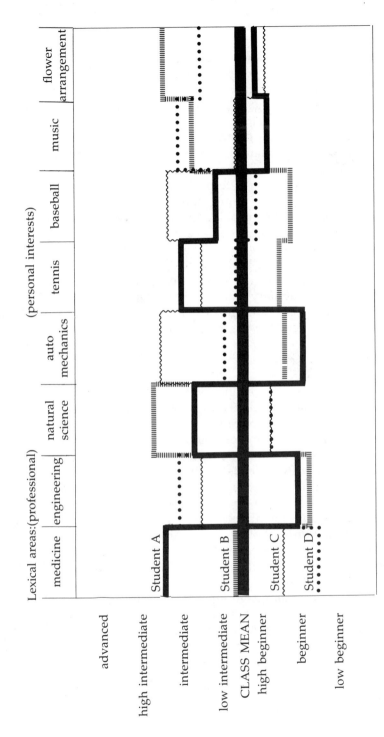

Figure 2. *Lexical levels by content area of four learners.*

215

same. Learners who have traveled abroad or who regularly meet native speakers often demonstrate greater strategic competence than those who have not had this experience.

Having discussed why games work, we can now turn our attention to several games. Any selection of games is necessarily limited and to some degree arbitrary. Most of the games suggested here were selected as means of developing language arts skills, particularly in the areas of vocabulary and structure, in a communicative context. The others were selected because they offer ways to personalize activities by giving learners input into the creation of game materials. I have found all of these games effective because they provide the learners with a communicative purpose and because the language developed through the games is useful outside the classroom. The games have all been used repeatedly with adult learners of a variety of backgrounds.

Three types of games will be considered: vocabulary, pair, and small group games. The vocabulary games may be used at any level. The specific pair and small group games presented are designed for beginning learners, but the models may be adapted for any level.

VOCABULARY GAMES

Perhaps more than any other single component, vocabulary is the "stuff" of language development. Even the most elementary learners, who know only a handful of structures or can carry out only a few functions, need large vocabularies in order to communicate. As the experiences of the learners with different skylines demonstrate, only interaction with others, or true communication, leads to the development of communicative competence. The foreign language classroom is usually rich with new vocabulary, introduced either by the teacher or by another learner, particularly when the class members are false beginners who, despite years of grammar-translation schooling, are unable to participate in a conversation if the subject is more complex than the color of pens.

Often when new vocabulary is introduced, the teacher writes the word on the board, the learners faithfully copy it into their notebooks (along with the native language equivalent), and teacher and learners turn their attention to the next classroom activity. As a result, the word is lost as quickly as it was found. Vocabulary games are one way of ensuring that new vocabulary is not lost, but that it is recycled until it is readily accessible to the learners. Though vocabulary games may take many forms, each of those described here involves the use of index cards.[2]

A large proportion of the vocabulary imposed by the teacher is likely to be either irrelevant or presented in frustrating quantities (e.g., "Today we're going to describe our houses. Here is a list of 45 adjectives."). The vocabulary items I identify for use in games tend to be those generated by the class members. Learner-generated vocabulary (i.e., vocabulary used first by a member of the class or supplied by the teacher in response to a learner's needs) is more likely to be remembered since it has fulfilled and can continue to fulfill a communicative requirement.

Slap. Depending on class size, between 20–40 cards, each with a different vocabulary item (e.g., "eggplant," "loan shark," "deposit," "withdrawal"), are placed face up on a table. Learners sit around the table, at arm's length from each card. One person chooses a word (e.g., "eggplant") and gives a clue as to which word was chosen (e.g., "It's a black vegetable"). The first person to identify the word calls it out, slaps the card, and collects it if the answer is correct. That player then chooses the next word and provides a clue. Players should try to give clues that are specific enough so that only one displayed word will fit the description. For example, the clue "money" could be associated with "loan shark," "deposit," or "withdrawal" and is thus too general. "I want to take some money out of the bank" is a better clue because it is related more directly to the desired target word. Slapping the card adds a physical component to the game, and also makes clear who found the correct word first. The player who collects the most cards wins. *Time:* 5–10 minutes.

Hint. This game is similar to *Slap,* except that it is played in pairs and the players do not see all of the words on the cards. Each pair receives a total of 15 cards, placed face-down on the table. The partners then take six cards each, without showing them to one another. The remaining three cards are placed face down between them in a pile. Players who have received unfamiliar words may exchange them for words from this pile at any point in the game. Player A looks at a card and gives player B a clue. B guesses what word is on A's card. If B's guess is correct, B wins the card from A, chooses a card and gives A a clue concerning the word chosen. If B guesses incorrectly, A gives another clue. The game continues in this manner until one team has correctly identified 12 words. *Time:* 5–10 minutes.

Dictionary. Each pair receives five cards. The object of the game is to create a dictionary-like definition for the words on the cards as quickly as possible. In the case of words with multiple meanings, players may use any of the accepted definitions. It may be useful to provide the following formula before the game begins:

Formula:

target word:	member of group *X*	*wh*-word	characteristics that distinguish this word from other members of group *X*

Example:

Loan shark:	*a money lender*	*who*	*charges very high interest rates*

This particular game is especially useful in technical ESP classes whose members will later have to teach processes and procedures to engineers from abroad. *Time:* 5–15 minutes.

Three card draw. Each pair selects a specified number of cards without looking at the words they contain. The pair is then given two or three minutes during which to create a short story using all three words. To encourage longer stories and less forced sentences, only one target word should be permitted to appear in a single sentence. Finally, each story is either read or pantomimed before the rest of the class. If the story is pantomimed, the class should be asked to guess the plot and the words that appeared on the team's cards. Note that while this game has no specific winner, it still qualifies as a game under our definition because the element of chance in selecting the words and guessing the plot contributes to motivation and enjoyment. *Time:* 10–15 minutes.

PAIR GAMES

Among the most useful of all game configurations are pairs. Pairs are particularly effective for games based on the principle of the information gap, in which one person possesses information that another person wants or needs. The usefulness of this strategy is twofold: (1) the density of the language involved requires learners to spend approximately 50 percent of their time interpreting and negotiating information, and the other 50 percent expressing information; and (2) the one-to-one situation focuses the learners' attention on being understood by a single individual and thus, allows for more finely tuned communication.

An abundance of pair work activities not originally designed as games can qualify as such if a time or pressure element is added to increase motivation and involvement in the activity. However, the teacher must be aware that such constraints can create frustration among the less able learners, often the very individuals who would benefit most from the activity. A more successful adaptation involves the insertion of an element of chance, e.g., the luck of the draw in a card game. While a time limit is included in the games presented here, note that it is not the primary game variable, but merely a guideline for the teacher.

The information gap has become a standard feature in communicative classrooms.[3] It is an effective tool because it clearly demonstrates to the learners both the specific task to be accomplished and also their measure of success in completing the task. This kind of feedback goes a long way toward building communicative confidence. An information gap activity may be converted into a game by adding an element of chance, an important feature of the *Map Gap*.

Double play map gap. (See Figure 3.) Traditionally, this game is played in pairs. Each partner holds the same map, but on each map different buildings have been labeled. The buildings labeled on one player's map are listed at the bottom of the other player's map and vice versa. One partner initiates play by asking, for example, "How do I get to the sta-

DUET-B   **HOW DO I GET TO . . .?**

Excuse me.	Is there	a hardware store near here?	Yes, there is.
			No, there isn't.
	How do I get to Where's	the First National Bank? Uno's Pizza?	
Go down Follow Take	River Road this street that street the second street	to across past	Second Street. the river. Hardy Street. the park.
Turn		right. left.	
It's	on the corner. on the right. the second building on the left. on River Road. on the northeast / southwest corner of River Road and Hardy Street.		

Here are the names of three businesses:
Softwrite Stationery Store/Stewarts Department Store/First National Bank
Choose three locations on the map and *WRITE THE NAME OF EACH BUSINESS* on the map. (Use only the *WHITE AREA;* do not write in the gray area.)

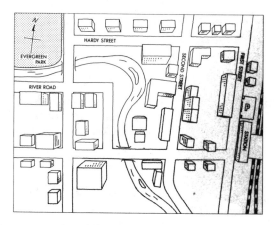

You are in *EVERGREEN PARK*. You would like to go to the following places:

___ the TBS Building   ___ a bakery   ___ Uno's Pizza Palace

Ask your partner for directions. Write the names on the correct buildings. Take turns.

(*Source:* M. Helgesen, T. S. Mandeville, and R. Jordan. *English Firsthand.* Ann Arbor, Mich.: Lateral Communication, 1986.)

Figure 3. *Double-play map gap.*

tionery store?" The other partner then gives directions that enable the first player to label the correct building "stationery store." Partners take turns asking directions and labeling buildings. *Time:* 20–25 minutes.

This version of the activity provides an excellent opportunity for communication, and it can easily be made into a game with the addition of a die. The students number the desired locations. On the die, "one" and "four" represent "location one," "two" and "five" represent location "two" and "three" and "six" stand for location "three." The same language is used, but requiring the players to roll the number of each shop in order to ask directions adds uncertainty and increases the challenge. By deciding which store is which the learners also play a direct role in creating the materials for the game. As a result, learners become a part of the entire process and feel an increased interest and sense of involvement in the activity.

GROUP GAMES

Group games offer the same advantages as pair games, plus the bonus of interaction with a greater number of people and exposure to a wider range of ideas and viewpoints, as well as a variety of pronunciations of English. However, the teacher must be aware of the possibility that one or two individuals may dominate the game and thereby make it less interesting and/or more frustrating for the others. In group games such as

20 Questions in which one individual addresses the entire group, the time all other individuals spend speaking is quite limited. For that reason, group games consisting of a series of pair interactions are preferable because each individual interacts first with one partner at a time and repeatedly changes partners.

The following games follow this model:

Heads or tails. For this game each pair needs a coin. The coin's head and tail (or in Japan, the Meiji Shrine and the number ten) represent "yes" and "no" respectively. Learners make a list of ten events and take turns inviting their partners to these events, one at a time. The invited player tosses the coin, and the result of the toss determines whether the player accepts or declines the invitation. Learners record the number of invitations accepted, and the player with the most acceptances wins. In the group version of this game, individual learners issue ten invitations to ten different players. This provides everyone with the opportunity to interact with a variety of partners. *Time:* 3–5 minutes.

Shop talk. (See Figure 4.) This game focuses on language use in situations in which learners need to ask for specific items or information. The class is divided into two groups, a group of customers and a group of store clerks. All members of each group receive a sheet of instructions containing a list of items in a variety of styles. The groups read their respective instructions, select individually one style of each item, and mark the information on their sheet. The clerks set a price for each item and log this information on their sheets as well. The shoppers ask the clerks for specific items in the styles marked on their sheets. If a clerk has the item in the exact style required the transaction continues. If the shopper decides to buy the item, its price is entered on the shopper's list. The shopper can purchase only one item from each clerk. (If class size does not permit this stipulation, the shopper can buy a second item from the same clerk but only after purchasing an item from another clerk.) If the first item requested from a given clerk is not available (i.e., the clerk does not carry that pattern), the shopper may request another item of the same clerk. Frequently, learners attempt to speed up the buying process by asking, for example, "Do you have any checked coats?" This strategy is acceptable since the point of the activity is the using of English to satisfy one's needs. The winner is the shopper who buys the most items at the lowest cost in the allotted time. *Time:* 15–25 minutes.

It should be mentioned that the conversation block at the top of Figure 4 is provided for those learners who may need some support at the beginning of the game. Because the language it supplies is so simple, those who choose initially to use it quickly abandon it.

SHOP TALK

SHOPPER			STORE CLERK				
I'm looking for a	jacket. shirt.	What	kind color size	do you want?			
Do you have any	skirts? suits?					SHOPPER	
Checked, Yellow, Size 28,	please.	Here you are.				Thank you.	
		Sorry, we don't have any	checked ones. yellow ones. size 28's.			Thanks anyway.	
How much	is it?	It's	$17.50.				
	are they?	They're					
I'll take	it. them.						
I think I'll look some more.							

Work as a large group (8 or more, if possible).
You are in a clothing store. Some of you are shoppers and some of you are store clerks.
Read your "role card" (for *SHOPPER* or *STORE CLERK*). Then begin.

SHOPPERS

You should try to buy as many pieces of clothing as you can.

Decide the items and the *STYLE* or *PATTERN* of the items you would like.

Circle your choices under the pictures of the items.

You must select each item from a different clerk. When you select an item, *WRITE THE PRICE ON THE PRICE TAG.*

You can spend only $100. Try to buy as many items as you can.

STORE CLERKS

You should try to sell as many of your items as you can.

Your store has *ONLY ONE STYLE OR PATTERN* for each item.

CIRCLE the style or pattern that you have.

Then write the price for each item.

When a shopper comes to you, say, "May I help you?"

coat
checked/solid

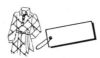

dress
striped/plaid

jacket
leather/down

necktie
solid/striped

Figure 4. *Shop talk.*

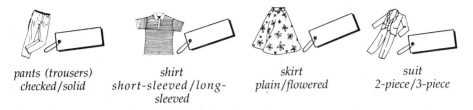

| pants (trousers) | shirt | skirt | suit |
| checked/solid | short-sleeved/long-sleeved | plain/flowered | 2-piece/3-piece |

How many items did you buy? ___Who bought the most items? ___

Which clerk had the lowest prices? _____

(*Source:* M. Helgesen, T. S. Mandeville, and R. Jordan. *English Firsthand.* Ann Arbor, Mich.: Lateral Communications, 1986.)

Figure 4. *Continued*

The "talk and listen" technique (Via 1976) is especially effective preparation for this activity although teachers will find it useful with other games as well. In this technique, two parts of a dialog are written on separate sheets of paper. Often each part of the dialog offers more than one option as a response. Pairs of learners then reproduce the dialog. They may refer to the text as often as they like, but whenever they speak, they must make eye contact with their partner. The issue of eye contact is important in working with Japanese language learners. Contrary to the stereotype, Japanese do make strong eye contact during informal conversations. It is in very formal situations or in interaction with someone of a clearly higher rank that strong eye contact is considered rude. Therefore, the "talk and listen" technique gives learners the opportunity to practice making eye contact in this latter type of situation when speaking English. This technique is also effective because learners are alerted by facial expressions to their partners' understanding or lack of it.

Three problems. Although originally designed for dealing with physical ailments (Schwartz 1983), this game is useful for developing the ability to describe problems and to ask for and offer solutions.

Each player folds a sheet of paper twice, first in half, then in thirds. In the top three boxes on the folded sheet, they write a physical ailment (e.g., a broken arm, a hangover, a burn). In the remaining three boxes, they write possible remedies or courses of action (e.g., go to the hospital, take some aspirin, apply cold water). The boxes are then torn along the fold lines, separated into problems and solutions, and given to the teacher or another designated individual. The problem and solution stacks are each shuffled and one problem and one solution are given to each player. Players must then talk to other players and find a solution to their problem. For example, the person with the burn may say, "I burned myself. What should I do?" If the player to whom this person has spoken has the appropriate remedy, (s)he will suggest, "How about applying cold water to it?" The partner with the ailment collects that solution and each partner receives a new problem or solution from the teacher. If the player to whom the problem is presented does not have the appropriate solution, an acceptable response is: "Sorry, I don't know what to do." The afflicted player then moves on to a new partner. The player who collects the most matches of problems and solutions wins. It should be noted that "You should go to the hospital" is an appropriate suggestion for any particular problem. Also, any proposed solution that a player can justify is acceptable. *Time:* 20–30 minutes.

CONCLUSION

I began this article with the claim that language development is itself a game because it meets the defined criteria: It is an active process; whether cooperating or competing, learners are decision makers; there is always an objective, a reason for speaking/listening; there are rules (grammatical, social, etc.); and there is always a significant element of chance, an opportunity to connect or to miss the mark. And if all goes well, language learning is fun.

I have offered a definition of games, a rationale for their use, and examples of some games I have found useful and successful in the classroom. However, I would like to emphasize that I do not view games, in and of themselves, as the definitive answer to the complex problems inherent in teaching and learning languages. Instead, games are a tool that can allow learners to learn language. Furthermore, and perhaps more importantly, they enable learners to use freely the language they are learning, and at the same time, to enjoy themselves because they are playing the real game: communication.

NOTES

1. A discussion of the role of language arts activities in the curriculum and additional suggestions for activities can be found in Savignon 1983.

2. For an excellent method of using vocabulary word cards for self-study, see Stevick (1982). Other vocabulary games are available in Bamford 1982 and Helgesen 1984.

3. For other examples of information gaps, see Watcyn-Jones 1981 and Olsen (1977).

REFERENCES

Bamford, J. 1982. "Vocabulary Building Using Index Cards." *The JALT Newsletter* 9:22–23.

Gibbs, G. 1978. *Dictionary of Gaming, Modelling and Simulation.* London: E. & F. Spon, Ltd.

*Helgesen, M. 1982. *Tricks for Individualizing EFL.* Washington. D.C.: U.S. Information Agency.

———. 1984. "Card Tricks for Vocabulary Building." *The Language Teacher* 6:35.

Kahn, H. 1971. *The Emerging Japanese Superstate.* Englewood Cliffs, N.J.: Prentice-Hall.

Krashen, S. 1981. *Second Language Acquisition and Second Language Learning.* Oxford: Pergamon Press.

*Lee, W. 1979. *Language Teaching Games.* Oxford: Oxford University Press. Second edition.

*Maley, A. and A. Duff. 1982. *Drama Techniques in Language Learning.* Cambridge: Cambridge University Press. Second edition.

*Olsen, J. 1977. *Communication Starters.* San Francisco: Alemany Press.

*Rixon, S. 1981. *How to Use Games in Language Teaching.* London: Macmillan.

Savignon, S. 1983. *Communicative Competence: Theory and Classroom Practice.* Reading, Mass.: Addison-Wesley.

Schwartz, J. 1983. "Games." Workshop presented at the January 1983 meeting of the Japan Association of Language Teachers, Tohoku.

Stevick, E. 1980. *A Way and Ways.* Rowley, MA: Newbury House.

———. 1982. *Teaching and Learning Languages.* Cambridge: Cambridge University Press.

Taira, T., and J. Sasaki. 1983. *The Ideal and the Real: English Language Education in Japan.* Tokyo: Kirihara Shoten.

Via, R. 1976. *English in Three Acts.* Honolulu: University of Hawaii Press.

Watcyn-Jones, P. 1981. *Pair Work.* Middlesex: Penguin.

Wright, A. 1982. "Games, Work and Language Learning." Paper presented at the 1982 Japan Association of Language Teachers Conference.

Wright, A., D. Betteridge, and M. Buckby. 1980. *Games for Language Learning.* Cambridge: Cambridge University Press.

---

*Game sourcebooks.

Glossary

ACHIEVEMENT TEST. A test that is based on the instructional content of a particular course or curriculum. Cf. PROFICIENCY TEST.

ACTFL. American Council on the Teaching of Foreign Languages, a professional organization.

AFFECTIVE (VARIABLES). Related to feelings and emotions; attitudinal, motivational, and personality factors in second language acquisition.

ALLOMORPH. A term used in structural linguistics to refer to a variant of an identified morpheme; that is, a morpheme may have two or more allomorphs, depending on the context in which it appears. The morpheme that expresses plurality in English, for example, appears in several variants: *hat-hats* /s/, *song-songs* /z/, *purse-purses* /əz/, etc.

ALLOPHONE.. A term used in structural linguistics to refer to a variant of an identified phoneme; that is, a phoneme may have two or more allophones, depending on the particular phonetic shape it takes in a given context. The English phoneme /t/, for example, includes the variants that occur in *eight* and *eighth*. Cf. PHONEME.

A-LM. *Audio-Lingual Materials* and, by extension, the audiolingual methods these materials promoted. Cf. AUDIOLINGUALISM.

ANOMIE. A feeling of social alienation, of not belonging to a cultural group.

APHASIA. Impairment or loss of the ability to use or understand spoken or written language as a result of brain injury or disease.

APPROACH. A set of assumptions about the nature of language and the nature of language teaching and learning; a philosophy or point of view. Cf. METHOD (OF TEACHING).

APTITUDE. Capability; innate or acquired capacity for something; an indication of the degree of success a learner is likely to have in a given educational setting.

ARELS. Association of Recognised English Language Schools, a British association of government approved private language schools.

ASTP. Army Specialized Training Program, an intensive language training program established in the United States during World War II.

ATTITUDE. A position that may be either physical, mental, or emotional; in relation to L2 learning, includes conscious mental position as well as a full range of often subconscious feelings or emotions.

AUDIOLINGUALISM. A language teaching approach based on structural linguistic theory and behaviorist psychology; methods of teaching language that emphasize habit formation and the production of error-free utterances.

BEHAVIORISM. A psychological theory that regards objective and observable facts of behavior or activity as the only proper subject for psychological study. An example is the stimulus-response theory of animal and human behavior elaborated in particular by B. F. Skinner and criticized subsequently by cognitive psychologists. Cf. COGNITIVE PSYCHOLOGY.

BILINGUAL EDUCATION. An educational program in which two or more languages are used in instruction.

BILINGUALISM. The use of two languages by an individual or by a social group. Cf. MULTILINGUALISM.

BODY LANGUAGE. *See* KINESICS.

BOTTOM-UP PROCESSING. A mode of processing information involving the use of specific features of the input data to build up meaning. Meaning is then checked against more general expectations. Also called data-driven processing. Cf. TOP-DOWN PROCESSING, INTERACTIVE PROCESSING.

CAPITAL-C CULTURE. The literary and artistic masterpieces of a civilization; major historical events. Cf. SMALL-C CULTURE.

CHANNEL. The form of communication, for example, spoken or written language, telegraphic signals, gestures (sign language).

CLOZE. The replacement of systematic deletions in a passage, proposed as a measure of the intelligibility or readability of texts and, subsequently, as a test of language proficiency.

CODE. A system of signs and/or signals used in communication.

CODE MIXING. The systemic mixing of linguistic units (words, idioms, and clauses) from two or more languages or language varieties in the course of a speech act or language activity.

CODE SIMPLIFICATION. Deviation from standard adult linguistic norms by a speaker or writer in an attempt to facilitate communications with a listener or reader presumed to be unfamiliar with these norms (e.g., a child, a foreigner).

CODE SWITCHING. Changing from one language or language variety to another in the course of a language activity.

COGNITIVE. Pertaining to the mental functions involved in perceiving, knowing, and understanding.

COGNITIVE PSYCHOLOGY. The study of mental states through inference from behavior. Cf. BEHAVIORISM.

COHERENCE. Ideas within a text; semantic links provided by meaning.

COHESION. The relationship of one linguistic item to another in a text; relations of meaning that exist within a text and that define it as a text; a means of achieving textual coherence. Cf. COHERENCE.

COMMEDIA DELL'ARTE. Italian popular comedy, developed during the sixteenth to eighteenth centuries, in which actors improvised from a basic plot outline; improvisation on a theme.

COMMUNICATIVE COMPETENCE. Functional language proficiency; the expression, interpretation, and negotiation of meaning involving interaction between two or more persons belonging to the same (or different) speech community (communities), or between one person and a written or oral text. Cf. LINGUISTIC COMPETENCE.

COMPETENCE/PERFORMANCE. A dichotomy proposed by Chomsky to distinguish between what an ideal hearer or speaker knows about the structure of his or her native language (competence) and the manifestation of this knowledge in actual language use (performance).

CONCEPTUAL LEVEL. A measure of an individual's cognitive complexity and interpersonal maturity.

CONSTRUCT. A mental ability, trait, or competence that is part of a theory of what it is that a test is supposed to measure. Cf. TRAIT.

CONTENT SCHEMA. Prior background knowledge of the content area of a text or discourse. Cf. FORMAL SCHEMA, SCHEMA.

CONTEXT OF SITUATION. Establishes the rules of appropriateness for the behavior of participants in a language event on the basis of who they are, where they are, and why they have come together, and gives meaning to that behavior.

CONTRASTIVE ANALYSIS (CA). The systematic comparison of structural features of two or more languages or language varieties.

CORRELATION. A systematic relationship between two or more observed variables without necessarily implying a cause and effect relationship.

CRITERION-REFERENCED TEST. Goal-referenced test; the evaluation of test takers in relation to their ability to achieve a particular level of performance, that is, a criterion; results are often expressed in terms of the percentage of correct answers in relation to the total number of items on the test. Cf. NORM-REFERENCED TEST.

CROSS-SECTIONAL (STUDIES OF L1/L2 ACQUISITION). Observation and comparison at a given time of the language performance of different groups representing different levels of development and/or contexts of acquisition. Cf. LONGITUDINAL.

CULTURE. See CAPITAL-C CULTURE and SMALL-C CULTURE.

CURRICULUM. A statement of both the content and process of teaching for a course or sequence of courses; a guide to selection of items and activities (British: syllabus); all educational experiences for which the school is responsible. Cf. SYLLABUS.

DEDUCTIVE. Refers to a method or approach to language teaching that reasons from general rules to particular cases; exposition of rules or principles. Cf. INDUCTIVE.

DEEP STRUCTURE. A term used in transformational-generative linguistic theory to refer to the sentence-level grammatical interpretation of surface structures. Cf. SURFACE STRUCTURE.

DIACHRONIC. See LONGITUDINAL.

DIALECT. A regional or social variety of a language distinguished from other varieties by features of pronunciation, grammar, or vocabulary; a variety of language defined in terms of the *user* (e.g., social class, caste, religion). Cf. REGISTER, VARIETY.

DIRECT METHOD. A language teaching method that makes exclusive use of the L2 without recourse to the learner's native language; inspired by the Natural Method but with claims for a more systematic approach to problems of L2 learning, particularly phonological; an American adaptation of this method is known as the "Cleveland Plan" by de Sauzé. Cf. NATURAL METHOD.

DISCOURSE. Connected speech or writing that extends beyond a single sentence or utterance.

DISCOURSE ANALYSIS. Analysis of connected speech or writing that extends beyond a single sentence or utterance; study of the pragmatic functions of language.

DISCOURSE COMPETENCE. The ability to recognize different patterns of discourse, to connect sentences or utterances to an overall theme or topic; the ability to infer the meaning of large units of spoken or written texts.

DISCRETE-POINT LANGUAGE TESTING. Separate assessment of isolated formal features of language; use of discrete-point response types (multiple choice, true-false, etc.). Cf. INTEGRATIVE LANGUAGE TESTING.

EGO PERMEABILITY. The permeability of a person's ego boundaries; the ease with which a person is able to acquire a new self-identification.

EMPATHY. A capacity for participation in another's feelings or ideas.

EMPOWERMENT. A term used in the educational context to describe the process of liberating learners from external controls to reflect on the forces that contribute to the problem solving and decision making processes.

Empowerment often leads to transformation of social and political environments so that they may better meet individual and community needs.

ERROR. A form that deviates from some selected norm of adult language performance; deviation from a prescriptive norm. Cf. GRAMMAR.

ERROR ANALYSIS. A listing or classification of learner errors.

ESL. English as a second language; teaching of English to nonnative speakers.

ESP. English for Specific (Special) Purposes, (e.g., academic purposes, science and technology); a component of ESL.

ETHNOGRAPHY. A field of study concerned with the description and analysis of culture.

ETHNOGRAPHY OF COMMUNICATION. A field of study that looks at the norms of communicative conduct in different communities from a multidisciplinary perspective as well as methods for studying these norms.

ETHNOMETHODOLOGY. A concentration on strategies of discourse interpretation.

ETS. Educational Testing Service, a developer and distributor of many large-scale standardized tests of aptitude, achievement, and proficiency, including the TOEFL.

EXTERNAL VALIDITY. The extent to which results of research or a test are generalizable to other groups and situations. Cf. VALIDITY.

FIELD DEPENDENCE/INDEPENDENCE. A measure of perceptual functioning indicating the extent to which a person is able to isolate elements from the context in which it appears.

FIRST LANGUAGE (L1). A language acquired in early childhood prior to, or simultaneously with, another language; native language; mother tongue; primary language.

FLES. Foreign languages in the elementary schools, a curricular development that gained momentum in the United States in the 1960s.

FOREIGNER TALK. Modifications (or simplifications) made in the speech of native speakers when conversing with nonnative speakers. Cf. CODE SIMPLIFICATION.

FORMAL SCHEMA. Prior background knowledge of the formal, rhetorical properties of a type of text or discourse. Cf. SCHEMA, CONTENT SCHEMA.

FOSSILIZATION. The process of stabilization in L2 acquisition whereby nonnative forms become a permanent feature of an individual's (or a group's) performance; the resistance of interlanguage features to further change. Cf. INTERLANGUAGE.

FSI. Foreign Service Institute, a U.S. government agency whose test of oral proficiency has been widely used in the Peace Corps and other language learning programs.

FUNCTION. The purpose of an utterance; the use to which a particular grammatical form is put (e.g., to request, to permit, to describe). Cf. ILLOCUTIONARY ACT, SPEECH ACT.

GLOBAL LANGUAGE TESTING. See INTEGRATIVE LANGUAGE TESTING.

GRAMMAR. A theory of language competence; rule-governed language behavior; any explicit characterization of language behavior (e.g., phase-structure grammar, transformational grammar, functional grammar); prescriptive norms, that is, a set of rules for "correct" or "proper" language usage, intended to preserve imagined standards and typically critical of socially stigmatized forms of the standard dialect. A PEDAGOGICAL GRAMMAR is a grammar intended for language teaching.

GRAMMATICAL COMPETENCE. Knowledge of the sentence structure of a language.

IDIOLECT. The linguistic system of an individual speaker.

ILLOCUTIONARY ACT. An act performed in saying something; function; speech act.

ILR. Interagency Language Roundtable, an association of U.S. governmental agencies (including the FSI) concerned with language training and testing.

IMMERSION. Use of the L2 as a means of communication with members of a surrounding community; participation in an L2 community as opposed to the classroom study of an L2 as a foreign language.

IMMERSION PROGRAM. An educational program for language acquisition in which the L2 is the medium of instruction; exclusive use of the L2 as a means of communication within the classroom or school.

INDUCTIVE. Refers to a method or approach to language teaching that proceeds from particular facts or examples to a general rule or principle; discovery learning. Cf. DEDUCTIVE.

INFERENCE. Interpretation of meaning based on assumptions regarding the context of a speech act.

INFORMATION GAP. A situation in which one participant in an exchange has information that others do not know and need to find out.

INSTRUMENTAL ORIENTATION. An orientation to L2 learning that emphasizes the utilitarian value of L2 proficiency such as getting a pay raise, a better job, or a good grade in school; the use of language as a tool for a specific goal (e.g., science, technology).

INTEGRATIVE LANGUAGE TESTING. Global assessment of effectiveness in terms of functional (semantic) criteria; use of an integrative response type (e.g., essay, interview, etc.). Cf. DISCRETE-POINT LANGUAGE TESTING.

INTEGRATIVE ORIENTATION. An orientation to L2 learning that reflects an openness toward another culture group and that may include a desire to be accepted as a member of that group.

INTERACTIVE PROCESSING. In reading, the constant switching back and forth between top-down and bottom-up processing of information currently viewed by theorists as the most effective and efficient type of processing.

INTERFERENCE. Presence of features of pronunciation, grammar, vocabulary that may be attributed to one's knowledge of another language. Cf. TRANSFER.

INTERLANGUAGE. The knowledge of an L2 that a language learner (user) has that approximates, but is not identical to, the knowledge of adult native speakers of the language; approximative system; a language system in transition; transitional competence.

INTEGRATIVE LANGUAGE TESTING. Global assessment of effectiveness in terms of functional (semantic) criteria; use of an integrative response type (e.g., essay, interview, etc.). Cf. DISCRETE-POINT LANGUAGE TESTING.

INTERFERENCE. Presence of features of pronunciation, grammar, vocabulary that may be attributed to one's knowledge of another language. Cf. TRANSFER.

INTERNAL VALIDITY. The extent to which the results of research or a test are affected by such factors as a decrease in the number of subjects or particular characteristics of the subjects. Cf. VALIDITY.

KINESICS. The study of body movements of all kinds including facial gestures, hand motions, leg movements, and shifts in overall posture; body language.

L1. *See* FIRST LANGUAGE.

L2. *See* SECOND LANGUAGE.

LANGUAGE FOR SPECIFIC PURPOSES (LSP). Instructional programs developed in response to specific adult professional, occupational or social needs, for example, English for Academic Purposes (EAP), English for Science and Technology (EST).

LANGUAGE LOSS. Attrition of language skills; forgetting a language through lack of use.

LATERALIZATION. Specialization of language function by one side (right or left) of the brain; cerebral dominance; loss of brain plasticity.

LEP.   Limited English Proficiency, a classification used in the description of the language skills of nonnative speakers of English in U.S. schools.

LEXICON.   The vocabulary of a language; a dictionary.

LINGUA FRANCA.   A language used for communication among speakers of different native languages.

LINGUISTIC COMPETENCE.   *See* GRAMMATICAL COMPETENCE.

LONGITUDINAL (STUDIES OF L1/L2 ACQUISITION).   Observation over time of the language performance of a single person or a group of persons with attention to changes that may occur. Cf. CROSS-SECTIONAL (STUDIES OF L1/L2 ACQUISITION).

MEAN.   Arithmetic average of a given set of values found by dividing the sum of the set by the number of values.

METALANGUAGE.   Language used to talk about language, (e.g., noun, verb, phoneme, speech act, cohesion).

METHOD (OF MEASUREMENT).   In testing, the technique used to measure a trait (e.g., multiple choice, interview, cloze). Cf. TRAIT.

METHOD (OF TEACHING).   Overall plan for the grading and presentation of material to be taught, based on an approach. Cf. APPROACH.

METHOD ACTING.   A theory and technique of acting in which the performer identifies with the character to be portrayed and renders the part in a naturalistic, individualized manner; the Stanislavski Method.

MLAT.   Modern Language Aptitude Test, best known example of a test designed to measure language learning aptitude.

MINIMAL PAIR.   Two words that sound alike in all but one distinguishing feature, denoting a difference in meaning, (e.g., *ship-sheep, cup-cop, watching-washing*). Cf. PHONEME.

MODULE.   An individual, multimedia teaching unit to supplement existing language programs. The unit may be content-based or activity-based.

MONITOR.   To give conscious attention to the form of linguistic production.

MORPHEME.   The smallest meaningful unit of a language; the smallest functioning unit in the composition of words. In English, for example, *unclaimed* consists of three morphemes: *un, claim,* and *ed.*

MORPHOLOGY.   The system of the word structure of a language; the study of the structure of words or word formation.

MOTIVATION.   Incentive, need, or desire.

MULTILINGUALISM.   The use of three or more languages by an individual or by a social group.

NATURAL METHOD. A language teaching method advocated in the nineteenth century, so called because its proponents claimed to follow the way in which children learn their native language, through conversation; characterized by a repudiation of books and grammar rules and the active demonstration of meaning through mime, gestures, and physical objects. Cf. DIRECT METHOD.

NDEA. National Defense Education Act, legislation passed in 1958 that gave support to foreign language study in U.S. secondary schools.

NEEDS ASSESSMENT. A survey of learner needs and interests as a basis for L2 curriculum and/or materials development.

NEGOTIATION. A process whereby a participant in a speech event uses various sources of information—prior experience, the context, another participant—to achieve understanding; the reciprocal efforts of conversational partners to maintain the flow of conversation; cooperation.

NEUROLINGUISTICS. Area of physiological research concerned with the relationship between human language and neural, or nerve, systems.

NEW KEY. A term used in the 1960s to refer to audiolingual methods of language teaching. Cf. AUDIOLINGUALISM.

NORMATIVE GROUP. A representative sample of the population for whom a test was developed (e.g., foreign student applicants, elementary school immersion students, native speakers).

NORMED-REFERENCED TEST. A standardized test that compares the performance of a test taker with the performance of a normative group and is designed to maximize individual differences. Results may be expressed in terms of a percentile rank. Cf. CRITERION-REFERENCED TEST.

NORMS. (1) In testing, the distribution of scores on a test; a descriptive framework for test score interpretation with reference to the characteristics of the normative group (e.g., age, grade level, sex, L1, etc.). Cf. NORMATIVE GROUP. (2) In linguistic theory, the standard practice in speech or writing with reference to a given speech community or a group within that community.

NOTION. A unit of meaning (e.g., time, space, quantity); a semantic unit.

NOTIONAL-FUNCTIONAL SYLLABUS. Organizes language content by semantic and functional categories within a general consideration of the communicative functions of language. Cf. SYLLABUS, PROCEDURAL-SYLLABUS, SITUATIONAL SYLLABUS, STRUCTURAL SYLLABUS.

PARALINGUISTIC. Pertaining to vocal signals or features outside the conventional linguistic channels (e.g., pitch, rate, volume, and nonspeech vocalizations such as laughter and coughs).

PHONEME. A minimum unit of speech sound that manifests differences in meaning, most often identified and represented through the contrast of words, or minimal pairs. In English, for example, the minimal pair *ship* and *sheep* may be used to demonstrate the distinction between the phonemes /I/ and /i/. Cf. MINIMAL PAIR.

PHONETICS. The science that studies human vocal sounds and the way they are produced (articulated) by the vocal organs.

PHONOLOGY. The sound system of a language.

PRAGMATICS. Concerned with the relationships between expressions in the formal system of language and anything else outside it; an interdisciplinary field of inquiry concerned with relations between linguistic units, speakers, and extralinguistic facts; roles and uses of language in social contexts; the science of language use.

PROCEDURAL SYLLABUS. Organizes the content of language teaching by tasks, or procedures, learners are to perform, rather than by discrete structural, semantic or functional categories of language. Cf. SYLLABUS, STRUCTURAL SYLLABUS, SITUATIONAL SYLLABUS, NOTIONAL-FUNCTIONAL SYLLABUS.

PROFICIENCY TEST. Any test that is based on a theory of the abilities required to use language. Cf. ACHIEVEMENT TEST.

PROXEMICS. Interpersonal space; the distance individuals stand or sit from one another.

PSYCHOMETRIC. Having to do with the measurement of psychological abilities or attributes and the statistical properties of such measurements.

RP. Received Pronunciation, the pronunciation traditionally characteristic of British public schools and the universities of Oxford and Cambridge.

REDUNDANCY. Repetition of subject matter already familiar to learners; availability of information from more than one source.

REGISTER. A special variety of language defined in term of its use in various professional contexts or settings (e.g., classroom, courtroom, pub, hospital); a variety of language defined in terms of its *use*. Cf. DIALECT, VARIETY.

RELIABILITY. The accuracy, consistency, or stability of the results (scores) of a test measurement.

SCHEMA (*pl.* SCHEMATA). A structured representation of knowledge stored in memory. Different schemata represent knowledge of various concepts: objects, situations, events, actions, sequences of events or actions, abstractions, linguistic objects, etc. Cf. CONTENT SCHEMA, FORMAL SCHEMA.

SECOND LANGUAGE (L2). A language learned after the basics of a first or primary language have been acquired; foreign language; "target" language.

SECOND LANGUAGE ACQUISITION. All nonnative language acquisition.

SEMANTIC(S). Pertaining to meaning in language; meaning; content.

SEMANTIC DIFFERENTIAL SCALE. A technique of attitude measurement in which respondents react to a concept or experience by placing an X along a series of bipolar response continuums, for example:

Father

happy ___: ___: _X_: ___: ___ sad
hard ___: _X_: ___: ___: ___ soft

SEMIOTICS. The study of both human and nonhuman signaling systems.

SIMULATION. Simplification of a real-world situation; a language learning activity that places learners in a situation or environment in which events and outcomes depend on their collective communicative competence.

SITUATIONAL SYLLABUS. Organizes language content according to situations or settings. Cf. SYLLABUS, STRUCTURAL SYLLABUS, NOTIONAL-FUNCTIONAL SYLLABUS, PROCEDURAL SYLLABUS.

SMALL-C CULTURE. Culture in an anthropological sense; the day-to-day living patterns of a group of people. Cf. CAPITAL-C CULTURE.

SOCIOLINGUISTIC COMPETENCE. The ability to use language appropriate to a given communicative context, taking into account the roles of the participants, the setting, and the purpose of the interaction.

SPEECH ACT. A functional unit of speech that derives its meaning not from grammatical form but from the rules of interpretation in a given speech community. Cf. FUNCTION, ILLOCUTIONARY ACT, INFERENCE.

STANDARD DEVIATION. A statistic that indicates the variability present in a group of measures (scores), based on the deviations of individual measures (scores) from the mean.

STRATEGIC COMPETENCE. The ability to compensate for imperfect knowledge of linguistic, sociolinguistic, and discourse rules or limiting factors in their application such as fatigue, distraction, inattention; the effective use of coping strategies to sustain or enhance communication.

STRATEGY. A particular method of approaching a problem or task; a mode of operation for achieving a particular goal.

STRUCTURALISM. An approach for the analysis and description of language; emphasizes the procedures by which linguistic items can be described as *structures* and *systems*. In the United States, this term is used with special reference to Bloomfield's emphasis on segmenting and classifying physical features of an utterance.

STRUCTURAL SYLLABUS. Organizes instructional material according to discrete structural, or formal, features of language. Cf. SYLLABUS, SITUATIONAL SYLLABUS, NOTIONAL-FUNCTIONAL SYLLABUS, PROCEDURAL SYLLABUS.

STYLE. Refers to the linguistic choices made by participants in a language activity, especially the level of formality (e.g., informal, formal).

STYLISTICS. A linguistically oriented approach to the analysis and description of situationally distinctive uses (varieties) of language; establishes principles and generalizations for the choices made by groups and individuals in their use of language; a school of literary criticism that attempts to go from a formal description of style to an interpretation of an author's personality or way of organizing experiences.

SURFACE STRUCTURE. The surface representation of a word or sound sequence with no reference to meaning or semantic value. Cf. DEEP STRUCTURE.

SYLLABUS. (1) British: specification of the content of language teaching; a structuring or ordering of that content in terms of grading and presentation. (2) American: A schedule of items or units to be taught; a daily or weekly program of material to be presented. Cf. CURRICULUM.

SYNCHRONIC. *See* CROSS-SECTIONAL.

SYNTAX. That part of grammar that is concerned with the arrangement of words in sentences, the distribution of words in constructions, and the systematic structural relations between sentences.

SYSTEM(IC). A network of patterned relationships constituting the organization of language.

TARGET LANGUAGE. The L2 being learned or taught.

TECHNIQUE. A particular device, strategy, activity used to accomplish an immediate goal. Cf. APPROACH, METHOD (OF TEACHING).

TESOL. Teachers of English to Speakers of Other Languages, a professional organization.

TEST. A sample of behavior; on the basis of observed performance on a test, inferences are made about the more general underlying competence of an individual to perform similar or related tasks.

TEXT. A "piece" of language relevant to a specific context; language in setting; transactions of various kinds such as tasks, games, discussions, etc.; a spoken or written passage that forms a unified whole.

THEORY. A formulation of basic principles supported by empirical evidence and open to confirmation or refutation by evidence yet to be discovered.

TOEFL. Test of English as a Foreign Language, a written test designed to test the English proficiency of foreign students applying for admission to U.S. colleges and universities, prepared and administered by Educational Testing Service.

TOP-DOWN PROCESSING. A mode of processing information in which predictions are made based on prior general knowledge and then checked against the input data for confirmation or refutation. Also called conceptually driven processing. Cf. BOTTOM-UP PROCESSING, INTERACTIVE PROCESSING.

TRAIT. In testing theory, the ability or attribute one is measuring. Cf. METHOD (OF MEASUREMENT).

TRANSFER. The carry-over into learner performance in a new language of features of pronunciation, grammar, and vocabulary, or discourse strategies that have previously been learned for another language. POSITIVE TRANSFER results when the two languages have features in common. NEGATIVE TRANSFER occurs when features do not coincide. Cf. INTERFERENCE.

TRANSFORMATIONAL-GENERATIVE (GRAMMAR). A linguistic theory concerned with the relation between the grammatical interpretation of sentences and surface structure as a means of discovering universal categories of grammar; Chomskyan linguistic theory. Cf. SURFACE STRUCTURE, DEEP STRUCTURE.

VALIDITY. The extent to which a test measures what it is supposed to measure and nothing else.

VARIETY (OF LANGUAGE). A situationally distinctive use of language (e.g., social, religious, professional). Cf. DIALECT, REGISTER.

Author Index